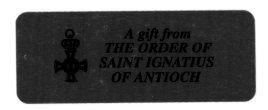

A gift from
**THE ORDER OF
SAINT IGNATIUS
OF ANTIOCH**

Ordained for Men in the Things of God

(Hebrews 5:1)

A COMMEMORATIVE COLLECTION

ON THE OCCASION OF

THE FORTIETH ANNIVERSARY

OF METROPOLITAN PHILIP'S

EPISCOPACY

EDITED BY JOSEPH ALLEN AND JOSEPH ANTYPAS

Ordained for Men in the Things of God:
A Commemorative Collection on the Occasion of the Fortieth Anniversary
of Metropolitan Philip's Episcopacy

Published by Conciliar Press
P.O. Box 76
Ben Lomond, California 95005

Printed in the USA

ISBN 10: 1-888212-85-3
ISBN 13: 978-1-888212-85-3

Manufactured under the director of **Double Eagle Industries**.
For manufacturing details, call **888-824-4344**, or email to **dane@publishingquest.com**

INTRODUCTIONS FROM THE CO-EDITORS

PART 1
THE THOUGHTS OF METROPOLITAN PHILIP

PART 2
IN THE VIEW OF ORTHODOX HIERARCHS AND CIVIC LEADERS

PART 3
IN THE VIEW OF HIERARCHS AND CIVIL LEADERS (SELECTIONS IN ARABIC)

PART 4
IN THE VIEW OF FAMILY, FRIENDS, CLERGY, AND CHURCH ADMINISTRATORS

INTRODUCTIONS

FROM THE CO-EDITORS

⬧ THE VERY REV. JOSEPH ALLEN

⬧ THE VERY REV. JOSEPH ANTYPAS

FROM THE CO-EDITOR

The Very Rev. Joseph Allen
Co-Editor, *Ordained for Men in the Things of God*

For Those Who Open These Pages

THESE WORDS ARE WRITTEN BOTH TO SAIDNA PHILIP and to all those who open the pages of this book.

Every reader should know that these words are written after reading and editing hundreds of pages—pages full of words by those who, after forty years, are desperately trying to express why this man is as he is. And even after that, each contributor is left feeling that there is still more to say, still more to explicate, still more to capture. As an Editor, I can understand the difficulty in exploring Saidna's heart and mind; this has not been my first endeavor to do such. The truth is that I have discovered in other of his works a heart and mind that is not easily captured.

Nevertheless, Saidna and friends, we have all tried to do so. We have done so not because we believe we can truly capture this high priest, this bishop, in our words; it is more a case of *our* need, a need for *us* to empty ourselves of the expressions of the great admiration held for the man. The fortieth anniversary of a personage of such legendary proportions is the perfect opportunity for us to make such an effort.

You should know that as the editors, Father Joseph Antypas and I had to have a *reason* to choose the contributors, knowing that there are hundreds of others who, given that same opportunity, would have also entered the struggle to express the inexpressible. If not, we would be editing thousands of pages in this Commemorative Collection!

But let the reader beware: this is not literary hyperbole, English or Arabic. These contributors mean what they say about the Metropolitan Archbishop; they are terribly truthful; they speak from their hearts. One gets the feeling in some of the entries that on this fortieth anniversary, it would even be painful *not* to express, or rather, painful to contain, these thoughts and words. And as future generations study this era, they will wonder: what kind of person *is* this, one who is called by these contributors: "great shepherd, teacher, preacher, administrator, builder, missionary, philanthropist, etc.?"

But let those same future generations read for themselves, not only words written *about* him; let them read words written *by* him. They should read his books *Feed My Sheep* and *And He Leads Them*, as well as his many other published articles. They will discover for themselves what captivates these contributors and why they use such lofty words to describe him.

For me, not only as an Editor, but also as the Director of Theological and Pastoral Education and the North American Chaplain of The Order of St. Ignatius of Antioch, I have certainly had enough experience with Saidna Philip (without which none of these programs would have succeeded) to know that any word or title I would use, would merely echo those which follow in this text. But, what I *can* say, and I know Father Joseph Antypas would agree, is that the title of this book encapsulates all we can express—all the titles, all the descriptions, all the good works, all the great theology. This man has truly been "ordained for men in the things of God" (Hebrews 5:1).

As you open the pages of this text, then, please let me offer my gratitude to my partner in editing, Father Joseph Antypas, especially for translating and editing the Arabic text. I also thank the many hierarchs and civil authorities for their contributions. And especially, I thank the many contributors who have taken this chance to express their thanks to the Metropolitan for the part he has played in their service to Christ.

And as for me, Saidna, what can I say? If there is anyone in these pages who needs to express gratitude, there is none greater than I. It has been by your creativity and energy that I have been able to travel down so many roads in the areas of ministry and education these past forty years. As for the rest, let each expression, each description and each word of gratitude you find in the text that follows, be multiplied in order to also speak for me.

It has been my greatest joy to fulfill what I believe the Trinitarian God—the Father, Son and Holy Spirit—has given to me to accomplish in the name of your extraordinary episcopacy.

—Father Joseph Allen, ThD, Editor

FROM THE CO-EDITOR

THE VERY REV. JOSEPH ANTYPAS
CO-EDITOR, *ORDAINED FOR MEN IN THE THINGS OF GOD*

WITHIN THE BODY OF THE WORK OF THE GREATEST GERMAN IDEALIST PHILOSOPHER, George Hegel (1770-1831), stands the fascinating idea of the "world historical individual." Hegel's goal and purpose was to explain the growth of cultures and societies, with the full awareness and appreciation of history that is possible only once every one hundred years.

To me, our beloved Metropolitan Philip, whose fortieth anniversary in the episcopacy we celebrate in 2006, is one such "world historical individual." I am not advocating a Hegelian model of interpreting history, as taught by this German idealist. To be fair to His Eminence, I would rather use Arnold J. Toynbee's research into the questions of how civilizations were created, why some flourished and why others failed. Toynbee discovered that challenges met by creative responses were the ideal conditions in which great civilizations developed. This expository principle of challenge and response summarizes the past forty years in the life of Metropolitan Philip Saliba, which has led us to the patterns that today characterize the Antiochian Orthodox Christian Archdiocese of North America.

The year 2006 marks my thirtieth anniversary in the Holy priesthood. In 1973 I came to the

Antiochian Archdiocese along with Archdeacon Hans, both of us being received by our beloved Primate. From that moment, we started to witness the love, support, vision and dynamic leadership of Metropolitan Philip. The Metropolitan is the source of inspiration to hundreds of priests, deacons and church leaders. He is perhaps the greatest American Orthodox leader who continues to proclaim the word of truth with integrity and courage.

I want to focus on four aspects of his archpastorate: his love to his clergy; his love to his flock in North America; his charismatic leadership in North American Orthodoxy; and his leadership in the Holy Synod of the Church of Antioch. In these four aspects one will note his worldwide engagement in issues, debates and creative contacts with individuals and institutions in the Mother Church. These remarks are based on my personal observations collected during his visits to the parishes I served, during conventions, conferences and seminars I attended in his presence and under his leadership, and during the five journeys I made with His Eminence to the Mother Church of Antioch.

His Love of Clergy
Metropolitan Philip challenges his clergy to live according to the priestly office of their divine calling. He encourages them to grow spiritually and to be men of prayer and action. His first and foremost priority is to know his clergy and their wives and children, and to extend to them his warmth and his loving paternal care. "You are not in the parish to dominate, but to serve, to discover and cultivate talent"; this is what he reminded the graduating class of 1981 at St. Vladimir's Seminary. Many archdiocese departments and institutions have been established in the past forty years, in which many clergymen have been able to cultivate their talents and to mature into good and productive soldiers in the Army of Christ. The following words to the clergy in the 1980 address continue to resonate in the hearts of many of our Antiochian clergy: "Don't forget that I love you and care for each and every one of you." To me, at least, this was not a simple verbal activity; it came from a good heart that was filled with the love of Christ.

His Love of the Flock

Metropolitan Philip's love of his spiritual flock is unwavering. This love includes all men, women and children. He recognizes them by their first names and they know him as their father and shepherd. Children are the real source of his inspiration. Throughout his entire ministry, he has invited his spiritual children to a life of service and genuine Christian communion. He wants them to learn and to become instrumental in their parochial worshipping communities. He also invites men and women to work side by side—to administer, to teach, to sing in joyful praise and to fully participate in the life of the Church.

I remember his words during the Second Antiochian Holy Year, when we were in Boston, Massachusetts, in the presence of our beloved Patriarch Ignatius IV, of thrice-blessed memory, asking whether we were prepared to face the challenges of the next century. A prophetic actor, however, does what the Lord dictates to him. In consequence, in early 1973 I witnessed the creation of the Antiochian Orthodox Christian Women, and the birth of The Order of St. Ignatius in 1976. I also witnessed, in 1985, the consecration of the Heritage and Learning Center in Pennsylvania. Today, the Antiochian Village is the nurturing home of the Antiochian House of Studies, the Cultural Library and the Heritage Museum, which all stand next door to the Antiochian Village Summer Camp. These form a hub for wonderful activities and programs that benefit all Orthodox jurisdictions, and many non-Orthodox institutions and organizations.

I was fortunate to have been chosen by His Eminence to be the Spiritual Advisor to the Antiochian Women of the Midwest for five years, the Spiritual Advisor of The Order of St. Ignatius in the Midwest for twenty-eight years and a mentor at the House of Studies for the past twenty-six years. Finally, in my capacity as pastor, my mission was to discover and cultivate lay members whom His Eminence could incorporate into service on the Board of Trustees of the archdiocese. These members continue to give their time and contribute generously to the needs of the Church as defined by our visionary leader.

His Charismatic Leadership

During the past thirty years of my ministry in the priesthood, I have witnessed Metropolitan Philip's challenges to North American Orthodoxy. In order to respond to the challenges of history, Metropolitan Philip wanted to introduce the concept of Church unity in a way that America would understand. As a Vice Chairman of the Standing Conference of Orthodox Canonical Bishops, he advocated that the Standing Conference must speak to America with one voice and one accord, in order to respond effectively to the moral and social challenges of our time. He has warned that a fragmented Orthodoxy in America can no longer be tolerated if we are to survive.

In 1975, I personally witnessed the Antiochian unification, arrived at with much enthusiasm and deliberation, in Louisville, Kentucky, uniting the New York and Toledo Archdioceses; this was a step toward Orthodox unity. Again, in 1987, I witnessed for the first time, at a National Convention in Dearborn, Michigan, the participation of the Evangelical Orthodox in the activities of the Antiochian Archdiocese. They have since become one united family. Finally, in 1994, His Eminence invited me to be amongst the Antiochian clergy when he hosted the first Orthodox Episcopal Conference, held at the Antiochian Village and Learning Center. That conference is known in history today as the "Legionaire Conference." This is what Metropolitan Philip has offered to America: 2,000 years of Orthodox Christian spirituality in a language that America understands.

His Leadership in the Holy Synod of Antioch

Last but not least, Metropolitan Philip impresses me as a man of vision and reason, combining a compassionate heart with common sense, especially when it comes to causes that affect people who are in need. In this regard, I must mention my experience and observation of the hundreds of orphans he touched, and the support he gave to St. George Hospital of Beirut, to the University of Balamand and to the task force formed to help the faithful in the Patriarchate of Jerusalem. His innumberable discussions at the Holy Synod and the many long hours he spent with the patriarch, metropolitans and friends prove his deep roots in the Antiochian soil.

I pray that the Lord God will grant Saidna Philip the strength to continue to lead us, and that the result of the establishment of the self-ruled status of the Antiochian Archdiocese will not lead to the same predicament as that of the Hegelian "world historical individual." My hope is that we will continue to receive guidance from our true shepherd, who will disperse and articulate the word of truth.

For Saidna Philip, the challenge will continue. We pray that God will grant him many more years of fruitful ministry and good health. May we, his flock, continue to be strong supporters of his dream of the One United Archdiocese in North America. The gates of hell will not overpower our relentless efforts and determination to be guided by both the love of God and the spiritual council of our beloved hierarch Metropolitan Philip Saliba.

AXIOS, AXIOS, AXIOS! On your fortieth anniversary!

—Archpriest Joseph Antypas

PART 1

THE THOUGHTS OF METROPOLITAN PHILIP

- ✦ ON THEOLOGY

- ✦ ON MISSIOLOGY

- ✦ ON ECCLESIOLOGY

THE THOUGHTS OF METROPOLITAN PHILIP

On Theology

I SEE THREE MAIN ISSUES which define our Orthodox Christian theology.

First, the doctrine of man in our theology is based on the biblical view which was fully defined by our Church Fathers. Man has all the potentialities for perfection, simply because he was created in the image of God. St. Maximus the Confessor states:

> Those who followed Christ in action and contemplation will be changed into an even better condition, and there is no time to tell of all the ascents and revelations of the saints who are being changed from glory to glory, until each one in order receives deification.

Man was not created to be a slave, neither to society nor to history, neither to science nor to technology, neither to communism nor to capitalism. Even though nature has limitations, these limitations can be overcome by the sacramental life of the Church. Each and every one of us can become Christlike through prayer, contemplation and action. St. Maximus further says:

While remaining in his soul and body entirely man by nature, he becomes in his soul and body entirely God by grace. Deification involves the whole human being.

All the ancient Greek dichotomy between body and soul disappears in St. Maximus. When God created man, He created him as a whole being, and when man collapsed, he collapsed not partially but as a whole being. Likewise, when man was redeemed, he was redeemed totally, body and soul. Through the sacrament of the Holy Eucharist, God enters into union with the whole man.

The second issue is the theology of hope. While other Christians have focused their eyes on Calvary, we have focused ours on the empty tomb. Do we not experience this reality every year on Easter morning when we shout, "Christ is risen from the dead"? In 1 Corinthians 15:14, 22, St. Paul says:

> If Christ has not been raised then our preaching is in vain and your faith is in vain. For as in Adam all die, so also in Christ shall all be made alive.

On Great Friday, there were tears, pain, agony and death, but on the third day, the darkness of Great Friday was dissipated by the bright light of the empty tomb. The new Pascha inaugurated the new age, the new being, and the new man. The Orthodox Church celebrates this joyful event every Sunday. The following are some of the hymns which we chant on the morning of the Holy Resurrection, which reveal to us this joy and this new being:

> Let us cleanse our senses that we may behold Christ shining like lightning with the unapproachable light of Resurrection, that we may hear Him say openly "rejoice," while we sing to Him the hymn of triumph and victory.
>
> Verily this day which is called Holy is the first day among Sabbaths, it is their king and lord, it is the feast of feasts, and the season of seasons.

Where are those like Sartre or Camus who say there is "no exit"? Let them gaze at the empty tomb. Our hope then is genuine because it is rooted in the reality of the Resurrection. It is not an empty utopian hope which ends in false security. It is the hope of the realization of God's kingdom first within us, and ultimately, beyond the veils of temporal existence.

The third issue of our Orthodox theology is the relevancy of our liturgical life. During the dark ages of Orthodox theology, our Church survived because of the richness of her liturgical life. If one understands our various liturgical services, one will understand the whole theology of the Orthodox Church. While others talk about liturgical poverty and liturgical renewal, as Orthodox, we must concentrate our efforts on liturgical understanding.

Any Liturgy which does not permeate the faithful with a strong feeling of the holy is a meaningless service. If one has a living priest, a living choir and a living congregation, then one will find oneself involved in a wonderful mystical experience. We cannot acquire a mystical experience in the Church if the Liturgy is nothing but a business meeting or another lecture. A few years ago I talked to a group of non-Orthodox students about the nature of our worship. One of them asked: "Why don't you preach in the Orthodox Church?" I said, "We do preach in the Orthodox Church, but we do more than that. We do not tell the faithful only what Christ said, but what He in reality did through the Sacrament of the Holy Eucharist." In the Liturgy of St. John Chrysostom, the priest prays during the Anaphora the following:

> Thou it was who didst bring us from nonexistence into being, and when we had
> fallen away didst raise us up again, and didst not cease to do all things until Thou
> hast brought us back to heaven.

In the Orthodox Liturgy, one can see God, man and nature in their proper perspective. Our Eucharist answers the central questions: Who are we? Where are we going? What is the meaning of life?

Who is God? The emphasis in the Orthodox Liturgy is first on being, then on doing. If our personality is disintegrated and if the image of God in us is distorted, then our actions will undoubtedly reflect this disintegration and that distortion.

—Edited by Father Joseph Allen, Th.D.

THE THOUGHTS OF METROPOLITAN PHILIP

ON MISSIOLOGY

OUR LORD HIMSELF WAS INDEED THE MISSIONARY PAR EXCELLENCE. In Matthew 4:23 we read: "And He went about all Galilee, teaching in their synagogues and preaching the gospel of the kingdom, and healing every disease and every infirmity among the people." And in the "fullness of time," the "Word became flesh" and entered time on a mission of salvation. He was sent by the Father to make us "partakers of the Divine Nature."

In John 20:21, Christ said: "As the Father has sent Me, even so I send you." The Church, which is the extension of Christ in time and space, was sent by Christ to missionize and evangelize. Evangelism means "to preach the Gospel." "Woe unto me if I do not preach," said St. Paul. After the birth of the Church on Pentecost Day, the Apostles and early Christians went about the *oikomene*, the known world at that time, preaching the Gospel and missionizing, despite their persecution and the monumental difficulties which they had to face. Although the Church was born in Jerusalem, Antioch became the greatest center for missionary activities. It was in Antioch that the disciples were first called Christians.

There are many stories about the missionary travels of the Apostles. It is clear, however, that Christianity did not spread throughout the entire Roman Empire until after the Edict of Milan. The Pax Romana presented what Michael Green describes as both opportunities and difficulties for evangelism.

Some of the opportunities were:

a. peace and unity;

b. philosophical hunger;

c. religious dissatisfaction.

Some of the difficulties were:

a. the cultural offensiveness of the Gospel, i.e., the Jewish communities and their Gentile adherents were openly affronted by the central language of the Gospel: God's Incarnation and death;

b. political considerations, i.e., the Christian unwillingness to participate in the state cult of the emperor was seen as political treason, and the closed nature of the Christian gatherings likewise led to charges of cannibalism.

After A.D. 313 circumstances changed radically, and organized missionary enterprises became normal. Metropolitan Anastasios divides the history of Byzantine missions into two major periods:

1. The fourth to the sixth centuries witness the Christianization of the empire and its immediate peripheries.

2. The ninth to the eleventh centuries brought Byzantium's classic outreach into the Balkans and Russia.

In the same way, we can missionize and evangelize America, but only if we unite. We pray that the mother churches will soon realize that we are no longer little children and that the Preparatory Commission for the Great Synod will stop discussing the Diaspora in absentia.

The truth is that America is searching for the New Testament Church. America is searching for the Church which was born on Pentecost Day. America is ready and waiting for us, but are we ready for America?

Let none of us forget these words from the Perfect Missionary, our Lord and Savior Jesus Christ.

> Do not say, "There are yet four months, then comes the harvest." I tell you, lift up your eyes and see how the fields are already white for harvest. He who reaps receives wages and gathers fruit for eternal life, so that the sower and reaper may rejoice together. (John 4:35, 36)

Unity in America: An Antiochian Perspective

To be more particular, I believe that the most difficult challenge which the Church will be facing in this new millennium is Orthodox unity in this hemisphere. I would like to state for history's sake that Antioch was never a stumbling block to Orthodox unity. Two of our illustrious and venerable patriarchs of this century have made crystal-clear statements on behalf of Orthodox unity in North America.

In 1977, the late Patriarch Elias IV, in an interview published in *A Man of Love,* was asked: "What do you foresee for the future of Orthodoxy in the Diaspora, particularly in North America?" His Beatitude answered:

> In preparation for the upcoming Great Council, the Antiochian Holy Synod has studied in depth the situation of Orthodoxy in the Diaspora. Our position is clear. There must be established independent churches in Eastern Europe, North America, etc. The possibility for such an autocephalous church is greatest in North America. However, the decision to create such a church must be done with the blessings of all mother churches which have dioceses on this continent.

We are all well aware of the canons of the Church which, among other things, say that there cannot be many bishops in one city. The Antiochian See is ready to do her part to rectify this unfortunate situation of Orthodoxy in North America. We affirm that in North America there should be an autocephalous church with its own patriarch and Holy Synod. However, all mother churches must agree on this point, and more importantly, the faithful in North America must do their part to make independence and unity a reality and not just a written Tomos.

In 1985, the position of Antioch was again stated on the pages of *The WORD* magazine by our beloved Patriarch Ignatius. In anticipation of the Great and Holy Synod, His Beatitude said:

1. The Orthodox Diaspora has reached such a maturity that it is necessary to consider it from a new viewpoint in such a way that leads to resolution.
2. We must see it as the vocation of the Orthodox Diaspora, not only to preserve the present, but to become a dynamic and creative element in its own environment.
3. It is desirable that the Council should recognize all the Orthodox churches in the Diaspora, provided there is no serious cause not to do so.
4. It is desirable that local synods should be created, comprising the bishops of the Orthodox churches of the area in question and their members. This should be realized especially in Western Europe, America, Australia and also elsewhere, as far as necessary.
5. Autocephaly should be granted to all the churches of the countries mentioned above. The local synods of the autocephalous mother churches should decide on it and determine its boundaries.
6. The traditional apostolic and catholic regulations of the Orthodox Church should be followed so that in each city there would be one metropolitan.

7. The relationship between the mother churches and the Diaspora churches are to be kept brotherly and cordial, as is natural to the Orthodox spirit and to the extent that all is for one and one is for all.

8. Within the churches, there should be preserved the cultural, linguistic and other national elements, insofar as they do not disrupt the unity of the local church or the wholeness of the local diocese.

I believe that these two explicit statements of our venerable patriarchs speak for themselves. My predecessor, Metropolitan Antony Bashir, was a staunch advocate of Orthodox unity in North America, and made many statements in this regard. In 1976, speaking in Pittsburgh, Pennsylvania, on the Sunday of Orthodoxy, I personally said:

> We Orthodox have a tendency to glorify the past and feel proud of ourselves. There is no doubt that the church of the Ecumenical Councils was glorious and courageous in responding to the challenges of her time. Have we responded to the challenges of our time? As individual jurisdictions, I believe we have succeeded in building beautiful churches, in educating young priests and organizing good choirs and church schools, etc., but collectively, we have done absolutely nothing.

An example of the problem is seen in the tragedy of Kosovo, which clearly revealed our nakedness and ineffectiveness as Orthodox in this country. We have no clout in Washington, D.C. whatsoever, because we are still speaking to the State Department and the White House as Greeks, Russians, Antiochians, Serbians, etc., instead of speaking to Washington with one voice. Even Madeline Albright refused to talk to us during the dark days of that unfortunate war. We cannot be agents of change in full obedience to the truth unless we transcend ethnicism and establish a new Orthodox reality in North

America. I am not asking anyone to deny his or her own history and culture. What I am asking is to blend the old and new cultures into some kind of integrated reality.

This focus on our missionary task was most noted when, in 1994, we in North America experienced a moment of transfiguration when thirty Orthodox bishops gathered at the Antiochian Village to know each other, pray together, and discuss common Orthodox problems. At that time, I delivered a paper on "Missions and Evangelism," and Metropolitan Maximos of Pittsburgh delivered a paper on "Orthodox Unity in North America." That was all. The news of this brotherly, long-anticipated and unprecedented meeting caused an earthquake in certain Orthodox quarters, which sent shock waves throughout North America, and beyond our shores. How dare we meet and say, "We are here in America to stay and we are not in Diaspora!"

I do realize that we are dealing here with a very complex problem. This multiplicity of jurisdictions is deeply connected to the self-evident reality of our various ethnic cultures. Such cultures cannot be eliminated by a statement from SCOBA or by an edict from some patriarch somewhere. Only time can take care of this problem. Despite this reality, however, we cannot consider this present Orthodox situation in America as final because, by so doing, we will betray Orthodoxy and her basic principles.

Finally, I firmly believe that Orthodox unity in North America is inevitable and such unity will strengthen the mother churches, spiritually and otherwise. No one can stop the wheels of history and no one can reverse the course of a mighty river.

Such a "mighty river" is the true metaphor of Orthodox missiology!

—Edited by Father Joseph Allen, Th.D.

On Ecclesiology

THE CENTRAL BIBLICAL THEME REGARDING OUR ECCLESIOLOGY is taken from the first Epistle of Saint Paul to the Corinthians 3:9-17:

> We are laborers together with God: you are God's field. You are God's building. But let every man take heed how he builds; for no other foundation can man lay than that which is laid, which is Jesus Christ. Every man's work shall be made manifest, for the day shall declare it. For it shall be manifest by fire, and the fire shall try every man's work, of what sort it is.

Certainly we do not organize for the sake of organization. We do organize in order to coordinate our efforts, so that our vision and dreams for a Christ-like Church might be fulfilled and realized. The purpose of all our organizations is to grow spiritually in Christ. If we fail to do so, then all our organizations and all our efforts will have been in vain. "Seek ye first the kingdom of God and His righteousness, and everything else will be added unto you"

For many years we have been administering our local parishes under a false dichotomy, under a dangerous and completely un-orthodox dualism. Thus, we have been preaching two kinds of theologies: one for the church upstairs, and one for the hall downstairs. We do not believe in this "upstairs-downstairs" theology. Nor do we believe in the existence of two classes in the parish opposing each other: namely, clergy versus laity. This kind of dualism has caused us many problems.

Some Orthodox clergy do not think that we need organizations and church councils. They think that they can administer the affairs of the parish without help from the laity. Furthermore, they believe that the councils are nothing but an American innovation in our Church and that we do not need them. We completely disagree with this trend of thinking. At the same time, there are some councils who believe that the priest can be hired or fired if he is not perfect. The question now is: what human being is perfect? If you are looking for perfect bishops or perfect priests, you are going to look, and look in vain.

We are very reluctant to transfer priests from one parish to another because someone does not like the way a priest combs his hair. We are very reluctant, also, to transfer a priest from one parish to another because his English (or Arabic) is not perfect. We are further reluctant to transfer a priest from one parish to another because of complaints that he asks questions about the financial affairs of his parish. Priests are appointed and transferred only by the Archbishop, on the basis of whether or not his ministry in this particular parish is still fruitful.

I believe that we have reached a state of spiritual maturity when we can look at the parish as the family of God, one which is bound together by the bond of love, and which works together for God's glory.

Saint Peter, in his first Epistle, chapter 2, verse 9, wrote:

> You are a chosen generation, a royal priesthood, an holy nation, a peculiar people, that you should show forth the praises of Him who has called you out of darkness into His marvelous light. Which in time past were not a people, but are now the people of God, which had not obtained mercy, but now have obtained mercy.

Thus, we are no longer living under the yoke of the law but in the grace and fellowship of our Lord and Savior Jesus Christ. There are no masters and slaves in the parish. The parish is the family of God. The priest who listens to your confessions, who leads you in prayers, who distributes to you the Sacrament of the Holy Eucharist, must be respected as such. At parish meetings, he must be given the place of honor. Councils must listen carefully to his comments and adhere to his recommendations. In his first Epistle to the Corinthians, Saint Paul wrote: "For though you have ten thousand instructors in Christ, yet you have not many fathers" (4:15). The priest, then, is a father to his family and not a dictator. He is the teacher of the Faith and must share in the administration of the parish. He must teach his children with love, carefulness, and patience. He must understand that the priesthood is a martyrdom for Christ's sake.

Charity, or *philanthropia,* is also critical to our Ecclesiology. In the *Didache* (an early Christian document), we read the following: "Thou must not refuse the needy but share everything with thy brethren. Say not that this is thy property, for if we enjoy together the eternal blessings it should be the more so with temporal ones."

St. John Chrysostom and St. Basil the Great were among the outspoken Fathers against social injustice and the monopoly of wealth:

> Say not I am spending what is my own, I am enjoying what is my own. No, not your own, but other people's. Precisely because you make an inhuman use of it and say I have a right for my personal enjoyment that which belongs to me. I maintain that those possessions do not belong to you. They belong together to you and your neighbors, just as sunshine, air, earth and all the rest. (St. Chrysostom, Homily 10 on Corinthians 1)

To this St. Basil the Great adds:

Who is covetous? He who is not content with what is sufficient. Who is a robber? He who takes away other people's property. Are you not covetous? Are you not a robber if you make your own that which has been given you in stewardship? He who takes another's clothing is called a thief, he who does not clothe the naked, although he could do so, deserves no better name. The corn which you store belongs to the hungry; the cloak which you keep in your trunk belongs to the naked; the shoes which are rotting in your house belong to those who go barefoot; the silver you hid in the ground belongs to the needy. (St. Basil, Homily 6:7)

The courage of the early Fathers in speaking against the indifferent and affluent upper class and injustice in society is quite amazing.

Our Ecclesiology must also include the relationship of our faith and our works. To St. James, our faith is not something abstract, nor is it an intellectual adventure, nor can it be reduced to a mere philosophy. In James' own words: "Religion that is pure and undefiled before God and the Father is this: to visit orphans and widows in their affliction, and to keep oneself unstained from the world" (James 1:27).

To this he quickly adds: "Be doers of the word and not hearers only, deceiving yourselves" (James 1:22). Therefore, if you have faith, translate it into concrete actions on behalf of your neighbor, for a dead faith can save no one.

What does it profit, my brethren, if a man says he has faith but has not works? Can his faith save him? If a brother or sister is ill-clad and in lack of daily food, and one of you says to them, go in peace, be warmed and filled, without giving them the things needed for the body, what does it profit? So faith by itself, if it has no works, is dead (James 2:14-17).

Metropolitan Philip, with the editors of this book, Father Joseph Antypas (left) and Father Joseph Allen (right).

Facing page:

Top left: Metropolitan Philip serving in Brazil with the late Patriarch Elias IV; Paschal season, 1978.

Top right: Metropolitan Philip at the Vatican with Pope Paul VI; Spring, 1968.

Bottom left: The Metropolitan bestowing the Antonian Gold Medal on the late Protosyngellos Ellis Khouri.

Bottom right: Ambassador George Tomeh, Syrian Ambassador to the United Nations, presenting Metropolitan Philip with a decoration from the Syrian government.

On this page:
In the chapel at the Englewood headquarters of the Archdiocese, and at St. Nicholas Cathedral in Brooklyn, New York.

Metropolitan Philip meeting with U.S. presidents and vice-presidents.

Facing page:

With President Dwight Eisenhower in Palm Springs, California; 1968.

With President Lyndon B. Johnson at the White House.

With President Jimmy Carter at the White House. From left: Father George Rados, Father Antoun Khouri, James Abourisk, President Carter, Patriarch Elias IV, Metropolitan Philip, and Metropolitan Ilyas Kurban.

This page:

With President Ronald Reagan at the White House.

With President George H. Bush at the 1991 Convention in Virginia.

With Vice-President Al Gore at the White House, for the signing of the Jordan/Israeli Peace Concord; July 1994.

With President George W. Bush.

Top left:
Addressing the
Archdiocese Convention.

Top right:
Greeting the Rev.
Jesse Jackson at the
Archdiocese Convention
in Chicago.

Bottom:
Dedicating the Cultural
and Athletic Complex
at the University of
Balamand in Lebanon;
June, 2002.

THE METROPOLITAN PHILIP
(SALIBA)
CULTURAL & ATHLETIC
COMPLEX

In his explanation of the Orthodox Faith, St. John of Damascus says: "Because faith without works is dead, likewise works without faith are dead, because true faith is tested through works." Some Christian denominations, unjustifiably, find contradictions between James and Paul. The Church, however, does not find any such contradictions. It is inconceivable that the emphasis of James on good works excludes faith, and by the same token, it is inconceivable that St. Paul's emphasis on faith in his letter to the Romans, Chapter 5, excludes good works. James and Paul wrote to two different communities with different needs. Concerning the "faith only" issue, I read and reread St. Paul's letter to the Romans and discovered, once again, that St. Paul never said that we are saved by faith alone. This is a critical distinction in our Ecclesiology.

St. James was concerned with the dead and legalistic approach to faith, while St. Paul was concerned with the self-righteousness of the Judaizing elements in the early Church. Their basic teaching was that salvation can be achieved through the legal piety of the law. St. Paul emphasized that we win salvation only through Christ and in response to divine grace, apart from the Mosaic Law. "Therefore, having been justified by faith, we have peace with God through our Lord Jesus Christ, through whom we have access by faith through grace" (Romans 5: 1, 2). There is a fundamental difference between the old law and the grace brought by Christ. "For what the law could not do . . . God did by sending His own Son" (Romans 8:3).

If we claim that we love God and our neighbor, but fail to translate this love into acts of mercy and compassion, we are living a false faith, a dead faith, and our Ecclesiology is left empty.

There were other Fathers who later taught this message. For example, St. Clement of Alexandria said: "When you see your brother you see God." Likewise, Evagrius taught: "After God, we must count all men as God Himself." Paul Evdokimov adds: "The best icon of God is man."

St. Anthony the Great put it this way: "From our neighbor is life, and from our neighbor is death. Therefore, if we win our neighbor, we win God, but if we harm our neighbor, we sin against Christ."

More profoundly, St. Basil the Great expands on this theme even more graphically, when he asks:

If I live alone, whose feet will I wash? What scope will a man have for showing humility if he has no one before whom to show himself humble? What chance of showing compassion, when cut off from the fellowship of other men? The Lord washed the disciples' feet. Whose feet will you wash?

I would like to reemphasize here that the purpose of all these quotations from the Fathers is not to impress on you that we are saved by good works alone. If good works are not a genuine response to the divine grace and an expression of our deep faith in Christ Jesus, then such good works are to no avail.

Professor John Karmiris can summarize this issue for our clear understanding of Orthodox Ecclesiology. He writes:

> Generally, then, we can say that man's justification and salvation is first and foremost an action and a gift of the divine grace; secondly, it is by the intention and free cooperation of man in the form of concrete faith and good works. While, to the contrary, a fall from faith and good works entails a fall from Divine Grace.

Our Orthodox Ecclesiology, then, entails the fullness of the Body of Christ, which means both the clergy and laity in a healthy dynamic, and then, together, fulfilling the ministry of that Body through common faith and philanthropic work.

—Edited by Father Joseph Allen, Th.D.

PART 2

IN THE VIEW OF

✦ ORTHODOX HIERARCHS
AND CIVIC LEADERS

 **IN THE VIEW OF**

His Eminence, Metropolitan Ilyas Kurban
Archdiocese of Tripoli, Antiochian Patriarchate

The Early Years

I HAVE KNOWN MY BROTHER IN CHRIST METROPOLITAN PHILIP FOR A LONG TIME: early forties! Both of us came from the same region in el-Matin, which is one of the most beautiful regions in Lebanon. I have known him as a son of a family that is committed to the cause of Christ. The monastery of St. Elias in Dhour Shweir, Lebanon, was the place where we used to meet, especially on the second day of the great Feast of the Resurrection of our Lord, and on the Feast of St. Elias on July 20th. On those days people come from all villages and regions to the monastery, where we celebrated together.

I had noticed a young boy, whose name at that time was Abdallah Saliba; he was good looking and strong. He used to ring the huge bell with one hand! God granted him a good voice with which he always praised God both in the Church and in his home.

As a novice in the Balamand seminary, he was always on top in his studies, and was the head of the volleyball team. He did not allow his team to loose in any encounter with other teams!

From his earliest years at Balamand, he used to write social, economic, and political articles, which were often published in many local newspapers and periodicals. He showed his interest in such matters very early in his life.

After Balamand

From Balamand he was transferred to Homs in Syria, to study in the Orthodox school there. After a few years in Homs, he went to Damascus to live in the Patriarchate. The late Patriarch, Alexander the Third, appointed him as his personal secretary and predicted then that the young seminarian Philip would have a bright future. Patriarch Alexander was indeed prophetic.

From Damascus Philip left for Beirut and joined the Archdiocese of Beirut as a Deacon. From Beirut he went to London where he improved greatly his knowledge of the English language. He came back to Beirut from where he finally decided to travel to America. In America, he joined the Holy Cross School of Theology. From Boston he was assigned to Detroit to serve the parish of St. George as a Deacon and was enrolled at the University of Michigan from which he graduated with a Bachelor's degree in literature.

His Service as a Priest and Episcopal Election

After Detroit Philip was ordained a Priest by Metropolitan Anthony Bashir and was appointed the pastor of St. George in Cleveland. He served this parish with great devotion, and during this time the parish experienced a great renaissance on all levels.

In February 1966, Metropolitan Anthony Bashir fell asleep in Christ, and the late Patriarch, Theodosius the Sixth, appointed me as *locum tenens* to the Archdiocese of New York and all North America. I immediately left for New York and did what I had to do, together with the Board of Trustees of the Archdiocese of North America.

After the funeral service that took place at the Cathedral of St. Nicholas in Brooklyn, we asked all the parishes of the archdiocese to send their representatives to a general meeting, which was convened at the Sheraton hotel in Manhattan. Four hundred representatives were present to nominate three candidates, in order for the Holy Synod of Antioch to elect one of them to be the new Metropolitan of the archdiocese. We asked all candidates to address the general assembly with a speech. When the turn came for Father Philip to speak, as he ended his talk, the hall exploded with applause and a standing ovation. It was clear that the Archdiocese of New York had chosen its new archbishop and leader.

The nomination took place and Father Philip took a huge majority of the votes. I had the list of names and submitted it to the late Patriarch Theodosios who in turn submitted it to the Holy Synod to elect one of the three nominees as the new archbishop.

At that time our Church was going through turbulent times and circumstances. The Holy Synod was divided into two parties; one party of the Synod wanted to elect its own candidate, regardless of who the people of America had chosen as their own candidate.

Several meetings of the Holy Synod took place, and nothing came of it. Finally, at one meeting, five of the bishops left the session, which was convened at St. Elias Monastery in Dhour Shweir.

With God's intervention, the remaining members of the Holy Synod elected Father Philip to be the new Archbishop of New York and North America. Immediately I telephoned New York and gave them the good news. The newly elected archbishop came directly from America to Lebanon, and a great ceremony took place at the Church in the Monastery of St. Elias. The Liturgy was presided over by the Patriarch, assisted by all present archbishops. Father Philip was consecrated the Archbishop of New York and all North America. A huge crowd came from all over America, Canada, Lebanon and Syria, to attend this historical ceremony.

His First Days as Archbishop

On the following day the Patriarch and the new Archbishop traveled to Balamand to place the corner stone of the Institute of Theology of St. John of Damascus. His Eminence, Metropolitan Philip did honor the will of his predecessor to finance the building of the Institute of Theology.

From there he left for America to preside at the Archdiocese Convention of San Francisco, California. Since that time the Archdiocese of North America has known a great renaissance. Great achievements were performed, the number of parishes grew from sixty to almost 250, and it is still growing as new churches, halls and centers of learning are being built. The Antiochian Village is one of the great accomplishments of Saidna Philip. Both Antiochians and other Orthodox come from all over to convene there: children, adults, men and women, etc. The center is used also by other non-Orthodox groups of all nationalities.

The Order of St. Ignatius, the Antiochian Orthodox Christian Women, the Society of Orthodox Youth Organizations (SOYO) and other organizations have "seen the light," thanks to Saidna Philip.

Everyone knows that he is an eloquent speaker, preacher and author of many books and articles in both English and Arabic. We can never forget his assistance in the Lebanese, Arab and Palestinian issues. We writers in this book can never give him in these articles all he deserves. He is a man of great vision and all his dreams have been fulfilled.

We ask Almighty God to grant him good health and length of days and many, "Many Years!"

Sincerely yours,

+ Archbishop Ilyas Kurban,

Metropolitan of the Greek Orthodox Archdiocese Tripoli, Koura

IN THE VIEW OF

His Eminence, Metropolitan Elia
Diocese of Hama, Antiochian Patriarchate

The Stages of Saidna Philip's Life

My Earliest Memories

Metropolitan Philip was known as Abdallah Elias Saliba. He was born in the village of Abu Mizan, an extension of the Shreen Village. Both villages were pastorally ministered to by the St. Elias Monastery, and Philip was 14 when he became a regular visitor of the Patriarchal monastery. I observed the growth of Abdallah, the student; he was distinguished in his studies, dignified, calm, melodious and tending to serve the church. I was one of those who always encouraged him to join the clerical life. That encouragement led to the beginning of his clerical life in the Monastery of St. Elias. As one of the clergy, I became aware of his vitality, obedience, intelligence, love for learning and enthusiasm to build a better future.

As a Deacon

His deaconate can be focused in two stages: his service at the Balamand Monastery in Lebanon, and his service at the Patriarchate of Antioch, in Syria. In Lebanon, Metropolitan Theodosius Abu Rjayle of

Tripoli chose him to serve and assist him in solving many problems of the archdiocese. As a teacher of Arabic Language and Literature at the University of Balamand, Philip gained the admiration and respect of his students and mates. He cared for everyone to the extent that he often gave his earnings to the needy students. Later, at the Patriarchate of Antioch in Damascus, he served as the secretary to Patriarch Alexander Tahhan. In this capacity, I consulted with him on many clerical issues of vital importance. We became closer and established a strong relationship, based on cooperation, respect and mutual understanding.

I remember him always as a man of courage and honesty. He faced obstacles and challenges with certainty and confidence. During his service in the patriarchate, Deacon Philip brought "life" to the faithful of the Patriarchal Cathedral; they came from everywhere to hear his melodious voice, as he praised the Creator. From Damascus, he moved to Homs and later to Beirut. Finally from Beirut he headed to London, England, in order to pursue his education.

As a Priest

His Priesthood was occupied by his life in America. He was ordained by the late Metropolitan Anthony Bashir, who appointed him as the pastor of St. George in Cleveland, Ohio. Father Philip excelled in his pastoral ministry, administrative capabilities and brilliant leadership. This prepared him for his greatest contribution: his episcopacy.

As a Metropolitan

Saidna Philip was nominated as a bishop in the United States of America, according to the Archdiocesan Constitution. In the summer of 1966, in the presence of many clergy and delegates from the Archdiocese of North America, he was elected and was later consecrated at St. Elias Monastery by the Patriarch and the members of the Holy Synod of Antioch. After his consecration he presided at the Archdiocesan National Convention in San Francisco, California. In this stage of his life, Metropolitan Philip faced new challenges, but he always dealt with them in confidence and wisdom, having in mind the unity of the archdiocese. I remember him telling me: "Challenges captivate and immunize my life; they enrich it and provide it with creativity and strength."

From his first day as an archbishop, he worked hard and developed all the pastoral and administrative aspects of the archdiocese. He created new organizations and charities, and encouraged many to contribute to their construction. His dynamic leadership and fatherly love continue to inspire many.

I would like to focus on three important aspects in the life of the Metropolitan which I have witnessed and which have left a huge impact on my memory and my life.

1. **Uniting the Archdiocese:** The first challenge Saidna Philip was faced with was the division of the archdiocese into New York and Toledo, Ohio. For years this painful division upset the whole Antiochian Patriarchate and created division in the Holy Synod. Metropolitan Philip suffered greatly from this painful experience, and came to the Synod with a solution that would resolve this division and unite the archdiocese in one body. With hard work, wisdom and leadership, the dream came true and the archdiocese was united as "the Antiochian Archdiocese of North America."

2. **My placement in North America:** I was a guest in the Archdiocese of North America and I was called to serve it for ten years. During that time, Metropolitan Philip's love, care, and generosity made me feel as if I was at home; I never felt as a guest. During the unfortunate health crises that Saidna Philip experienced after his heart surgery, he was asked to reduce his travels. He then delegated me to represent him in some pastoral visits and duties. This stage was most useful, as I gained tremendous administrative and pastoral experience. I learned more about the archdiocesan structure, its parishes and organizations. The directions of His Eminence, and his sharp personality inspired me in many aspects. We met every evening to exchange discussion, experience and knowledge. I carried that experience

to the Archdiocese of Hama, where I tried to create a smaller "model" of the Archdiocese of North America in my own archdiocese.

3. **The Self-Ruled Status:** After more than two years of complicated and dynamic meetings between the Archdiocese of North America and the Patriarchal Holy Synod, the Archdiocese of North America was granted the status of self-ruled. The revised Archdiocesan Constitution, adopted during the special General Assembly, was approved by the Holy Synod. I would like to conclude my brief memories with these words: *Congratulations* to my brother, Metropolitan Philip, on this occasion. I ask the Lord to grant him health and length of days. If I had to write everything I know about Saidna Philip, I would have to write hundreds of pages to cover all of his accomplishments. Metropolitan Philip's sharp personality and rich knowledge have accompanied him in all stages of his life, as a layman and as a clergyman. His love and care for everyone around him reflects his great faith and purity of heart.

 **IN THE VIEW OF**

His Eminence, Metropolitan Elias Audi
Diocese of Beirut, Antiochian Patriarchate

Saidna Philip, Our Teacher and Exemplar

Brethren, I count not myself to have apprehended; but this one thing I do, forgetting those things which are behind, and reaching forth into those things which are before.
(Philippians 3:13)

Eyes
are always glued to sunshine,
and yet they never get satisfied
(Fouad Rifka)

IN CHILDHOOD I ENCOUNTERED THE UNSETTING SUN. This dream accompanied me when the Spirit of the Lord moved me, saying unto me: "Come let us depart from Lebanon and seek the land yonder." In that far region I met father, Metropolitan Anthony Bashir, who took me in as a son and helped my little buds to blossom. But no sooner did I enjoy his love and comfort, then the Blessed One took him away.

"My heart is firmly established in Thee, O God, for your mercy is greater than the heavens." This was, indeed, my plight.

Later, God did send another angel to me and to His Church, Metropolitan Philip Saliba, who took me in as a son, so that I may continue to do that which is appropriate to His Holy Name. This new angel became my refuge; in him I found love and care. His home became mine and a home to my peers in the ministry. Because of his love, my habitation became like a great tree beneath which we enjoyed the fruits and the shade, and worked together so we may discover that which builds up the soul and establishes joy in the heart. His compassion eliminated despair and toil; his presence filled our souls with warmth and eliminated all boundaries, which are created by the Enemy in our hearts.

His suffering was nourishment in the pursuit of virtues, revealing the splendor known to those who persevere and who are bathed in the light. Never did he take a step backward, and his eyes were always focused upon Him to whom he dedicated his life. Never has he stifled a ray of light or broken a fresh branch. He nourished what he planted with compassion, without bragging. Suffering had tested him, and yet he was calm. He was a comrade to us and through us, always steadfast and persevering.

He encouraged me to pursue the beautiful dream of the unsetting sun, and our love was translated into service: tending the wounds and washing the feet of the brethren of the Lord. He became our teacher and exemplar. He accepted what the Lord gave, keeping joy in his heart and repeating the words of St. Paul: "Rejoice in the Lord always; and again I say rejoice" (Philippians 4:4). I spent six years under his wings, getting my training in ministry, wisdom and love in order to tend to the flock of the Redeemer. In the midst of this undertaking, the Lord called me to return from whence I came. For obedience in the Lord brings comfort, while premature understanding and imperfect knowledge render only weak intelligence and shaky love. In time man shall realize that Love, and only Love, which is beyond time and space, can become the womb of all life, at any age. This is what I have witnessed in the person of my mentor and father, since the Lord chose me to become his co-worker. Love is his habitation and his comfort in our struggles; he is always ready for love, service and sacrifice.

This is the image of Saidna Philip I carry with me in my heart, and whenever I reflect on it, it brings a prayer of thanksgiving to my lips, that the Almighty will grant to him His good and perfect gifts.

# IN THE VIEW OF

His Excellency, General Emile Lahoud
President of Lebanon

On the occasion of his fortieth anniversary in the episcopacy, His Eminence Metropolitan Philip does not only create a special nostalgia, he makes Lebanon, the country of Faith, completely full of nostalgia in anticipation of this event. In the life of those who have come to know him and love him, he has a heart full of generosity. His words sparkle with the Spirit—an uplifting language that leaves in us some of his faith in the Absolute.

Saidna's Faith

To understand faith is a difficult task, and living it may be most intricate; however, the simplicity and completeness of Metropolitan Philip's faith make one realize that eternity resides in us. When that happens, our entire dimensions are filled by the power and depth of love.

Since I have known Metropolitan Philip, his visits to Lebanon have become a focalpoint of a nation with a message. He has made himself a champion of humanity, in whom the dialogue among cultures is realized. As I have known him in the Land of Cedars, which embraces the sky, I have seen in him a balanced thinker. His speech is the discourse of the Spirit. With him one realizes how to incorporate faith and thinking in order to discover the way to the truth. He who believes knows who is the way and the life, and also knows the truth that liberates from oppression.

His Witness Throughout the World

Metropolitan Philip has carried his archpastoral staff all over the world. He has become the witness of the One who has saved the world. His message in Lebanon, and in the United States as well, is a song of honor and praise, planted in the vineyard of God. But there is no evidence of weary toil on his brow, nor any sign of exhaustion in his steadfastness. Many minds have been enlightened by him, and many hearts have become enlightened by the divine light. And those who have listened to his words were able to read the brightness of truth in his eyes, establishing hymns of righteousness.

Metropolitan Philip is Lebanon's apostle in the United States. He is the fearless voice of the Arabs; always articulating the truth and executing what truth is. This is what he has taught: do not be intimidated by the dimensions of geography and history, but say and do the truth.

Dear Saidna Philip, may your words always be the voice of truth, and may the coming years be crowned with the peace which you bring to us and to the whole world—a message of unending love. May you continue to celebrate this anniversary, one after another, enriching the Faith in which we triumph over every weakness. May we continue to be jubilant in people like you.

—General Emile Lahoud,
President of Lebanon

 **IN THE VIEW OF**

His Eminence, Archbishop Demetrios
Greek Orthodox Archdiocese of America
and Chairman, Standing Conference of the
Canonical Orthodox Bishops in the Americas

My dear concelebrant in the Lord!

What a great joy it is to address you on the occasion of your fortieth anniversary as chief shepard of the Antiochian Orthodox Christian Archdiocese of North America. Both on behalf of the hierarchs, clergy and faithful of the Greek Orthodox Archdiocese in America, and on behalf of the members of the Standing Conference of Canonical Orthodox Bishops in the Americas, I offer thanks to Our God for the spiritual leadership you have provided for your flock in North America.

During these forty years, we have experienced several wars, significant natural disasters in various parts of our globe, many changes in the Roman Catholic and Protestant Churches, numerous changes in the lifestyle and values of the society in which we live and many developments and challenges within our own Orthodox world, both here and abroad. Through all this turmoil, you have provided steadfast guidance and direction for your own flock, and as Vice Chairman of SCOBA, for all Orthodox Christians in North America.

We all pray that God will enable us, for many years, to continue to benefit from your experience.

We have all watched as you worked to reconcile factions within the Antiochian community, and as you sought to expand the outreach of your archdiocese by welcoming new generations of persons into our Orthodox Christian family.

We know that your Mother Church, the Holy Patriarchate of Antioch, which elected you forty years ago to head the Antiochian Orthodox Archdiocese, must surely be rejoicing with us in recognizing your many accomplishments and your contributions to the growth of Orthodox Christianity in America.

With great love and high esteem in Christ,

Your Brother in Him,

    + Demetrios,

    Archbishop of America

 IN THE VIEW OF

His Eminence, Metropolitan Herman
Archbishop of Washington and New York, and Metropolitan of All America and Canada, The Orthodox Church in America

Your Eminence, dear Brother and Concelebrant of the Holy Mysteries:

Your fortieth anniversary as chief shepherd of the Antiochian Orthodox Christian Archdiocese of North America is an occasion for celebration in your archdiocese. The accomplishments of your archdiocese under your guidance and leadership have been historic. You have placed your many talents at the service of the archdiocese, making it a strong and effective Orthodox presence and witness in the United States and Canada.

The significance of your fortieth anniversary cannot be contained within the Antiochian Archdiocese. Your vision, your forceful and articulate witness to the Orthodox Faith in North America, your preaching of Orthodox unity in season and out of season, have inspired Orthodox people of North America, challenging them to overcome complacency and narrowness, asking them to bear witness to Christ and the Orthodox Faith before all who live in North America. You have often described Orthodoxy as the "best kept secret in North America," inviting Orthodox to bring our Faith to everyone in our societies.

There is a special bond between you and your archdiocese and the Orthodox Church in America.

Together, we build our ministry and mission in North America on the foundation laid by such witnesses and leaders as Saint Raphael (Hawaweeny) of Brooklyn, New York. Together, we look to the future in light of our common vision for a united Orthodoxy in North America—united for witness and united for mission. This means that we are together in the present, of one mind and one heart in our conviction and experience that the Orthodox Faith is for all people, times and civilizations. It is not only for our Orthodox brothers and sisters who live in the traditional centers of Orthodoxy in the Middle East and Europe, but equally for Americans and Canadians.

At this time of joyful celebration on your anniversary, let us all renew our commitment to act together for Orthodoxy in North America, in the conviction that acting together for Orthodoxy in North America is also action for the worldwide family of Orthodox Churches.

May God grant you Many Years!

With love in Christ and brotherly affection,

+ Herman

 **IN THE VIEW OF**

His Eminence, Metropolitan Maximos
Greek Orthodox Metropolis of Pittsburgh

To Many More Years, Brother and Master

FORTY YEARS OF HOLY EPISCOPACY IN THE UNITED STATES is a great accomplishment in itself, especially when most of them are years of service in one of our major Orthodox jurisdictions as the ranking bishop, and so as one of the major leaders in the Orthodox world. I am especially happy and pleased that I was given the task of offering my remarks on the occasion of this anniversary of my older brother and bishop, our beloved Metropolitan Philip, the head of the Antiochian Orthodox Christian Archdiocese of North America.

My Sincere Admiration

I am very thankful to my colleagues at the Antiochian House of Studies in Ligonier, Pennsylvania: the Very Rev. Dr. Joseph Allen and the Very Rev. Dr. Joseph Antypas, the editors of the commemorative book on this august celebration. I have always admired Saidna Philip as a church leader and as an Orthodox Christian bishop. It was a great joy for me to be invited to represent my diocese at the

Congresses and Assemblies of the Antiochian Archdiocese in our area and other places in the United States. I will never forget his leadership when it came to discussing contemporary Orthodox unity, or to foreseeing the future of this Orthodox unity in the Western Hemisphere. We can trust that with leaders like Saidna Philip, Holy Orthodoxy will finally enjoy full and complete visible unity; that is, not only in faith and sacramental life, but also in episcopal administration.

Before the famous meeting of all Orthodox canonical bishops, which took place in Ligonier, Pennsylvania, at the Antiochian Village Cultural Center in 1994, the Metropolitan had frequently expressed his views regarding Orthodox unity in the United States at intro-Orthodox meetings. I do remember the location of several of these meetings: at the Saint Vladimir's Theological Seminary, the Holy Cross Seminary in Brookline, Massachusetts, the Ligonier Antiochian Cultural Center, and the Greek Orthodox Archdiocese Biennial Congress. At each of these events Metropolitan Philip spoke up with regard to the need for pan-Orthodox unity in the land. It is the hope of all of us who would like to see this unity realized that his efforts will bring forth fruit at the time that the Lord has appointed.

Serving All the People of God

In addition to his efforts toward the creation of visible administrative unity among the Orthodox jurisdictions in the Western Hemisphere, Saidna Philip will be known in history for the restructuring of his own archdiocese. This archdiocese is now comprised of several dioceses and is serviced by a synod of bishops within the archdiocese. This new structure enhances the service of the Church to God's holy people, which is the primary purpose of the Church's existence. The adage "charity begins at home" applies to the Church as well; if the Church wants to serve all of God's people, it is appropriate that it should begin with serving its own people. All the other Orthodox in the Western Hemisphere should rejoice at this restructuring.

We cannot be the authentic Church of Christ if we are not interested in other churches and Christian denominations around us. In addition to his interest in other Christian groups, through the participation of his archdiocese on the ecumenical agencies, Saidna Philip will be known in history for accepting into the Holy Orthodox Church, through his archdiocese, the former "Evangelical Orthodox Church." I was witness to the hospitality extended to this church and its reception into the bosom of Holy Orthodoxy by His Beatitude Patriarch Ignatius IV of Antioch and Saidna Philip at Seven Springs, and later in Ligonier, Pennsylvania. All the Orthodox, not only the Evangelical Orthodox, should be grateful to Saidna Philip and Patriarch Ignatius for making it possible for these brothers in the Lord to join Holy Orthodoxy. I, at least, am one of those who is very grateful to them for their open-mindedness and Orthodox spirit of hospitality to all Christians. There is no doubt that the wish of the Leader of the Christian Faith, the Lord Jesus, that "they all may be one" (John 17:21) does not apply only to the Orthodox; but, rather, to all Christian Churches and denominations, as well.

Saidna's Keen Interest in Theological Education

The last of the main and important things for which I am personally indebted to Saidna Philip is his interest in theological education for all Orthodox clergy. He himself studied in both main Orthodox seminaries in the land—Holy Cross Theological Seminary and Saint Vladimir's Orthodox Theological Seminary. Saidna Philip realized how important it is for as many deacons as possible to serve in the Orthodox Churches in the Western Hemisphere. The Antiochian Orthodox Heritage and Learning Center in Ligonier, Pennsylvania, became the center for the Saint Stephen's Studies program, which is instrumental in educating hundreds of deacons and prospective deacons not only for the Antiochian Archdiocese, but also for other Orthodox jurisdictions in the Western Hemisphere, and throughout the world. It is heartwarming to hear their enthusiastic comments as they graduate from the program, or the comments they make privately on how much they appreciated such a program; and, of course, how thankful they are to the Antiochians, and especially to Saidna Philip, for establishing such a fine program.

The Antiochian Village, besides hosting the summer camp program for the younger members of the Antiochian Archdiocese, is a meeting place for clergy retreats, including the clergy of the Greek Orthodox Metropolis of Pittsburgh, Pennsylvania. This Metropolis also held many of its clergy-laity assemblies there because the Antiochian Village was the best place for the assemblies to meet, away from the noise and distractions of today's world.

Most importantly, over the past ten or more years, the Antiochian House of Studies has become a "University Without Walls" (UWW), as it is fondly called by those who appreciate the fine higher education that it provides for different categories of students. These UWW students include the theology students of Holy Cross and Saint Vladimir's, the priests who take its courses as a continuing theological education and the candidates for the Doctoral Degree in Ministry, a program in partnership with Pittsburgh Theological Seminary.

My Personal Engagement

I am personally very pleased and thankful to Metropolitan Philip and the Antiochian Archdiocese for such a fine place of higher learning, for which not only the Antiochians, but also the entire Orthodox Church may be very proud. I have been involved with the Antiochian Village from the beginning of my service in Pittsburgh, twenty-seven years ago; and for more than the past ten years, thanks to Saidna Philip, I have been directly involved with the Ligonier, Pennsylvania, "University Without Walls."

My personal engagement with the program of theological studies allows me to discuss theological topics of relevance, Orthodox spirituality, and ecumenical studies. I have found that it is of paramount importance for the students to be kept abreast of developments in the ecumenical dialogue between our Church and the other Christian Churches and denominations, especially those with which our Church is in dialogue. I am very impressed with the special interest and concern that our students have expressed regarding these topics. My foundation of studies is in Orthodox patristic theology, contemporary Orthodox dogmatic theology and Orthodox applied theology.

All these things would not have been possible without the fine spiritual and administrative guidance of Saidna Philip during his forty years of service to our Holy Orthodox Church and God's holy people in the Western Hemisphere. As a bishop serving the same Church, I am personally indebted to Metropolitan Philip for his leadership, and I am edified by his love for the Holy Orthodox Faith and Orthodox unity.

It is my prayer that the Lord may give him many more healthy years of fine service and leadership to the benefit of God's holy people and to the greater glory of God's Holy Name.

IN THE VIEW OF

His Eminence, Archbishop Nathaniel
Romanian Orthodox Episcopate of America

"Lord! O Lord! Look down from heaven"

Your Eminence Philip,

Dear Brother and Concelebrant of the Holy Gifts:

The pious clergy and faithful of the Romanian Episcopate join me in offering to you our sincere congratulations on the occasion of the fortieth anniversary of your consecration into the Holy Episcopacy, giving thanks to God for your pastorate in North America!

It is almost four decades since I met you on the occasion of a National Conference of the Holy Archdiocese held in Detroit, Michigan. To be present among the clergy and faithful gathered under your wing as the Antiochian Christian Archdiocese was an event that expanded my experience of Holy Orthodoxy. The same Faith, although with various traditions; the same worship, although with different languages; the same witness, even though fragmented.

An Open Heart to America

You had been recently elevated to be the ruling Hierarch of the Ancient and Venerable Church of

Antioch in North America, and were gathering the reins of your far-flung archdiocese into your capable hands. Your heart was open to North America as wide as are the Great Plains of Mid-America. Being on a fruitful visit to the Parish of Saint George the Great Martyr in Wichita, Kansas, I was greatly moved in observing that these faithful were certain that you would expand, even more, the work of the "Great Commission," which your worthy and honorable predecessor, Anthony Bashir, of thrice-blessed memory, had carried on from his own predecessors. Among these is our Holy father among the saints, Raphael, Bishop of Brooklyn in New York. They saw in you strength, youth, wisdom and love to carry on the work of bringing the scattered sheep of Christ and those who were not yet of his flock, into the sheepfold of eternal salvation.

Now, forty years after I first met you, we remain in the same Faith expressed in various traditions, the same worship expressed in different languages, the same witness in need of administrative unity, of "defragmentation". Four decades ago the word "defragmentation" was hardly known, let alone used as much as it is today. I think that it still may not be very familiar to some who are also called to administrative unity. Through forty years, you have been the leading hierarch for a unity of witness in North America, and it is our prayer that before the conclusion of this outstanding, milestone celebration, your efforts will come to fruition—that defragmentation will be complete!

At the time of our meeting, you were a new member of the SCOBA taking part in its efforts to bring some kind of mutual recognition between the various jurisdictions in North America. Now, with experience and sagacity, you are the strong voice crying in the wilderness of disunity for fulfillment of the re-unification of all Orthodox Christians in North America, as it existed in the time of Saint Raphael. This saint, and model for our own pastorates whose presence was experienced by some still living witnesses, did not shirk from the formidable pastors tasks of his day. His work encompassed exhaustive and uncomfortable travel, the establishment of new communities of immigrants, a "leap of faith" into a yet young and rather wild America and the constant search for and re-uniting of his fellow believers to the Holy Sacraments and to a worshiping community dear to their hearts.

Our Labor Continues

Faces changed, communities expired and communities expanded, communication is made almost instant—but the labor of the shepherd is ever the same, though the path is ever new, as he leads the flock to "safely graze." Through your courage, tempered by wisdom, you opened the sheepfold to those who were searching for the green pasture and the still waters. With your pastoral staff you cracked the isolation of the water-retaining rock to let flow the promise of the Living Water to quench the thirst of a new people, thus refreshing the breadth and width of North America. You send out the invitation: "Come, see and taste how good the Lord is!"

You have provided a home for those who have desired to bring the familiar tents in which they worshiped with them, gracing them with patience and understanding. By your paternal openness you have filled their hearts with peace and refreshment. This cosmopolitan stance brings forth its own fruit and reminds us that, indeed, we worship God in spirit and in truth. New pastors have been set aside to serve this part of your flock and they bask in the order and discipline of love and understanding. They have found the rock of safety.

In SCOBA, in your Synod, in the archdiocese, in *The WORD* and in public addresses, you have not ceased to speak out words of recognition of the joy in our Holy Sacramental Communion. But you have also exhorted all to reconciliation and to a unity of order within their local territorial Church of Christ, that we might enwrap the Church in North America with the un-torn mantle with which she was once adorned. You are a voice, indeed, crying aloud amidst the raucous clamor of our day, a voice reassuring the faithful, strengthening the pastors and echoing in the Synods of North America and abroad.

Through the years, now twenty-five for me as hierarch, we have met and embraced; we have looked into each other's eyes and recognized the pastoral concern for our flocks, for the dignity of Christ's Holy Church, for the illumination of this land into which the Holy Spirit has carried the Holy Orthodox Faith. And then we have each one returned to his sheepfold, to continue the same work of care, of chiding, of reconciling, of lifting, of cleansing, of renewal and of trust and hope in Him who did not leave the apostles and disciples as orphans.

Four Decades Later

Moses accompanied his people forty years through the desert; our Lord tarried with his apostles and disciples forty days after His holy resurrection; and you have walked in front of your people, with them, among them, for them and because of them, for four decades. I recall on various occasions watching you give the hierarchal blessing with the *dikiri, trikiri*, listening to the sonority of your archpastoral exclamation, your plea and prayer, "Lord! O Lord! Look down from heaven. Look at this vine which Your own right hand has planted, visit it and strengthen it." This was the voice of a true pastor, of one who loved his flock and was carrying it back to the Father.

Your Eminence and dear Brother, some shepherds were very young, as were Apostles Titus and Timothy, others were old as Hierarchs Polycarp and Nicholas, each one having received the "grace which fulfills that which is lacking," as his staff of support along the road of his pastorate. Along with this heavenly grace, the Good Shepherd of our souls entrusted you with faithful sheep and pastors, giving human support and love, encouragement and delight, pains and sorrows, tears and sighs. The divine and the human, the weft and the warp shuttling back and forth, day by day, sometimes hour by hour, weave a unique cloth—the gift of your life, your talents, your growth and love. This you give to the Child in the manger, to the Son of Man who has no place to lay His head, to the wounded, pierced Body, to the resurrected Bridegroom, to the ascended Glorified Humanity and to the awesome Judge to come. May He find it an acceptable offering, and may He bestow on the giver the reward of a faithful servant for a work well done!

"Many Years! Many Years! Many Years!"

+ Nathaniel, Archbishop of Detroit, Romanian Episcopate, OCA

Various photos of Metropolitan Philip with His Beatitude, Patriarch Ignatius IV of Antioch.

Below:
In Damascus, with Patriarch Ignatius, Father Joseph Antypas, Fawaz El-Khoury and Dr. George Farha.

Left:
Metropolitan Philip presenting a donation to Father Alexander Schmemann of St. Vladimir's Orthodox Seminary. From left: Mr. Theodore Mackoul, Mr. Zoran Milkovich, Metropolitan Philip, Mr. Mansour Laham, Fr. Alexander Schmemann, Fr. Daniel Hubiak, Bishop Elia, Father Cyril Stavrevsky and Bishop Antoun Khouri.

Below:
Metropolitan Philip with the Evangelical Orthodox clergy when they joined the Antiochian Archdiocese in 1987.

Left:
Meeting of Orthodox bishops in Ligonier, Pennsylvania; November 30, 1994.

Below:
Celebrating the Liturgy with fellow hierarchs at the Archdiocese Convention; 1995. From left: Bishop Demetri, Bishop Basil, Metropolitan Abad, Bishop Antoun, Metropolitan Shadrawi, Metropolitan Philip, Metropolitan Dumit, Bishop Nifon, Bishop Joseph and Metropolitan Damaskinos.

Above:
Metropolitan Philip meeting with Patriarch Alexi of Moscow; September 1997. From left: Dr. George Farha, Fr. Thomas Zain, Patriarch Alexi, Metropolitan Philip, Mr. Robert Koory and Mr. Robert Laham.

Left:
The Metropolitan with Bishop Nifon (the Antiochian Patriarchal Vicar to Moscow), Mrs. Mona Hrawi and May and Raymond Audi.

Above:
Metropolitan Philip with members
of the Holy Synod of Antioch; June 2002.

Left:
Metropolitan Philip with Pope John Paul II in the United States.

Top:
The Metropolitan with all the hierarchs of the Americas and the Archdiocese Board of Trustees.

Bottom:
Metropolitan Philip with students attending the Antiochian House of Studies at the Antiochian Village.

Above: A meeting of the Arab-American delegation of ADC, with Secretary General Kofi Anan and Metropolitan Philip at the United Nations.

Top right: With Metropolitan Elias of Beirut and M.P. Atef Mijdlany, in Beirut, Lebanon.

Middle right: With the President of Syria, Dr. Bashar Al-Assad, and Fawaz El-Khoury, Dr. George Farha and Father Joseph Antypas.

Bottom right: Metropolitan Philip presenting the Antonian Gold Medal upon the Deputy Prime Minister of Lebanon, Isam Fares, and his wife Hala.

Below: With the president of the University of Balamand, Dr. Elie Salem, and Fawaz El-Khoury, at the Archdiocese.

Left:
Metropolitan Philip with all of the Antiochian hierarchs at St. Nicholas Cathedral in Brooklyn, New York; June, 2005.

Bottom left:
Metropolitan Philip with Metropolitan Paul of Australia at the Archdiocese Convention; 2005.

Bottom right:
Metropolitan Philip with Metropolitans Antonio Shedroui and Sergios Abad.

IN THE VIEW OF

His Eminence, Metropolitan Nicholas
Metropolitan of Amissos,
Carpatho-Russian Diocese of the USA

Glory to Jesus Christ!

Beloved Brother in Christ:

I was delighted to learn of festivities marking the fortieth anniversary of your consecration to the episcopal office.

I am certain this historic event will provide you with many memories of clergy, loved ones and friends who were present at your Consecration. The gathering of your brother hierarchs, clergy and faithful will also provide a beautiful panorama of an evolving Orthodoxy in the world and, in particular, North America during these last forty years. This is the memory that you, as well as all Orthodox bishops, will cherish all the days of our lives.

May our great God strengthen you for continued service to the church in the years to come! Our vocation is not an easy one today, and we are sorely tried by the world. I pray that the Holy Spirit bless you with discernment, that all things be made clear and that through your episcopal ministry His Name may be glorified and His will be done.

Wishing you much spiritual joy, and greeting you fraternally as co-worker in the Lord, I remain:

Most sincerely yours in Christ,

+ Metropolitan Nicholas

IN THE VIEW OF

His Grace, Bishop Antoun
Diocese of Miami and the Southeast,
Antiochian Archdiocese

I met Metropolitan Philip in December 1945 at the University of Balamand. For more than sixty-one years of my life I have known this man. When I met him, I did not even know his name. He played a joke on me when we first met. I went to the bishop at the time and told him what this man was doing to me. From that time forward we began to foster a relationship that would last a lifetime, one that is closer than either of us even have with our own families. From those simple and humble beginnings on that beautiful hill in Lebanon, neither of us could have imagined that both of us would come to the U.S and work together many years later.

Different Paths, Same Ending

After our years at Balamand, we found ourselves serving as deacons in the Patriarchal Cathedral of the Dormition in Damascus. Then he left and went to London to study and later returned and taught at the Balamand. All the while I was still in Damascus and teaching in the local Orthodox school.

Later, he decided to immigrate to the United States through Archbishop Samuel David with our friend Father Emil Hanna. This would be a journey that would move him from his birthplace for the rest of his life. I went to Beirut to say goodbye to them, not knowing whether or not our paths would cross again. From 1945 to 1955 I knew him as a young man who was very ambitious, and I can say that, from the beginning, I saw in him the qualities of a leader that I have never seen in any other man.

We communicated while he was in America. After his departure, I went to Brazil and served for a time as a deacon. Not satisfied with my theological education, I asked and then was granted permission to come to the United States to study at St. Vladimir's Seminary. Soon after my arrival, while he was a priest in Cleveland, he called me and asked me to come and see him. I asked him how far it was and he just told me to get on the bus and say "Cleveland," and the driver would tell me where to get off—not to worry. So I took the bus and I kept asking every time the bus stopped, "Is this Cleveland?" It took more than twelve hours on the bus. When I arrived I said to him, "Why did you do that?" He said, "If I told you how far it was, you would not come." He and his parishioners were so generous to me that they sent me back to New York by plane! This was in September, 1959. I was still a deacon and he was a priest at that time. On Epiphany the following year, I returned to Cleveland. The relationship between the two of us is one of a lifetime friendship. If I start to enumerate every step of my life with Metropolitan Philip, I personally would have to write a book.

His Election and Early Episcopacy

After Metropolitan Antony fell asleep in Christ, we were all wondering who would replace him as leader of this vast Archdiocese of the United States and Canada. Among a few of the clergy, who had great trust in him, we talked and decided that the right man to replace Metropolitan Antony was Father Philip Saliba. We voted that he would become the Archbishop of this archdiocese. While his nomination and eventual election were not without problems, as was often the case during that period of our Antiochian history, I truly believe the Holy Spirit acted and chose this young Archimandrite. He called me on August 5, 1966, after the Holy Synod of Antioch met, to tell me he had been elected as the new Metropolitan. He asked me to go with him to Lebanon for the consecration; however, at that time I didn't have the proper legal papers to travel, so I could not accompany him. Nevertheless, I was thankful to God that they elected him to shepherd this archdiocese.

The day after his consecration on August 14, 1966, he went to the Balamand to celebrate the Feast of the Dormition—the main Church's patronal feast day there. They also broke ground for the new theological school. Both of us love the Balamand very much and have such beautiful memories and stories of that place, which we could talk about for years to come.

Suddenly with great zeal and determination, the new Metropolitan decided he wanted to visit every parish of the archdiocese during the first year of his episcopacy, and he killed himself trying to do it. In January 1968, he had his first heart attack. I was a priest in Toronto, Ontario at the time and I couldn't believe it when I heard the news. How could this strong man I knew, the one who used to ring the bells at the Balamand with just two fingers, be stricken like this? For two weeks I couldn't accept it, and in January of that year I flew to New York and took the train to Washington, D.C. I entered the hospital and saw him lying on the bed. I couldn't help but cry for joy that he was still alive. Thank God, with help, he regained his health and in 1969 we invited him to come and visit the parish of St. George in Toronto. After receiving the invitation, he called the parish council chairman at that time and told the chairman to have me, Fr. Antoun, call him back. I called him and he said to me that he had some work for me to do. "By August, I want you to come here and help me in the archdiocese." I couldn't say no to him.

I came to Brooklyn, New York, and worked with him. That same year, I met a young lady named Kathy who moved from San Francisco to become his new secretary. Kathy is still with us in the office after all these years. She can also testify to the work we did in that old house, with the old typewriter that she used. He said to me one time: "Antoun, we hope to build a new headquarters for this archdiocese." This is where Mr. Ted Mackoul began going to New Jersey and looking for a place. Finally, we found a place and moved from Brooklyn to Englewood, New Jersey, in 1971.

From Heart Attack to Vision

In New Jersey, in 1972, he decided to have open-heart surgery. He checked around for different doctors and finally decided on the Miami Heart Institute, in Miami, Florida. I must share a story about the Miami Heart Institute. The night before the operation, in September 1972, he asked me to bring the Bible to him. We were alone in his room. He asked me to read Psalm 50 to him. I looked at his face and he said to me, "I put my hand in the hand of the man who calmed the sea—Christ. If he wants me to live, it is up to him and if my mission is finished, be strong, don't ever give up." Thank God, the next day the doctors called me to go to his room alone. I saw those tubes as he tried to talk to me. I knelt and thanked God; this was something that made my faith stronger because the man I saw in the bed had such a strong faith. Thank God he gained his health back.

After his operation in 1972, he was "dreaming dreams." No one thought that these dreams would become reality in this archdiocese. This man had a vision. Christ wanted him to live and to continue his mission in this archdiocese. After he returned to health, he began organizing the archdiocese into departments and traveling again from parish to parish. In 1977, he invited Patriarch Elias IV, of thrice-blessed memory, to the United States. This marked the first time in history a Patriarch of Antioch set foot on the shores of North America. He later raised money for the Balamand in honor of the late Patriarch Elias IV whom we loved very much.

How could I write or tell all he has done? If one wants to know all he has done, go around the country and see. When he started, we had sixty-five or seventy parishes maximum. Because of his vision and determination, this vast archdiocese has grown and prospered over the years.

A burning issue in the 1970s was the disunity of our Antiochian people in North America. He had seen the dead fruit of such divisions in the old country and read about them in the history of the Church. He felt it was his sacred responsibility to try to unify the two archdioceses in North America. He did indeed unite the two archdioceses, New York and Toledo, together with the late Archbishop Michael. Archbishop Michael became the auxiliary archbishop in 1975 and Metropolitan Philip was the Primate.

Another thing that was foremost in his mind was to better organize the growing archdiocese. It was quickly becoming evident that this was no longer a small one-man operation. In 1973, when we had the archdiocese convention in Atlanta, Georgia, he formed the Antiochian Orthodox Christian Women of North America. He organized them and they wrote a constitution. He worked very hard to have every parish form a chapter. All these women gladly served under his leadership. And without these women in the parishes we couldn't have what we have today. They started to collect money for married seminarians as their first project. That project continues to this day. At Christmas time, each married seminarian receives a check from the ladies. This is but one of the many organizations and departments he developed to help serve the needs of the people of the archdiocese.

Not long after developing these organizations for the ladies, the youth and various departments, he was dreaming about another organization for the entire archdiocese: The Order of St. Ignatius of Antioch. Many people mentioned to him that he would be lucky if he got fifty or sixty members. He said fifty or sixty are better than nothing. He worked very hard and today there are over 3,000 members, all because of his leadership and because this money goes for projects and charities. I never thought that this Order would really become a charitable corner stone of this archdiocese for many reasons; I was surprised!

Shaping History

Around this same time, he entered into negotiations to buy the Antiochian village from the Presbyterians. Many people criticized him saying, "What's that crazy bishop doing buying all that land in the middle of nowhere?" Well, let me tell you he proved them wrong once again and a revolution happened! Today, that place has planted the seeds for many lay leaders, future priests and countless young people who would meet each other and eventually marry. Three years later he built a center with a library, a chapel and 50 rooms. Later on, 50 more rooms were added. If you don't believe it, come and see. This is my motto: "Come and see," like St. Thomas. You cannot imagine today what the Antiochian Village is all about. It is all due to his determination and the love he has for the children and the youth. This is what the Village is all about.

In 1987, he made the decision to accept the Evangelical Orthodox Church. Many jurisdictions in this country said he committed a big blunder by accepting them. Since that time, the Missions Department started in earnest. More than 75 parishes and missions exist today because of his challenge to America to "Come home, America" to the Orthodox Church. The challenge he put to them to establish Churches and bring converts is now a common experience. When I first came to this country, I very seldom saw people converting to our Faith. Today, however, it is happening all the time because of his commitment to evangelization.

In 2000, he experienced his second heart attack in Florida. I was with him and rushed him in my car to the hospital. People said he had little chance, and, in fact, the doctor told me to give him "last rights." I promptly told the doctor we do not have last rights in the Orthodox Church and I will pray for his recovery. Thanks be to God, he recovered again and he survived to continue his dream.

I pray that his health stays strong after his third life-threatening experience of October 2005. Thank God he is back and determined more than ever to finish the work he has set out to do. I am very proud to have been his assistant, as a priest and later as a bishop, in this archdiocese all these years. I pray that God will give him long life so that he may continue to dream dreams and fulfill his Spirit-filled visions.

His life-long friend and co-worker in the Lord's vineyard,

+ Antoun

IN THE VIEW OF

CLOVIS MAKSOUD
DIRECTOR, CENTER FOR THE GLOBAL AMERICAN UNIVERSITY,
WASHINGTON, D.C.

Saidna Philip: A True Statesman

SAIDNA PHILIP'S INFLUENCE GOES FAR BEYOND HIS BELOVED PARISHIONERS. They are the blessed recipients who have become the advocates and practitioners of reconciliation. His commitment—reinforced by devotion, knowledge and openness—has endeared him to the wider Arab-American and the Muslim-American communities. In time of crisis—and there were many—Saidna Philip was the healer, the hopeful and inimitable catalyst who kept the community here in the USA from mirroring the tragic fragmentation abroad. Thus, he planted the seeds of unity and national harmony into émigrés thoughts and beliefs on how things ought to be. While an official in the UN and Washington, I have witnessed his endeavors, his corrective role and his salutary impact in shielding his broad constituency from discriminatory laws and practices.

Uniting New York and Toledo

I vividly remember how he responded graciously to restore the unity of the Orthodox Diocese from the endemic split and thus the magnificent sight at the Louisville Convention in 1976, when the late Archbishop Shaheen enabled the long sought unity to be realized. I was there, at this landmark convention, when what seemed elusive became fulfilled. In a way, that tenth anniversary of Saidna Philip set the stamp of his ongoing legacy.

During the eighties of the twentieth century, when Lebanon was in the grip of conflict—sectarian and otherwise—he presided over the most sizeable interfaith board, which has continued to enrich and maintain the stamina required for unity among all faiths. After September 11, 2001, this stamina was put to the test. While certain tensions ensued, Saidna Philip's spiritual resourcefulness and built-in wisdom continued their healing role.

And Today

On his fortieth year of accession, Metropolitan Philip retains the freshness of his creative and inspiring leadership. In a way, the challenge for all of us is to render the quality of his dynamic, positive and progressive role contagious. This is especially important to the nation that he came from, so that the unity and the culture of human liberation and sustainable development that he promotes in his country of adoption would also be Saidna's gift to the patrimony of our forefathers in Lebanon.

In one sentence: Saidna Philip has rendered the term "Saidna" not only his deserved religious title, but also one that all of us accept spontaneously and enthusiastically. His endearing presence among us all is a binding contract that emboldens and enriches our lives and provides us with incentives to follow his path.

     —Clovis Maksoud

     Director, Center for the Global South, American University, Washington, DC

IN THE VIEW OF

SHEIKH SAMI MERHI
CHAIRMAN, THE DRUZE COUNCIL OF NORTH AMERICA

And He found Philip and said to him, "Follow Me." (John 1:43)

ON THE OCCASION OF THE FORTIETH ANNIVERSARY OF METROPOLITAN PHILIP, I take this opportunity to congratulate His Eminence and the Antiochian Orthodox Church of North America, and convey my best heartfelt feelings of commonality and brotherhood.

A Man of Unity

It has been over a quarter of a century since I first met His Eminence. Over the years we have become as close as blood brothers. Very few people we meet in our lifetime become instantly as close as family. My working relationship with His Eminence started after the break of the civil war in our beloved Lebanon, which was anything but civil. Then came the brutal invasion of Lebanon by Israel in 1982. We mobilized our human and material resources for Lebanon's salvation. Through the Standing Conference of Christian and Muslim Leaders in North America, which represented the entire Arab-American family, Metropolitan Philip was elected the Chairman of the conference, and I served as its secretary. Over the years we held meetings with United States Presidents, Secretaries of State and members of the United States Congress in order to bring an end to the suffering of the people of Lebanon under occupation. Numerous resolutions and statements were jointly signed by all members of the conference in a show of unity, which sent a message to the world that the Lebanese people and Lebanon were victimized by a biased media that portrayed the Lebanese War as being based only on sectarianism, i.e., a war between Christians and Muslims. The solidarity of the members of the Conference was a vivid demonstration of unity, tolerance and cooperation, and that is the perennial reality of Lebanon.

I can unequivocally say that Metropolitan Philip's leadership and compassion qualify him as the Metropolitan of all Arab-Americans, and that is what makes him not only unique, but very special. In 1985, the American Druze Society (of which I was serving as National President at the time), was holding its annual Convention in Los Angeles, California. This Convention coincided with a visit of his Beatitude, Patriarch Ignatius IV of Antioch in California. I called Metropolitan Philip and shared with him my thought that it would be a great idea for the Patriarch to come to the Druze Convention to bless and officiate the grand opening of the Convention. Metropolitan Philip reflected on the idea and said: "Sami, it's a good idea." While considering the situation on the ground in Lebanon (specifically the events of the war in Mount Lebanon involving the fighting between the various sectarian militias), we came to the conclusion that it was just *because* of this sectarian fighting that we should-and must-come together as a community to demonstrate our understanding of tolerance and cooperation. We had to do this so that we would be a genuine example of exactly the opposite of what was being portrayed about us. Needless to say, the Patriarch, joined by Metropolitan Philip and six other bishops, came to the Convention, and were welcomed by the ADS Board of Elders, myself and members of the Board of Directors. A standing ovation by over 500 members of the ADS greeted the guests in the Grand Ballroom. After being introduced, the Patriarch stood up to speak and made the most humble statement by a head of a Church to a Druze gathering by announcing that he was the student of the late Sheikh Nassib Makarem. Once again, the Assembly stood up in a huge applause. He gave a short speech, advocating our belief that we are a family of one, and that this is how the Lebanese should live their lives: in togetherness—for that would be the only salvation for Lebanon. The Patriarch and Metropolitan left thirty minutes later and to this day I believe we made history together. We showed the world the good values of the Arab family when the media reported this event by announcing: "Orthodox Christian Patriarch blessed and officiated the Druze Convention in Los Angeles." That was an historical day Metropolitan Philip helped to make happen.

Trips Abroad

In August of 1990, a close friend of mine called me from Liberia and told me of a grave situation on the ground: a group had captured over a hundred Lebanese and Syrian nationals and were holding them hostage, while there were also hundreds of people caught in the crossfire of the war and who were without food, water and medical assistance. I immediately called Metropolitan Philip and advised him of this tragic situation. He asked me to call members of the Standing Conference for an emergency meeting at the archdiocese. After the meeting, a joint statement was signed and was sent to the White House requesting President Bush to intervene, to bring an end to this battle and to free the hostages. Then the Metropolitan got on the phone and spoke to Governor John Sununu, who was the Chief of Staff for President Bush at that time. Within forty-eight hours, the United States Marines intervened and helped rescue and evacuate seven hundred and ten citizens by helicopter and ship from Monrovia, Liberia to Freetown, Sierra Leone. Under his leadership, the Standing Conference made history that day.

In 1991, his Eminence asked that I join him and members of the archdiocese on an official visit to Syria and Lebanon. We arrived in Damascus to an official welcome, and he was received as the equivalent of a head of state. One day we traveled to a beautiful village called Ma'aloula. This village is built inside a rocky mountain and as we visited one of the oldest churches, I walked into a historical bookshop where I spotted one of the oldest and most beautiful icons I have ever seen. The sales lady said this icon was over 150 years old, and one of the most valuable icons they carried. I said, "Name your price." To make a long story short, I was able to buy that historical piece of artwork and went to present the Metropolitan with it as a belated birthday gift. I said, "Your Eminence, I don't think I could ever present to you a better birthday gift," and as he looked at it, his eyes lit up and a tear was touchingly observed. He said to me as we hugged, "Thank you very much: this icon will take its place at the Antiochian Village in Pennsylvania."

During the four-day trip to Damascus, we had a private meeting with President Hafiz Asad. The meeting was scheduled to take place in Damascus, but due to the President's illness, he sent a private aircraft to take us from Damascus to Latakia. As we sat across from each other in the plane writing our notes for the meeting with the President, the Metropolitan leaned over and said: "Sheikh Sami, what things do you think we should be discussing with the President?" Surprisingly, when we compared notes, it was as if the same person wrote them. Our sense of nationalism, responsibility and deep care for our people and our country were similar.

After a four-hour meeting with President Asad, I thought we gave the most sincere and compelling ideas on how to end the Lebanese conflicts. On our way to Damascus, *en route* to Lebanon, which we were supposed to travel by car, the United States Ambassador to Syria advised us against traveling to Lebanon because of the fighting that was taking place that week. We then contacted His Eminence Metropolitan Elias Audi in Beirut, to ask his opinion about this new development and to seek the advice of the American Embassy. Metropolitan Audi replied via a fax encouraging us to come and promising that if anything happened to any of us, he would have a royal funeral. While laughing at the text of his facts, we headed for Lebanon and fortunately for Metropolitan Audi, he was saved the expense of a royal funeral!

Memorable Moments

The late and beloved Hala Salam Maksoud, who was the President of ADC in 1998, invited the Metropolitan to be the keynote speaker at the Convention of the ADC in Washington, D.C. She asked me to introduce him to the Assembly. Our plane to Washington, D.C., was delayed for hours on end until finally we were told we could not take off due to poor weather *en route* to D.C. Unfortunately, we were not able to attend the event. The Metropolitan asked me to join him for dinner in his residence. We faxed over his speech to Mrs. Maksoud, and his brother, Doctor Najib Saliba, read his speech. When we arrived at his home in Englewood, the Metropolitan told me, while holding his speech in his hand: "You know Sami, I had written a wonderful speech, let me read it to you." I told him: "No, please stop, let me first introduce you." So as we sat there, just the two of us, I formally introduced him and he formally read his speech!

There are many memorable moments that we shared over the years that remain a sustaining factor in our ongoing friendship.

I would like to end this tribute by affirming that we, as a people and a nation, are blessed by the Almighty God, who gave us one of the most compassionate persons, Metropolitan Philip, whom we have the privilege of knowing. As a man who left his beautiful village of Abou Mizan in 1955, on his journey to the United States, I am sure he will forever remember when his blessed late mother, Saleema, grabbed onto the side of the car that Metropolitan Philip was seated in, and said to him: "I want to see you again." This historical journey continued as he embarked on a mission to serve humanity and write history. He excelled at both. I know that he has always been motivated by a quote from the Holy Bible that reads: "To whom much is given, much is required." May God bless him and give him many, many years of health and peace of mind.

When the righteous are in authority, the people rejoice. (Proverbs 29:2)

—Sami Merhi

# IN THE VIEW OF

Beshara Merhej
Former Minster of the Interior, and Former Member of Parliament, Lebanon

The Inspired Philip Saliba

The Inspired One

METROPOLITAN PHILIP SALIBA HAS A SPECIAL PLACE IN MY HEART. I confess having been deeply influenced by his distinguished personality and by his most daring and open positions, as well. Such positions have inspired me and have given me incentives to make some important and difficult decision in my own life. I have followed his journey and struggles since he returned to Dhour Shweir, Lebanon, in 1966, at the Holy Synod meeting, which convened at the St. Elias Patriarchal Monastery. That day, my dad, who is closely related to the Metropolitan, had affirmed to me that the Synod would elect Father Philip "Metropolitan for North America." I told my dad: "How can you anticipate this decision?" He answered: "I read that in the eyes of the big delegation from America. Their love for him is immeasurable. They are certain that the Synod will take their feeling into consideration and will consequently respond to their wishes, as the delegates represent, truly, the clergy and laity of the North American Archdiocese." The monastery's bell tolls announced the election of its venerable son, Philip, as Metropolitan of North America. This was music in the ears of the members of the delegates, which soon spread to the surrounding villages and towns. I learned then the meaning of collaboration and planning. Since that day, the more I became acquainted with Metropolitan Philip, his deeds and accomplishments, the more my love and appreciation for him have increased.

A True Antiochian

Metropolitan Philip was the object of severe criticism on many occasions. Some even expressed doubts about his Antiochian commitment and the desire to sever relations with the Mother Church. I found myself, without being asked to do so and without any planning, opposing such doubts. And this occurred because of my deep confidence and conviction of Saidna Philip's genuine belonging to the Antiochian Church, and his having lifted her banner high in America. Later the truth was revealed to all those vulnerable to superficial doubts. Naturally, Metropolitan Philip forgave those who trespassed against him, gaining the love of those who are far and near.

Metropolitan Philip Saliba is a shining historic figure in the life of the Antiochian Church and is worthy of this unique position. Because of his additions and contributions, the Antiochian Archdiocese experienced a renaissance. Established by his righteous predecessor, and continued by Metropolitan Philip, this has become a vast archdiocese, with many institutions, and holds a remarkable and effective presence in the new continent. His care is not limited only to his children in religious and social levels, for he has also assisted and contributed to those who live in the Middle East. He worked to reconcile the crises that emerged from the civil war. It is important to point out that Metropolitan Philip, like other great leaders, spear-headed his team worker—focusing on planning, executing and maintaining. He knew how to inspire his assistants and spiritual children in order to instill in them the importance of responsibility, productivity and excellence of work. He showed them how construction is an ongoing experience, maintained by stewards, who incorporate beauty of service with an admiration of belonging.

The secret behind his efforts, which made such contributions of the spirit tangible for all to feel, is Metropolitan Philip's faith and hope, which is expressed with a message, a vision and a determination. This truth is revealed in him as a bright light that scatters the surrounding darkness of those who toil and are afraid, and opens a wide gate to those who return in repentance and faith. It is not unusual for someone who possesses all these virtues to transcend the norm, and to ascend from one height to another while invincibly performing good deeds, witnessing to the holiness of pursuit and the determination of will.

A Person of Hope

Despair and stillness have no place in his prestigious gathering. There, life emanates as from a vineyard producing oil and wine; these are the gifts, given to those who toil in the vineyard. In this respect, Metropolitan Philip rejected all ritualism as being fossilized and repetitious. He preferred to follow the school of the Master, rebelling against thieves and merchants of the Temple. It is true that he has lived in the United States most of his life; nevertheless, he did not lose his deep roots. He has been firm in his love for being Lebanese and an Arab by culture. He became a hopeful refuge to all Arabs in America, especially to the Palestinians, who knew his commitment and faith towards *al-Quds* (Jerusalem) and for their national and human rights.

From the perspectives of faith and adherence to heritage, Saidna Philip took many risks, which became the property of his generation. He grew up in a family which experienced needs, though it continued to build and plant the seed. He realized that perseverance and struggle are both needed in order to transform rocks into "living stones," which can erect an elegant structure.

Productive but Not Arrogant

From his youth, then, Metropolitan Philip realized that life was a gift, which cannot be taken for granted. He moved forward in education and perseverance. He reached a high position in church ministry. His spiritual children and those who know him have witnessed his dignified presence and the humility with which he washes the feet of his peers, expressing his constant dependence on his Redeemer. He works in all places and all times to bring forth religious awakening, encouraging his spiritual children at every gathering to set aside self interest and close-mindedness. This is the reason why he is abundantly productive without being arrogant. His main mission is to care for the future generations, leading them to the lofty Christian virtues and the pure springs of the Eastern message, establishing their faith in their Redeemer. In this way, he is expressing his passion for the stones of *al-Quds*, the bells of Bethlehem and the footsteps of Nazareth. His joy is to see the youth adopt the Message, to rid themselves of extremism, disintegration and vices, which rob societies of their spirit, shake their faith, damage their thoughts, falsify their will and transform them into monsters that exploit the poor and are motivated only by their desires. God has given Saidna Philip many gifts and placed a great mystery in him. This is indeed the gift that transforms individuals into organic units, working together in remarkable coordination for well-being and goodness.

How bright is the gift of giving in every time, and how beautiful is the grace of a worthy recipient.

 **IN THE VIEW OF**

Ghassan S. Skaf, m.d.
Department of Surgery, Division of Neurosurgery,
American University of Beirut

It was both a blessing and a pleasure to meet with His Eminence Metropolitan Philip in Lebanon in the 1960s through my late uncle and his dear friend, the Metropolitan Archbishop of Hama, Athanasios Skaff. Back then I was a growing child, but every time we had a chance to meet, he always made me feel loved, welcomed and, most of all, very comfortable in talking to him, about any subject, despite the age difference. His words of encouragement have driven me since: "Always aim high. Work hard and you will get there somehow…but always aim high." From then on, my fate to become a surgeon became less a matter of chance, and more a matter of choice and personal character. As my parents and late uncle Archbishop Skaff recognized and supported my desire and potential to become a physician, I carried this notion of "aiming high" into every aspect of my life: my education, my social circle, my meticulousness in daily activities, and most certainly, in practicing medicine. The resonance of his calm and reassuring words are still echoing in my mind. While I never awoke on a given morning realizing I was going to become a surgeon, a true realization of the degree of my determination for personal advancement led to my acceptance for training in neurological surgery in the United States. There, Metropolitan Philip soon became a very dear friend, a mentor and a spiritual father.

A Christian Wise Man

Our beloved Metropolitan Philip has made me realize that Christianity means the creation of holy bonds of love and friendship with God and people, and not only those with which we deal. These bonds have led His Eminence to seek my opinion of his medical problems and helped me develop abilities to both lead and serve. We all know that he has a valuable circle of trustworthy friends and parish councils. As such, he has set an example for me of how "a wise man will hear, and will increase learning; and a man of understanding shall attain unto wise counsels" (Proverbs 1:5), for "in the multitude of counselors there is safety" (Proverbs 11:14). In this process, he has also shown me how to respect and seek the insight of even "one's much younger children."

"The disciples were called Christians first in Antioch" (Acts 11:26). Our Antiochian heritage is a blessed holy gift from God, manifested also in great openness to different civilizations, cultures and religions.

Through the grace of God, the continuous enlightenment of the Holy Spirit and the guidance, love, and prayers of the holy fathers of our Faith, we have been blessed with a spiritual revival in the East, and with new groups joining our Church in the USA. Part of the revival in the East was due to the genuine moral and material support of Saidna Philip to the University of Balamand and other institutions. The creation of these new institutions has been a blessed fruit of the "marriage" of the work of the Holy Spirit with the wise vision and missionary leadership of Metropolitan Philip.

Growth in North America

The spiritual and cultural richness of our Orthodox Christianity is, as a Russian theologian said, "not a warm oven but a nuclear reactor which stimulates great achievements. However, that depends on the reaction." For a nuclear reaction to happen, one needs first to clean and remove un-needed elements. Then one needs to create the right and proper conditions by bringing the elements very near to each other and then applying the right energy for the reaction to start.

The growth that was achieved in our Church in North America has been a clear example of such a successful reaction. Our beloved Antiochian Orthodox Church at large has most of the elements need and a great potential to actually create such a nuclear reaction. If we blend the spiritual and humanistic wealth of our Eastern Christian heritage with the missionary and organizational talents of our dedicated and beloved North American members, wonders can occur. We could offer a potent Orthodox medication and an Orthodox treatment to an ailing modern world, thirsty for the true Spirit.

Being Led by the Holy Spirit

As St. Augustine said: "Love God and do what you want."

This was, is and how we would like the Antiochian Orthodox Church to be: a Church of love, which effectively and creatively serves its children, who are dispersed all over the globe. We would like our Holy Antiochian Church to be always light and agile, carried and led by the Spirit to where the Spirit desires.

I do believe that such agility, effectiveness and creativity have been demonstrated to a great extent during the past forty years in our Church in North America, thanks to the efforts of our beloved Metropolitan Philip.

I have lived in North America and am now working in an American institution in Lebanon, the American University of Beirut (AUB). At AUB, I see a challenging task of applying advanced modern management practices in the Middle East. This also makes me think about globalization and the power of the multinational institutions that apply advanced management tools in any country in which they work.

Saidna Philip has been blessed with a holy gift from God and this has led to the expansion of our beloved Church in North America. His successful and effective management of our Church in the US and Canada, and the dynamic interaction between clergy and laity is an example from which to learn. Our situation and our environment in the Middle East are very challenging. Just as the Protestants and

Catholics had a call to come to the Middle East and found successful institutions, I believe that our Orthodox Church in North America has a similar call: of humbly helping our Church in the Middle East improve its managerial practices and its missionary work.

On another dimension, there is the need to establish effective bonds and cooperation amongst the different Orthodox Christians—both in North America and worldwide. This is another challenge, which I believe has always been in Saidna Philip's mind and heart.

It seems that God has entrusted the Antiochian Church, since its foundation, with the task of blending different cultures and ethnicities, using Christianity as the only bonding force. Today, it remains a gigantic and daunting task, and probably the Antiochian Orthodox Church is still called to be the active catalyst in creating new Orthodox bonds.

The Way I See You

My dearly beloved Metropolitan Philip, I am both proud and thankful that such a compassionate leader leads the Orthodox Church of North America, possessing spiritual and moral qualities, together with strength, love and justice for all. This is truly the way I see you.

God has given you talents and already the talents have been multiplied; yet we and, we are sure, God would like to see more! My eyes keep looking in two directions: one eye on some of the current and future challenges and potentials that are facing our Church, and another eye on your great achievements.

Words fall short of expressing the great love and appreciation I hold for you, and my gratitude to God for giving you as a gift to both the Church and to me.

May the holy seeds that you have planted, and which have already given fruits, grow more and more, spread more and more, and bear more and more fruit during your earthly life and beyond. What you planted is deeply rooted in Christ.

May every new day of your earthly life be full of growth in holiness and glory, and may God grant the same growth to our beloved Orthodox Church through your wise guidance in the Holy Spirit.

—Ghassan S. Skaf, MD, FRCSC, FACS

Head, Division of Neurosurgery, Department of Surgery

American University of Beirut; Beirut, Lebanon

IN THE VIEW OF

NADIM SHWAYRI
FOUNDER OF *AL KAFAAT*

The Righteous Son of America

PHILIP, THE RIGHTEOUS SON OF ANTIOCH:

It is axiomatic to say that the Holy Church is in a continuous state of being under God's care. The Church may experience periods of vulnerability, and may live through crises of deterioration, stillness and captivity; however, the divine providence surrounds her in the person of a "savior" who moves her in the direction of her sacred mission.

Philip the Reformer: What He Has Accomplished
Metropolitan Philip Saliba is a reformer who is representative of this line of rare and distinguished "saviors". He has produced and witnessed action throughout the forty years of his episcopacy. So, "come and see."

I do confess my inability to cover all aspects of Metropolitan Philip's accomplishments. However, I am certain, and convinced, that what he has accomplished has indeed enriched Orthodoxy, via its

Antiochian Gate; he has brought Antioch to the everlasting spring of life, through his example in North America. His legacy puts Antioch in line with contemporary life; he takes his responsibility for the universal Church.

Saidna Philip granted great value to the laity, and made them an essential partner in the life of the Church. He has created a return to the Antiochian legacy, which enriches the intellectual, spiritual and material direction of the faithful. Without such input and lay participation, says Saidna Philip, the Church will lose its holy and genuine character; its sacramental and liturgical services will become useless. The Church is not the people, alone, on the one hand, and the priest as shepherd on the other hand. The Church becomes alive only in as much as there is creative interaction between the shepherd and the people, bringing forth fruit, energy and love. Without interacting and collaborating, the parish will reach mediocrity, and become frozen in some traditional, barren and dry "clericalism". The Church as lived by Saidna Philip is a workshop of continuous labor, in communion with God's grace; like bees, each one has a role to fulfill and a contribution to make within active and serious parochial ministry. In such a creative and dynamic understanding, the parish becomes the unity of life. Its active members demonstrate their love of God by living like Christ and enriching all potentials for serving men.

His Struggle

Philip has struggled throughout the years of his episcopacy in a practical way: he works to reach a high level of integration and to bring real partnership in establishing parishes. No wonder that in forty years the number of parishes quadrupled. These parishes brought together the Antiochian youngsters in North America through building the Antiochian Village. They also established the House of Studies, preparing pastors to gain theological education with high spiritual and ethical standards, and enabling them to successfully work with the laity in order to develop and improve parochial life. The building of parishes—furnishing them with people and material needs—takes on a true spiritual dimension when we realize that the goal behind all this work is to actualize the principle of the "Church as servant." This can be done only through deeds rendered unto men. Metropolitan Philip's motto, and his principle of fulfilling his social, spiritual and cultural goals during the years of his episcopacy, have permeated the scope of his archdiocese and reached the Mother Church of Antioch. This includes countries and nations stricken with poverty and decadence, as well as regions afflicted by severe natural disasters. All this stems from his reading of Matthew 22:40: "You shall love your neighbor as yourself. On these two commandments depend all the law and the prophets." Love of God and serving man are treated on the same level.

Evangelization and Practical Ministry

Metropolitan Philip is exemplary in combining evangelization within the framework of practical ministry. The Order of St. Ignatius, which he founded, stands today at almost three thousand members, who are working together and fulfilling their ministry under his care. The Antiochian Orthodox Christian Women also continues to financially support diverse projects in Latin America and in the Middle East.

By all these life accomplishments, Metropolitan Philip launched a renaissance in the Church of Antioch, connecting it with its remarkable past. Ministering to men is our Church's great and suffering legacy. St. Basil the Great established health centers in Cappadocia, and St. John Chrysostom did the same thing in Constantinople; both of them were emulated by Islam in the East and by Latin Europe during the middle ages.

The depth and maturity of Saidna Philip brought him into contact with the legacy of Antioch, and led to his openness to orthodoxy as a whole. He welcomes all those who are seeking salvation in Christ. In Antioch the disciples of Christ were first called Christians. It is obvious that this visionary, this man of great faith, should have called the Standing Conference of the Canonical Orthodox Bishops in the Americas (SCOBA), where each hierarch has an independent administrative structure under the united mandate of the Mother churches. He has called them to work together towards an apostolic and united church, based on mutual love, and abiding by the principle of respecting their unique liturgical particularities. He has often called them to quit being an expression of some polemical 'orthodoxies,' as expressed by the French Orthodox theologian, Olivier Clement.

Bringing Forth a Renaissance

The religious, social and diverse cultural activities that have flourished in the past four decades under the episcopacy of Saidna Philip have given the Antiochian faithful, wherever he may be, a deep and pure sense of belonging to the Church. We hope that this renaissance will reach all the regions of the Church of Antioch. This will bring into focus the level of challenge that has been met in the example of the Antiochian Archdiocese in North America. With good efforts, the Church of Antioch can establish an ecumenical mission of building bridges and strengthening relations with the Mother Church of Constantinople and with the world of Orthodoxy as a whole, i.e., to enrich the Church and deepen its legacy.

I do not exaggerate if I say that Church history will bestow Saidna Philip's name to this era in the history of the Church of Antioch. He is a leader among those who have worked for many centuries and who continue to awaken the Church from its captivity, those who resurrect its ministry and service and those who protect the glorious Antiochian heritage in its march to the heavenly Father.

—Nadim Shwayri

IN THE VIEW OF

HIS GRACE, BISHOP JOSEPH
DIOCESE OF LOS ANGELES AND THE WEST
ANTIOCHIAN ARCHDIOCESE

Metropolitan Philip's Profound Leadership in America

ON THE OCCASION OF THE FORTIETH ANNIVERSARY of His Eminence's consecration to the episcopacy, I cannot help but reflect upon the great legacy he has built up for future generations, both in America and throughout the world.

Saidna's Place in the Antiochian Legacy

In America, I have witnessed the foundations being laid for an ever-growing archdiocese that will change the face of America. Beginning with the ministry of St. Raphael almost one hundred years ago, the Antiochian presence in North America has steadily grown, both in number and influence. This ministry, which was once limited to the immigrant Orthodox, has grown under the direction of Metropolitan Philip. He has taken up the mantle of leadership amongst the various Orthodox communities.

Beginning with the decision of the late Metropolitan Anthony Bashir, of thrice-blessed memory, to translate the services of the Church into English, the Antiochian Archdiocese became committed to serving the people of America. When he passed into a Place of Rest, the Holy Synod of Antioch elected a young, missionary-oriented priest to take the lead.

It is a great challenge to work with His Eminence to balance out the needs of immigrants and their descendents with those of the ever-rising number of converts and non-Orthodox Americans marrying into Orthodox families. This trial often causes lesser hierarchs to fail, as they support one group to the detriment of the other. Metropolitan Philip's vision of Orthodoxy in North America is one of inclusion, not exclusion.

Unity, the Fruit of Inspiration

Unity is not something imposed; it is the fruit of inspiration. His Eminence has succeeded in inspiring people to share their talents and resources with the Church, and we have developed ministries that are seen nowhere else in the Orthodox Church. From the Antiochian Village (by far the largest and most successful summer camping program in the Church) to the St. Stephen's Program (bringing modern American directed reading learning into the Orthodox education experience), along with many other departments and organizations, our ministries are setting new standards in ministry.

As we celebrate this joyous occasion, we must remember that God has given us many blessings for which we are grateful. In gratitude to Him, we must be faithful to our Antiochian heritage and the path set forth by our beloved Archbishop Philip. We must continue to move forward as a missionary community, inspired by our Metropolitan's visionary leadership. Though we are certain to have more necessary changes in how we do things, what we strive for must never change. Our calling is to continue to preach the Good News to this great nation and bring those who hear this message to God.

Openness to Change

Our growth necessitates change. Certainly we cannot grow from a little over sixty parishes in 1966 to over 260 parishes now and not expect our ways of doing things to change. Our Metropolitan realized this and initiated the process, which led to our newly granted self-ruled status. With the establishment of dioceses and the consecration of new bishops for North America, the Metropolitan has built up a Synod of hierarchs who will continue to work with him in the vineyard of this archdiocese for years to come.

Since 1966 Metropolitan Philip has added greatly to the talents given to him by the Master of all. He has united the separated Antiochian communities into a single family and has built up the infrastructure of our archdiocese. He has worked hard to encourage the work of SCOBA, to spread the unity of our archdiocese to the rest of the churches in North America.

Saidna's Commitment and Mission

When His Eminence recommended to the Holy Synod of Antioch that I come to America, I knew of His Eminence mostly by his reputation in the Middle East. There he is known as a leader who has maintained close bonds to our beloved Patriarchate and the people there. He has been ready to lend a helping hand to many institutes and organizations, and he has been very supportive of His Beatitude Patriarch Ignatius IV. He was also key in the creation and sustaining of the University of Balamand, one of the great educational institutes in the region. As I got to know him here, however, I became more and more aware of his acute sense of leadership in North America.

His greatest mission is to bring America to Orthodoxy. Following the footstep of Saints Peter and Paul, Metropolitan Philip's mission is to *reorient the American culture towards Orthodoxy.* As the Bishop of Los Angeles and the West, I have been blessed to co-work with His Eminence in implementing this mission in the heart of a diocese in which the process of conversion was initiated by a group of beloved clergy and laity.

I believe the key of His Eminence's success has been his commitment to the Gospel of our Lord Jesus Christ and to the Apostolic Tradition of Antioch. By never forgetting that we are an Orthodox

Christian community, rather than a member of this or that ethnicity, he has been able to minister to all the varieties of needs of our diverse communities. However, relying on His Eminence's vision of universal ministry and fearless evangelization, we find that outreach is not a difficulty for us. We keep "first things first," never compromising the Gospel for the temptations of self-indulgence that has brought down so many others.

This bond of trust is the backbone of our Local Holy Synod. The cannons of the Church call the bishops and the metropolitan to be of "one mind," which can only be if we trust the Lord and one another. I believe that our confidence in one another, and our Metropolitan's trust in us, is central to the continuation of the good works the Lord has wrought in our archdiocese.

As do all the faithful of this God-protected archdiocese, I pray that His Eminence enjoys many more years of good health and fruitful ministry in North America!

With thanks to God,

+ J oseph

Bishop of Los Angeles and the West

Antiochian Orthodox Christian Archdiocese of North America

 **IN THE VIEW OF**

His Grace, Bishop Basil
Bishop of Wichita and the Diocese of Mid-America
Antiochian Archdiocese

So Many Miracles!

IT'S STRANGE. I CAN RECALL WITH ABSOLUTE CLARITY (something that seems to get rarer and rarer for me with each year—clarity of recollection, that is) so many moments when the mighty river we know as His Eminence Metropolitan Philip overflowed the levy and came rushing into my life. Here are but a very few:

On first Hearing Saidna's Name

It was Sunday, August 23, 1966, when, for the first time, I heard his name elevated during the divine services at my home parish of St. Michael in Monessen, Pennsylvania. "For our Father and Metropolitan Philip, for the venerable priesthood, the deaconate in Christ, for all the clergy and the people, let us pray to the Lord." Having served at that holy table for thirteen years (ever since my paternal grandfather, Giddoo Slabey, first took me into the sanctuary when I was four years old) I had never until that moment heard any other name elevated as "our Father and Metropolitan" except that of the late Metropolitan Antony, of thrice-blessed memory.

It was not very long after that that the new "Father and Metropolitan" of our archdiocese was coming for his first archpastoral visit to southwestern Pennsylvania—not to our tiny parish in Monessen, but to our sister parish of St. Michael in nearby Greensburg, Pennsylvania. Since the Esseys made up a good portion of the choir in Monessen, none of my family could go to Greensburg for the Hierarchical Divine Liturgy, but my Godfather (my paternal Uncle George), Uncle Emil and other uncles and aunts invited me to go along with them for the grand banquet. I can still see the banquet room with the young and vibrant bishop (until then I thought one had to be old to be a bishop). I can even still see the thick black frames of his eyeglasses—thick black frames were way cool in 1966! And most of all, I can still hear his clear voice booming to the furthest reaches of that vast banquet hall. I remember that I hung on every syllable and wished that he would never stop speaking those words of Holy Orthodoxy!

My First Meeting with Him

It was on Saturday, July 4, 1970 that I traveled to the Eastern Region SOYO Convention (the title hadn't yet been changed to Parish Life Conference) at the Seven Springs Resort in southwestern Pennsylvania to be interviewed by Metropolitan Philip concerning my desire to enter St. Vladimir's Seminary that fall. I was so nervous—after all this was the Archbishop of New York and AAAAAAAAAALL North America—that I couldn't drive myself, so I asked Afif Elias, son of my parish priest, to go with me.

I remember the drive there; I remember waiting in the hotel lobby and purchasing a three-barred silver neck cross for my father; I remember going up to and into the Metropolitan's suite; I remember seeing him sitting on the couch, and then I remember leaving Seven Springs. For the life of me I can't remember one second of the interview itself! You'll say, "After all, that was thirty years ago," and you'd be right. But I clearly remember that even when I was driving away from Seven Springs those thirty years ago, I had no idea what he had said to me or what I had said to him. To be honest, I didn't even remember breathing while I was with him.

As a Seminarian and Youth Director

Fast-forward to early November 1970, and I recall so very clearly driving with other Antiochian seminarians from St. Vladimir's Seminary to the old archdiocesan chancery at 239-85th Street in Brooklyn. We went down Henry Hudson Drive, past two very tall buildings that had just been built (the 'Twin Towers' of the World Trade Center) and large sheets of ice blew off the upper floors of those buildings and onto our windshield. I remember going through the Brooklyn-Battery Tunnel and pulling up to the modest house where we were warmly greeted by His Eminence Father Antoun Khouri and Miss Kathy Meyer. We first went upstairs (was it to the third floor?) where in the tiny chapel we chanted Vespers. We then retired to the dining room on the first floor for what was to be my first "Seminarian Dinner" with Metropolitan Philip.

I clearly remember the day (June 10, 1975) I arrived at the new archdiocesan chancery in Englewood, New Jersey, to work for His Eminence as the first director of the Department of Youth Affairs. He sat me down in the living room and said: "You are welcome to live here with Father Antoun and me, but we live a very simple life like monks. Since you are a young man, you should have your own apartment." I did find my own place on East Edsall Avenue in nearby Palisade Park—and twenty-eight years later I was tonsured a monk!

Other Recollections

Like so many others who know and love Metropolitan Philip, I could go on and on with personal recollections—like that summer day in 1976 when, during a lay-over at Chicago's O'Hare Airport, His Eminence (at that time the sole bishop serving our archdiocese) shared with me his vision that one day a synod of bishops would serve our Antiochian Archdiocese; or his announcing to me in August of

1979 that I was to be ordained a celibate deacon on September 30 during the first St. Thekla Pilgrimage at the Antiochian Village; or my ordinations to the subdeaconate, the deaconate, the priesthood, my elevation to the episcopacy; or that wonderfully liberating conversation with him in his suite at the Village about my desire to be tonsured a monk.

So many memories! Memories of a young Metropolitan who over the past forty years has become the most venerable and esteemed leader of Holy Orthodoxy in our nation, and memories of a young college student who over the past forty years became a devoted son and now serves as a fellow bishop with him whose name we all still elevate with love at each divine service—"Our Father and Metropolitan Philip." May the Lord God remember his High Priesthood in His kingdom always. Many years, Saidna, "Many Years!"

+ Basil

# IN THE VIEW OF

His Grace, Bishop Thomas
Diocese of Oakland, Pennsylvania and the East
Antiochian Archdiocese

Metropolitan Philip is one of the great leaders of our Church. During the last century into this century there have been many great men and women of faith. But none of them have done more to further the cause of Christ than this bishop, who was born in Lebanon. Trying times require the best *of* men and the best *from* men. That is exactly what the Church has gotten from Metropolitan Philip. During our times the Church has faced insidious heresy, and during our times this man has done combat against it. On several occasions his great struggle for truth has brought him near peril. However, such was not God's will. Instead he has spent the last forty years of his adult life in a courageous fight for the truth. He is one of the great Fathers of Orthodoxy. During his lifetime he has written several books, many of which were penned as pastoral works. His biography is a best seller. As one of the greatest leaders of our time his legacy, like a beacon, continues to shine.

To speak of and admire him fully would perhaps be too long a task. Metropolitan Philip is noble in action, humble in mind, unapproachable in virtue, very approachable in conversation, gentle, sympathetic and sweet in words, angelic in appearance, more angelic in mind, calm in rebuke and persuasive in praise. His disposition has sufficed for the training of his spiritual children with very little need for words. His life and habits form the ideal of a bishop.

To his spiritual children, whatever he thought, was law, and whatever, on the contrary, he disapproved, they renounced. His decisions have been to us the tables of Moses and we have paid great reverence to him. Let all of the Antiochian Archdiocese praise him in our prayers. Let all the Antiochian faithful of this archdiocese thank him for his tirelessness. Let the archdiocese thank him for his support of the needy. Indeed let us thank him for his unyielding stance toward the powerful and for his condescension to the lowly. Let the virgins celebrate the friend of the Bridegroom. Let the unfortunate celebrate their consolation. Let the simple folk celebrate their guide. Let the contemplative celebrate their theologian. Let the elderly celebrate their staff. Let the youth celebrate their instructor. Let the poor celebrate their resource. Let the wealthy celebrate their steward. Even the widows I think praise him as their protector. I know the orphans will proclaim him their father. The poor proclaim him as their benefactor. The strangers proclaim him as their host. The sick proclaim him as their physician.

And now as he reaches the fortieth year of his episcopacy he is gathered to the fathers of the Church: Patriarchs, Prophets, Apostles and martyrs who contend for their faith.

+ Bishop Thomas

# IN THE VIEW OF

HIS GRACE, BISHOP MARK
DIOCESE OF TOLEDO AND THE DIOCESE OF THE MIDWEST ANTIOCHIAN ARCHDIOCESE

YOUR EMINENCE,

Christ is in our midst! He is and ever shall be!

Thanks be to God that you accepted the call to come to North America! Your ministry over the past forty years has set the standard for Orthodox Christian Missions and Evangelism. When I consider your vision for Orthodox Christianity and your accomplishments, I realize that I have had the privilege to serve alongside an Apostle to America! As one who came late to the scene, all I saw was Metropolitan Philip, the administrator. Over the past two years, I have discovered Metropolitan Philip—the theologian, missionary and apostle to North America.

Words cannot express the gratitude that one feels at being graciously accepted into the One, Holy, Catholic and Apostolic Faith. For those of us who have made this journey, a warm and hospitable "welcome home" was sweet to our ears. We are deeply grateful that you have removed the cultural and linguistic barriers, while preserving the Apostolic Faith intact. You have truly sought to make the Ancient Faith incarnate in this new land. You have made room in this God-protected archdiocese for those seeking the fullness of the Holy Orthodox Church, and you have treated them as one of the family.

Our meager words of thanks pale in comparison to the wonderful gift you have given to North America. Thank you for giving of yourself so tirelessly over these forty years. Thank you for giving us the Faith of the Prophets, the Faith of the Apostles and the Faith that has established the universe.

Your unworthy brother in Christ,

+ Bishop Mark, Bishop of Toledo and the Diocese of the Midwest

IN THE VIEW OF

His Grace, Bishop Alexander
Diocese of Ottawa, Eastern Canada and Upstate New York
Antiochian Archdiocese

Saidna as a Man of Courage and Determination

I FIRST HEARD OF SAIDNA DURING HIS FIRST TRIP TO THE HOLY SYNOD as Archbishop of New York. He and his entourage were on the plane headed to Beirut. Dr. George Malouf became alarmed when the skin color of the Metropolitan's face turned to blue. He checked his pulse; there was none. The Metropolitan gasped for oxygen. It sounded as if he was breathing his last. He was only thirty-something of age, and had just begun his ministry as Archbishop. The doctor asked for oxygen and oxygen was brought.

When the plane landed in Turkey, Dr. Malouf informed the Metropolitan that he had just had his first heart attack, and that he should be taken to a local hospital. Of course, Metropolitan Philip refused saying that he had to go to Lebanon because everyone was expecting him. This was his first participation in the Holy Synod, and there were some important issues concerning the North American Archdiocese to be discussed. To show weakness was not acceptable to him. His life was not important; if he died he would have done his best. With God's blessing he would make it to Beirut, and he did.

A local doctor was summoned. He insisted on keeping him in Turkey and wanted to give him an injection of sorts. Dr. Malouf said no to the injection and signed a document bearing responsibility for any consequences to the rejection.

Upon arrival in Beirut, Metropolitan Philip was secretly taken to a hospital where he underwent an electrocardiogram. The ECG confirmed the heart attack. Again, he refused bed rest and went on to attend the Holy Synod. No one in the Synod knew about the attack. It was the best-kept secret at that time.

This is Metropolitan Philip. Selfless! Courageous! A man with a strong conviction of a mission! A man with an unwavering determination to bring this archdiocese to its current status! A leader *par excellence*!

May God grant him "Many Years!"

+ Bishop Alexander Mufarrij

Diocese of Ottawa, Eastern Canada and Upstate New York

PART 3

IN THE VIEW OF

✧ CLERGY AND CIVIC LEADERS
(ARABIC SELECTIONS)

كــما يــراه

ســـيادة المـــتروبوليت إلياس قـــربان
مــتروبوليت طرابلس والكورة وتوابعهما

معرفتي بسيادة الأخ الحبيب فيليب متروبوليت أمريكا الشمالية تعود إلى الماضي البعيد إلـــى أوائـل الأربعينات فكلانا نأتي من نفس المنطقة في المتن الشمالي وهي من أجمل مناطق لبنان عرفته ابنــا لعائلــه متجذرة بالأيمان كان دير مار إلياس في ضهور الشوير هو الذي يجمعنا في اثنين البــاعوث وعيـد النبـي الياس كان الفتى عبد الله قوي البنية بهي الطلعه يربع جرس الدير بيد واحدة وكان صوته الجميل يتردد فـي حنايا الوديان والتلال في المنطقه

ثم عرفته مبتدئا في اكليريكية البلمند فكان على رأس التلاميذ كما كان يرأس الفريق الرياضي و كان ممنوع على فريقه أن يخسر في لعبة مع أي فريق آخر في المنطقة ظهرت مواهبه الأدبية باكرا فكان يكتـب المقالات و المواضيع الاجتماعية و السياسية والأدبية و ينشرها في أهم الصحف و المجـــلات انتقـل إلــى المدارس الغسانية في حمص و بعدها إلى دمشق و نال حظوة عند البطريرك الكسندروس الثالث حيث إتـسم منه خيرا و تنبأ له بمستقبل زاهر و ذلك للمواهب التي حباه الله فيها

و من دمشق انتقل إلى بيروت و بعدها إلى لندن حيث قضى فيها سنة كاملة لدراسة اللغة الإنجليزية و بعدها رجع إلى بيروت و خدم كشماس في أبرشية بيروت و منها انتقل إلى الولايات المتحـدة الأمريكيـة و انتمى إلى معهد الصليب المقدس اللاهوتي لدراسة اللاهوت و منها انتقل إلى رعية ديتـرويت يخدمها كشماس و التحق بجامعة Wayne State University و نال منها الإجازة في الآداب و بعدها نال ســر الكهنــوت المقدس على يد المطوب الذكر المطران انطونيوس بشير و عيّن راعيا على كنيسة القديس جورجيوس فـي كليفلند فخدمها بإخلاص و تفان و عرفت الرعية في عهده نهضة اجتماعية روحية و عمرانية

و في شباط 1966 انتقل المطوب الذكر المتروبوليت انطونيوس بشير إلى الاخدار السماوية و علـى إثر ذلك عينني غبطة البطريرك ثاودوسيوس الثالث معتمدا بطريركا على أبرشية نيويورك و سائر أمريكا

الشمالية فانتقلت على الفور الى نيويورك و عملت بما كان مطلوب مني و من مجلـس أمنـاء الأبرشيـة و الجمعية العامة للأبرشية و دعونا إلى اجتماع عام لممثلين الرعايا في الأبرشية في شهر آذار

فحضر الاجتماع ما يقارب الاربعماية مندوب و كل كهنة الأبرشية طلب من الذين يريدون الترشيح أن يوجه كل واحد منهم كلمة إلى المجتمعين فتقدم المرشحون الواحد تلو الآخر

و لما أتى دور الأب فيلب صليبا و قال كلمته فجذب أنظار الجميع و دوت القاعة بالتصفيق و الهتاف و هذه كانت العلامة الفارقة بأن الأب فيلب هو مرشح الأكثرية الساحقة ممن يعرفونه شخصيا و ممـن لـم تسنح لهم الفرصة للتعرف عليه و جرت الانتخابات فنال الأب فيلب الأكثرية الساحقة من الأصوات

حملت الأسماء و قدمتها إلى صاحب الغبطة و لما كانت أحوال الكنيسة مضطربة تأجل انعقاد المجمع المقدس أكثر من مرة بتدخل الهي و من النبي الياس صاحب الدير حيث كان المجمع يعقد اجتماعاته في تلـك الفترة خرج من الجلسة ستة ومطارنة مناوئين و لهم خططهم و اتجاهاتهم لإملاء الأبرشيات الشاغرة و منها أبرشية أمريكا فأخذ الحاضرون الذين بقوا في الجلسة للمبادرة بانتخاب الأب فيلب صليبا مطرانـا علـى نيويورك و سائر أمريكا الشمالية و سيادة الأسقف اغناطيوس هزيم مطرانا على اللاذقيـة أخبـرت أمريكـا بالأمر فحضر فيلب من أمريكا و جرت سيامته مطرانا على نيويورك و سائر أمريكا الشمالية فـي كنيسـة الدير بحضور وفود كبيرة أتت من المنطقة و من كل أنحاء لبنان و سوريا و الولايات المتحدة و من ديـر مار الياس توجه غبطة البطريرك و المطران الجديد غلى دير سيدة البلمند حيث وضع الحجر الأساس لمعهـد القديس يوحنا الدمشقي و أكد سيادة المطران الجديد بأنه سيقوم ببناء المعهد و من البلمند انتقل المطران فيلب إلى أبرشيته و ترأس مؤتمر الأبرشية و منذ ذلك الوقت دخلت أبرشية أمريكا مرحلة جديدة هي رحلة بناء و تبشير و نمو على كل الأصعدة

و مما هو جدير بذكره إن المطران الجديد استلم من سلفه ما يقارب السبعين رعية و في عهده حتـى هذا الوقت ارتفع العدد إلى 250 رعية و العدد يزداد سنة بعد سنة

إن الإنجازات التي قام بها سيادة المتروبوليت فيلب كبيرة و مهمة أعاد تنظيم الابرشـي المتراميـة الإطراف على أسس جديدة و حديثة و من ابرز ما قام به بالإضافة إلى بناء مئات الكنائس الجديدة و القاعات و مراكز التعليم و الإرشاد و بناء المطرانية الحالي في نيوجرسي و إيجاد القرية الانطاكية التي تشغل مساحة كبيرة من الأرض و أقام عليها أبنية جديدة للاجتماعات و النشاطات و اللقاءات على شتّى أنواعها و أصـبح

هذا المركز نقطة اللقاء للشعب الانطاكي الأمريكي و للكندي المنتشر على كامل الأراضي الأمريكية و الكندية لا سيما الأطفال و الشباب كما أصبح هذا المركز يستقطب الكثيرين من غير الانطاكيين

كما أسس منظمة القديس اغناطيوس الانطاكي التي تدعم الأبرشية ماديا و معنويا و كـذلك منظمــة الامرأة الإنطاكية و غيرها من المنظمات

و من اهم ما قام به هو إقناع أهل توليدو بدمج الأبرشيتين، ابرشية نيويورك وأبرشــية توليــدو فــي أبرشية واحدة

و في السنتين الأخيرتين انتزع من المجمع قرارا بان أبرشية نيويورك و أمريكا الـشمالي أصبحت تعرَف بأبرشية نيويورك و أمريكا الشمالية ذات الحكم الذاتي و بناءا لطلبه أضيف إلى الأبرشية ثلاثة أسـاقفة جدد تمت سيامتهم في الكاتدرائية المريمية في دمشق باحتفال ولا أروع و لا أجمــل و اصــبحت للابرشية الواحدة اسقفيات في الشرق و الغرب و في كل المناطق الأمريكية و الكندية لا يمكننا إن ننـسى مواقـف المطران فيليب الوطنية في دعم قضايا لبنان و سوريا و فلسطين و لقد فرض احترامه على كل الناس و على رأسهم رئيس الدولة في سوريا و رئيس الدولة في لبنان

لا يمكننا إن نعطي سيادته حقه في هذه العجالة فهو كاتب و مبدع و خطيب مفوه يتلاعب بعواطف الجماهير

إنجازاته كبيرة و تطلعاته تذهب إلى المدى البعيد إلا أطال الله بعمره إلى سنين عديدة

كما يراه

سيادة المـــتروبوليت إيــــليا صليبا

ميتروبوليت حماة وتوابعها

علمانيا قبل الرابعة عشره من عمره هو عبد الله الياس صليبا من قرية أبي ميزان التابعــه 1
لدير مار الياس شويا ألبطريكي وكان لهذه القرية امتداد يسمى قرية شرين في منطقه علويــة مــن
منطقه الجليل الذي تقع أبو ميزان في سفحه وكنت شخصيا مسؤولا كنسيا عن هذه القرية المزدوجة
أبو ميزان شرين واتابع مراحل حياة الطالب عبد الله في صغره وكان بالفعل من المبرزين فــي
صفه رصينا هادئا رخيم الصوت ميالا لخدمه الكنيسة وكنت من المشجعين له للانتماء إلى الحيــاة
الاكليريكية وكان لنا جولات في بعض النشاطات المدرسية

ميتدئــا بدا حياته الاكليريكية في دير مار الياس شويا وكنت اكليريكيا فيه ولاحظت فيــه 2
النشاط والطاعة والذكاء رحب العلم والطموح إلى مستقبل زاهر وكنا في تعاون

شماسا انجيليا في حياته الشموسيه اكتفى أن أتطرق إلى بعض الخطــوط العريضة فــي 3
مرحلتين عاشهما في بيتين كنسيين احدهما في لبنان والاخرى في سوريا أي في البلمند الكورة
لبنان الشمالي وفي البطريكية دمشق وكان مطران طرابلس والكوره وقتئذ ثيودوسيوس أبو رجيلي
فيما بعد البطريك ثيودوسيوس السادس يختاره للخدمة معه ويعتمد عليه في حل الكثير من المشاكل
المعتقدة في الابرشيه وكأستاذ للغة العربية والأدب في البلمند كان ناجحا إلي ابعد الحدود وموضــع
إعجاب تلامذته وزملائه ولا اخفي شيئا هاما كان يصدر عنه اذ كان يوزع راتبه علــى الطــلاب
الفقراء ويشتري ثيابا وغذاء لهم والاهم من ذلك وبالرغم من وجود رئيس للدير والمدرسة كان وهو
شماس يشغل مركزا فيها وموضوع ثقة وتقدير رئيسهما

اما مرحله وجوده في البطريركية فقد كانت حافلة بالعطاء والتحديات وكشماس كان يشغل مركز أمين سر البطريرك الكسندروس طحان وموضوع ثقته ومرجعا لمعظم أموره الاداريه وبالرغم من كوني كاهنا في البطربركيه فقد كنت ارجع اليه مع كهنة آخرين في كثير من الأمور كممثل للبطريرك وفي هذه المرحلة ازداد التقارب والتعاون والانسجام أكثر بيننا وكان يغلي صراحة وجراه في مجابهة التحديات التي تعترضه وكثيرا ما كانت جرأته ودفاعه عن الحق يجعلان أن يصطدم مع كبار المسؤولين في البطريركية حتى مع البطريك نفسه وبتابع مجابهة حتى الوصول إلى العادل وكانت مرحله حياته في البطربركيه صاخبة ومليئة بالتحديات التي كان يجابهها بقوة ويتغلب وقد حدث هذا الامر مرارا وكانت النتيجه له لا عليه ويبقى شامخ الراس مرفوع الجبين وكنت مرافقا له في كل هذه الازمات وتولدت بيننا اخوه وصداقه الى ابعد الحدود والشماس فيلبس في هذه المرحله كان يحاور الكتاب والشعراء ويقرض الشعر وله العديد من القصائد والكتابات اثناء وجوده في دمشق خلق حياه في البطريركية و الكاثدرالية المريمية التي كانت تغص بالمصلين لسماع صوته الرخيم ولإتقانه للخدمة و رافق هذه الحياة الصاخبة ببرائة و تواضع و انسانية فياضة بالمحبة و الكرم والتهافت على خدمة الآخرين و امام الحاح مطران بيروت و حمص إيليا الصليبي و الكسندروس جحا صرف مدة من الزمن في حمص و بيروت و تعامل مع المسؤولين الكبار و الصغار فيهما بنفس روح المسؤولية و الصفات الانسانية التي تحلى بها و كانت ترافقه و يجسدها بتمامها مع المتعاملين معه و في هذه الحقبة من الزمن سافر الى لندن لمزيد من التحصيل العلمي و التعمق في معرفة اللغة الانجليزية و الدراسات الكنسية و كنت متابعا لتنقلاته و التواصل مستمر بيننا و بنفس الوتيرة من الاخوة و الصداقة

4 **كاهنا** هذه المرحلة عاشها في امريكا الشمالية التي استدعته الرئاسة الروحية اليها كشماس ثم شرطن كاهنا بوضع يد المثلث الرحمات انطونيوس بشيرا و عين كاهنا لرعية كليفلنـد ارهايو الانطاكية التي لمع فيها و رفعها الى الاوج نشاطا و عطاء في كل مجالات الحياة الكنسية كان لـه دوره الفعال في كل نشاطات الابرشية و مؤتمراتها و مركز استقطاب و اعجاب اخوته الكهنـة و المؤمنين و يشغل دائما مركز القيادة في كل مجال و يشكل املا كبيرا في خلافـة المتروبوليت السلف و لا انسى مواقفه الجريئة الصامدة في سبيل وحدة الابرشية و العمل المخلص لارتباطهـا

القوي بالكنيسة الام انطاكية   كان انطاكية بدمه و مواقفه و كل ما فيه   و مواقفه في هـذا الاتجـاه واضحة و معروفة و مشهود له فيها

5   **متروبوليتـا**   جرى ترشيحه اسقفا في الولايات المتحدة حسب دسـتور الابرشية   و تـم انتخابه من المجمع الانطاكي المقدس في دير مار الياس شويا في صيف 1966   و حضر هـذا الحدث وفد من كهنة ابرشية امريكا و مجلسها الابرشي   و كنت وقتئذ امينا لسر المجمع الانطـاكي المقدس و بعد سيامته سافر توا الى سان فرانسيسكو لترؤس المؤتمر العام للابرشية   و تفاصيل هذه الاحداث تعرفها ابرشية امريكا بكهنتها و مؤسساتها   ومع هذه الاحداث بدأت التحـديات القويـة و استمرت من خلال هذه المسيرة الاسقفية   و كانت سيادته يجابه هذه التحديات بما اعطـاه الله مـن امكانيات و مؤهلات   و يتغلب عليها   و لا ازال اذكر عبارته الشهيرة لي و انا اشاركه بعض هذه التحديات إذ قال   التحديات تصقل حياتي و تعطيها مزيدا من المناعة و الإبداع و الصلابة و القـوة حتى صرت راغبا في خلقها   إذ كانت غير موجودة   و الجدير بالذكر انـه منـذ اليـوم الأول لأسقفيته باشر عمله الأسقفي بزخم قوي و بمختلف حقول النـشاطات الرعائيـة مؤسسا رعايـا و إرساليات جديدة و مجالس و لجان كثيرة و مؤسسات خيرية عديدة لتدعم العمل الرعائي   فزاد عددها أضعاف ما كانت عليه و أصبحت الأبرشية كخلية نحل تعمل بتوجهاته الديناميكية سائرة في طريـق التقدم المستمر و الازدهار المتواصل وبدافع الاختصار أريد أن أركز على ثلاثة مراحل هامة فـي حياة الاسقفيه شهدتها واشتركت فيها وحفرت عميقا في ذاكرتي وحياتي

أ   **توحيد الأبرشية**   ورث المتروبوليت فيلبس انقساما حادا في أبرشية أمريكا الشمالية باسم نيويورك وتوليدو   هذا الانقسام قض مضجع الكرسي الانطاكي بكاملة وخلق الكثير من الحزازات والتـشنجات والانقسامات حتى بين أعضاء المجتمع المقدس واستمر هذا الوضع عدة سنوات   وكان المتروبوليـت فيليبس يعاني الكثير من هذا الواقع المؤلم وبحلم بوضع حد له وتحقق الحلم بالتئـام الجـرح ولحـم الانقسام بمساعيه وقيادته الحكيمة وكنت وقتئذ ضيفا عليه وفي دار المطرانية التـي أسـسها وكـان تأسيسها وإيجادها حلقة في سلسلة التحديات التي كانت ترافقه   وبعد جهد وتعب تغلب علـى تحـدي

117

الانقسام ووحد الأبرشية وصارت تعرف بأبرشية أمريكا الشمالية وتفاصيل هذه المرحلة تحتاج إلـى مئات الصفحات ويعرفها الجميع

ب إقامتي في أمريكا الشمالية إستمرت هذه الإقامة طيلة عشر سنوات تقريبا سببتها ظروف كنسية قاهرة في الوطن الأم ونظرا للجو الأخوي الذي خلقه ألأخ المتروبوليت فيليبس لم أكن بأنني أشعر ضيف بل صاحب البيت مغمورا بفيض من المحبه والترحيب والاهتمام والعطاء السخي مـن قلبـة وجيبه ووضع في تصرفي كل ما كنت أحتاج إلية وصادف اثناء وجودي فـي امريكـا خضـوع المتروبيليت فيليبس لجراحة قلبيه اضطرته إلى تخفيف نشاطه الرعائي واسفاره البعيد فانتدبني لتمثيله في بعض الواجبات الرعائيه التي افادتني كثيرا ومكنتني من التعرف علـى كـل رعايـا الابرشيه ومجالسها ومؤسساتها ونشاطاتها ومؤتمراتها ألعامه والخاصه واكتسبت خبره واسعه علـى صعيد التنظيم ومعالجه الامور المعقده ولم يخل نشاط ما دون مشاركته لي فيه وكانت كل تحرياتي فـي اطار توجيهات سياديه والتعاون معه بشخصيته نفسها الغنية بالمحبة والتواضع والصراحة الاخويـه والحوار البناء وصفاء القلب والنية وكنا نلتقي يوميا مساء لنتحاور ونتبادل ألمعرفه والخبرة وهذا ما اكسبني الكثير الكثير على صعيد التنظيم والاداره والإخلاص الاخوي ظهرت آثار هذا الاكتـساب في أبرشيتي التي أرعاها حاليّا حماة اذ صارت من حيث التنظيم ماليّا واداريا وتعليميّـا ورعانيـا صورة مصغرة لأبرشية أميلركا الشمالية

ج الاداره الذاتية موضوع الاداره الذاتية واسع ومتشعب وعقد في سبيله الكثير من المجتمعـات على صعيد الأبرشية الامريكيه والمجمع المقدس واستغرق من الوقت في جو صاخب ومعقد في حدود السنتين وكانت النتيجة أن حصلت الأبرشية على قرار مجمعي بمنحها الاداره الذاتية ووضع تنظيمها في دستور جديد تبناه المؤتمر العام للابرشيه في بتسبرغ ونقحه وصادق عليـه المجمـع المقـدس وتفاصيل هذه المرحله واضحة ومعروفه لدى القيادات ألروحيه والمؤمنين في جميع أنحاء الكرسـي الانطاكي المقدس وابعد من ذلك إلى بقية الكراسي الارثوذكسيه والعالم المسيحي واختم هذه النبذة من الذكريات بثلاثة أمور في غاية الاقتضاب

1 تهاني الاخويه الخالصة للأخ المتروبوليت فيلبس بهذه المناسبة سائلا له العافية الكاملة والعمر الطويل والإنتاج المستمر

2 إذا أردت أن أسجل معرفتي وخبرتي في المتروبوليت فيلبس وبقليل من التفصيل فاني احتاج إلى مئات الصفحات

3 المتروبوليت فيلبس بشخصيته الجذابة وغناها الإيماني العلمي الأخلاقي هي نفسها التي كان يتحلى بها علمانيا واكليريكيا في مختلف الدرجات ولم تتغير أبدا ثابتة وممثله بصفاته الانسانيه وتفرعاتها في ديناميكية وتواضع وكرم وصفاء قلب ومحبه حضانة للجميع

كــما يــراه

سـيادة المـتروبوليت إليـاس عودة
مـيتروبوليت بيروت وتوابعها

ولكني افعل شيئا واحدا اذ انا انسى ما هو وراء وامتد الى ما هو قدام   فيلبي 3:13

أبدأ

بالشموس تلتصق العيون

ولاتشبع

فؤاد رفقة

منذ الطفولة إلتقت عيناي بالشمس التي لا تغيب، والحلم كان رفيقي إلى ان رافقت السحب الى حيـث هبّ بي روح الرب قائلا هلم معي من لبنان الى البلاد التي هناك في تلك الربوع البعيدة التقيت أبا إتخذني إليه إبنا إتخذني إليه لكي تتفتح براعم حلمي المبارك وما لبثت ان إغتسلت في راحتي محبته، على ضـفاف قلبه، حتى إتخذه المبارك إليه وما تركني وحيدا ثابت قلبي يا الله ثابت قلبي   لأن رحمتك قد عظمت فـي السنوات   هذا كان لسان حالي

ثم اتى إلي من جعله الله ملاكا لكنيسته واحتضنني إبنا أستقر و استمر فيما هو لمجد القدّوس

هذا الملاك صار لي من ألتجىء إليه وأجد عنده المحبة والاهتمام بيته صار بيتي وبيت رفاقي فـي الطريق التي نحن عليها تحول المكان في عيني الى شجرة كبيرة نستظلها، نأكل أثمارها و نشترك معا فـي حرمة الحديث الذي يبني ويزرع الفرح في القلوب

حنان يزيل التعب واليأس وحضور يملأ النفس دفئا، ويذيب ثلوج التساؤلات ويحطم كل جـدار بنـاه المحارب في قلوبنا

121

آلامه كانت غذاء في جذور الفضائل، تكشف فيه ضياء عرفه الصابرون وأدركه من تعمد بالنور لـم يلتفت يوما الى الوراء عيناه شاخصتان أبدا الى من نذر نفسه له

فتيلا لم يطفيء وغصنا ما كسر سقى بالرفق ما زرع وما جعل الماء تشمخ على ما روت هـدوءا عرفناه إختبر الوجع كان رفيقا لنا و بنا وهو على الصلابة و الصمود

دفعني ان اساير الحلم الجميل لكن محبتنا اتخذت للخدمة ولغسل جراح إخوة الرب وأقدامهم كان لـي المعلم و القدوة في تقبل ما يرمي الرب في أيدينا وما يسمح به لنا، و في المحافظة على الفرح ترتـاح فيـه قلوبنا وكأنه يردد قول الرسول بولس افرحوا بالرب كل حين وأقول أيضا إفرحـوا في 4:4 أمـضيت السنوات الستة في كنفه أتدرب وأعتاد على الحكمة والدراية والمحبة لرعاية الفادي

وفيما أنا في خضم ما انا عليه في خدمة احبائه وفي تلقف ما قد يفيد رسالتي، دفعنـي الـرب الـى الرجوع من حيث أتيت لأتمم ما يريد لي أن اتمم الطاعة للرب تعزي ولكن الفهم غير الناضج والمعرفة غير المكتملة تجعلان الادراك ضعيفا والمحبة مضطربة الى أن يعلم الانسان ان المحبة وحدها لا تخضع للزمـان والمكان وانها وحدها الرحم الذي يبقى ولو شاخ الانسان هذا ما رأيته في معلمي و أبي عندما إختارني الرب ان أكون شريكا له بقي مستوطنا في المحبة التي جمعتنا تعزية للجهاد الذي نحيا فيه، مستعدا للمحبة والخدمة والتضحية

هذه صورة تبقى لي معلقة في محراب قلبي، كلما إلتفت إليها تستنهض دعاء شكورا الى العلي ليمـنح من عليها اجمل ما يطلب منه

كمـا يـراه

العمـاد اميـل لـحود

رئيـس الجمهوريـــة اللبنانيـــة

في ذكرى سيامته الاسقفية الاربعين لا يصنع لنا سيادة المتروبوليت فيليبس ذاكرة خاصة،بل هـو يصنع لبنان، بالايمان، مستقبلا هو كل الذاكرة

له في كل من عرفه واحبّه نبض من حياة، ودفق من عطاء، وكيف للذي في كلماته وهج الروح، لغة تسام ألا يترك في كل منا بعضا مما في الايمان مطلق؟

قد يكون فهم الايمان من اصعب الامور، وقد يكون عيش الايمان من اكثرها تعقيدا، الا ان ما يختزنه المتروبوليت فيليبس من رضى وبساطة تجعلك تدرك، لا بل ان تلمس ان المدى كيان يستقر فينا، وهو متى فعل ذلك تملك كل ابعادنا بقوة المحبة وبعمقها

انني مذ عرفته، في لبنان في زيارات هي له نقطة عبور الى وطن رســالة، جعـل نفسـه محطـة انتظارات الانسانية به تتحقق حوارات للحضارة، مذ عرفته هنا في وطن الارز المعانق رحابة السماء، عرفت فيه مفهوما متكاملاً حديثه حديث الروح معه تدرك ان الفكر متى تكامل مع الايمان يصبح طريقا للحق ومن آمن يعرف من هو الطريق والحياة، ويعرف ايضا الحق حيث هو محرّر من كل ظلم

لأربعين سنة، حمل سيادة المتروبوليت فيليبس عصاه الراعوية على دروب العالم، حتى اقاصيه، فكان خير شاهد لمن خلّص العالم

بين لبنان والولايات المتحدة الاميركية رسالته نشيد تسبيح واكرام، زارع هو في كرم الالوهـة فـلا تعب يترك اثره على جبهته، ولا ارهاق يضعف من ثباته كم من عقول به استنارت، وكم من قلوب اهتـدت بفضله الى انوار البهاء الالهي

لطالما اصغى اليه من عرفه وقرأ في عينيه اشعاع الحق وزهو الكلمة، وهو يرصف فوق كل هامـة اناشيد الاستقامة

للبنان هو رسول في العالم الامريكي، وللعرب هو الصوت الذي لا يخاف ان يقول ما هو حــق، وان يفعل ما هو حق هي تلك الواقعية التي يعلّمها   الا تخاف من ابعاد الجغرافيا ولا من سطوة التــاريخ، لقـول الحق وفعله

فيـــــا سيـــــادة الـــمتروبوليت،

لتبق اقوالك صوت الحق الذي لا يُعلى عليه

ولتبق السنوات تأتي وتروح وانت متوج بالسلام، تحمله الينا   والى العالم، رسالة محبة لاتنتهي

ودمت، من يوبيل الى يوبيل ذخر الايمان به ننتصر على كل ضعف فنزهو مثلك

كـمـا يـراه

بشارة مرهج

وزير الداخلية اللبنانية سابقا وعضو سابق في المجلس النيابي اللبناني

ألمــــلهـَم

للمطران فيليب صليبا مكانة خاصة في قلبي واعترف اني تأثرت عميقا بشخصيته الفذة كما الصريحة والجريئة التي حفزتني والهمتني لاتخاذ قرارات مهمة وصعبة في حياتي تتبعت مسيرته وكفاحه منذ ان عــاد الى ضهور الشوير عام 1966 لمواكبة المجمع المقدس المنعقد في دير مار الياس شويا يوم ذاك اكــد لـي والدي الذي تربطه بالمطران صلة قرابة ان المجمع سينتخب الأب فيليب مطرانا على اميركا الشمالية قلت له من اين لك ان تستبق الأمور؟ قال لقد قرأت ذلك من عيون اعضاء الوفد الكبيـر القـادم مـن اميركـا ان عاطفتهم تجاهه لايمكن وصفها انهم مجمعون عليه واكيد ان المجمع سيأخذ ذلك بعين الاعتبار ويتجاوب مـع رغبة الوفد لاسيما وان الوفد يمثل الأبرشية اصدق تمثيل وعندما قرعت اجراس الدير مؤذنة بانتخاب ابنـه البار فيليب مطرانا على اميركا الشمالية عمت الفرحة الوفد المرافق كما كل القرى والبلدات المحيطة تعلمت في تلك الحظة الرائعة معنى التضامن والتصميم ومنذ ذلك اليوم كلما عرفت المزيد عن المطران فيليب وعن اعماله ومآثره كلما ازددت حبا له واعتزازا به

في مناسبات عدة تعرض المطران فيليب الى انتقادات حاده حتى ذهب البعض الى التشكيك بإلتزامـه الانطاكي والحديث عن رغبته في الاستقلال عن كنيسة الأم وجدت نفسي دون تخطيط او تكليف أتـصدى لذلك التشكيك أدحضه بناء على ثقتي العميقة بالرجل ويقيني بانتمائه الصادق الى الانطاكية التي رفع راياتهـا عاليا في اميركا ثم مرت الايام وتبين للجميع سذاجة التشكيك وهزالته وكعادته سامح المطران من اساء اليـه فغمرته محبة القاصي والداني

المطران فيليب صليبا اسم تاريخي لامع في حياة الكنيسة الانطاكية وهو استحق هذه الصفة النادرة لانه اعطى واضاف نهضت على يده مطرانية اميركا الشمالية لتصبح، تأسيسا على جهود السلف الصالح، ابرشية مترامية الاطراف، متعددة المؤسسات لها حضورها الكبير والمؤثر في القارة الجديدة هذا الحضور لا يقتصر اشعاعه على ابناء الأبرشية في حياتهم الايمانية والاجتماعية فحسب، وانما يفيض ايضا على الشرق مؤازرة واسهاما واقالة من العثرات خصوصا في زمن الحرب والازمات ويكفي المطران فيليب انه كان على رأس هذا النهوض التاريخي، تخطيطا وتنفيذا ومتابعة، شأنه في ذلك القادة الكبار الذين يعرفون كيف يلهمون معاونيهم ويدركون كيف تكون المسؤولية مشاركة وانتاجا واتقانا، ويحرصون على ان تكون عملية البناء مستمرة ومحمية بجهد المؤتمنين الذين عندهم جمال الخدمة يقترن بروعة الانتماء

وسر الجهود التي تحولت انجازات على الارض ملموسة ان الرجل المفعم بالايمان و الامل هو صاحب رسالة ورؤية وارادة، وكلها اقانيم في حقيقة واحدة تتجلى في نفسه نورا ساطعا يطرد عتمة الطريق امام الخائفين و المتعبين، ويفتح ابوابها واسعة امام العائدين الى فضاء التوبة والايمان

ومن اجتمعت في نفسه هذه الفضائل ليس غريبا عليه ان يخترق المألوف ويتجاوز الممكن الى رحاب اوسع فأوسع، ويرتقي من ذروه الى اخرى نضالا لا يلين لترجمة الايمان اعمالا صالحة تتوالد كل حين لتشهد على قدسية المسعى وصلابة الارادة

اما القنوط و العقود فلا مكان لهما في مجلسه الاثير حيث الحياة نعمة تفيض بالزيت والكرمة يستحقها العاملون تحت اشعة الشمس في هذا السياق رفض المطران صليبا طقوس التحنيط والاجترار وآثر الالتحاق بمدرسة السيد ثائرا على اللصوص وتجار الهيكل

صحيح انه عاش في العرين الاميركي معظم حياته لكنه لم يفقد اصالته بل ازداد تمسكا بلبنانيته وعروبته فأصبح مرجعا لكل العرب في اميركا وبخاصة ابناء الشعب الفلسطيني الذين يعرفون عن عمق ايمانه بالقدس وحقوقهم الوطنية و الانسانية

من موقع الايمان والتمسك بالتراث جازف بأمور كثيرة فسجل مآثر اصبحت ملك جيله هكذا شب وشهد في عائلة غالبت الشقاء وزرعت السنابل وشيدت البنيان مدركة ان الصخور قبل ان تتحول الى حجارة صالحة للبناء تحتاج الى جهد وعناد، وقبل ان تتشكل عقدا يتباهي به الدير والدار تحتاج الى مهارة وعناء

فهم منذ يفاعته ان الحياة نعمة مثلما هي استحقاق فاخترق الصفوف وارتقى الدرجات بالعلم والسهر حتى بلغ اعلى المراتب في الكنيسة كما في عيون ابنائه ومحبيه وعارفيه يفخرون به قويا في حضرة

السلطان، متواضعا يغسل ارجل التلاميذ، متكلا على المخلص في كل حين، عاملا في كل زمان ومكان ليقظة إيمانية تشرك ابنائها في الحصاد بعد ان تحضهم على اللقاء وخلع ثياب الانانية والانغلاق

ولا غرو فصروحه حصينة تتكاثر على الارض كما حبات الحنطة وتتكسر عند أسوارها كل ريح غرور همه رعاية الاجيال يهديها الى الفضائل المسيحية والينابيع المشرقية الصافية فيترسخ إيمانها بالفادي ويشتد طوقها الى حجارة القدس واجراس بيت لحم وأدراج الناصرة

سعادته رؤية الشباب يتتكبون الرسالة يقاومون من خلالها الغلو والانحلال وكل الافات التي تسعى لسلب المجتمعات روحها وزعزعة ايمانها وتعطيل فكرها وتزييف ارادتها وتحويلها الى اسواق تعصر الفقراء او قطعان تحركها الغرائز

حباه الله مواهب كثيرة وأودع فيه سرا عظيما لقد خصه الله بنعمة تحويل الافراد الى جماعات تتحو الى الخير والصلاح وتعمل في تناسق بديع

ما أبهى العطاء في كل مكان وزمان ما أجمل النعمة لمستحق

Facing page:

Metropolitan Philip with the Former President Amin Gemayel of Lebanon, and His Eminence Metropolitan Elias Audi.

This page:

With President Amin Gemayel of Lebanon; September, 1987.

This page:

Metropolitan Philip with
King Hussein of Jordan.

Facing page:

With President Elias
Haraoui of Lebanon;
September, 1991.

Metropolitan Philip with President Emile Lahoud of Lebanon.

Top: With the former Minister of the Interior of Lebanon, His Excellency Beshara Merhej, and Mr. Mansour Harek.

Bottom left:
Guests and benefactors who attended the *Al Kafaat* Luncheon on May 22, 2006. From left to right: Archdeacon David Nimmer, Dr. Anis Saliba, Ms. Myriam Shwayri, Mr. Nadim Shwayri, Mrs. Lourdes Zac Zac, Metropolitan Philip, Mr. George Zac Zac, Sheikh Sami Merhi, Very Rev. Joseph Anytpas and Mr. Fawaz El-Khoury.

Bottom right:
At the same luncheon, with Ms. Myriam Shwayri (*Al Kafaat* Director of Communications and Publication Relations) and Mr. Nadim Shwayri.

Top: With President Hafez Al-Assad of Syria, in the Presidential Palace, Damascus, Syria; October, 1996.
Bottom: With President Bashar Al-Assad of Syria, in the Presidential Palace, Damascus, Syria; Fall, 2004.

كمـا يــراه

السيد نديم حبيب شويري

رئيس مؤسسة الكفاءات للتأهيل في لبنان

فيـلـيـبوس – أبن أنطاكية البـار

من البديهي القول أن الكنيسة المقدسة هي في حالة استفقاد دائمة من الله تراهـا تمـر فـي فتـرات ضمور، وقد تعيش أزمات موجعة من تفكك وخمول وضياع وفجأة ترى العناية الالهيــة تحيطهـا باطلالـة مصلح فذ يأتيها منقذا، فيدفعها من جديد في خط الرسالة المقدسة

سيادة المتروبوليت فيليبوس صليبا هو من سلالة هذه القلة النادرة من المصلحين الأفّذاذ، بشهادة مـا حقق وأنتج سحابة الأربعين سنة من عمر أسقفيته الفاعلة فــ تعـالوا وانـظـروا

أعترف باستحالتي الاحاطة بكافة جوانب ما حقق فيليبوس وأضاف في خط آباء الكنيسة ولكني أعتقد جازما، بكل قناعة، أن ما أنجزه قد أغنى الأرثوذكسية من ضمن بوابتها الانطاكية، مساهما بارجاع أنطاكيــة الى مناهل الحياة، عبر أنموذج ما فعله لها في شمال أميركا، حيث وضعها على سكة الحياة المعاصـرة، ثـم دفعها للأخذ بمسؤولياتها تجاه الكنيسة الجامعة

في اعطائه القيمة الكبرى للعلماني، واعتباره شريكا أساسيا في حياة الكنيسة، رجوع الـى الأصالـة الأنطاكية، واغناء فكري وروحي ومادي في مسيرة الجماعة المؤمنة مـن دون شـراكة العلمـاني، يقول فيليبوس، تفرغ الكنيسة من معناها الأصيل المقدس، وتصبح خدمات الأسرار والليتورجيا غير ذي جـدوى الكنيسة ليست العامة أو الشعب من جهة، ورجل الدين أو الراعي أو أمير الكنيسة مـن الثانيـة هـي كنيسة حيّة بمقدار ما هي تفاعل خلاق بين الراعي والشعب العلماني في تثمير ما عند الاثنين مـن طاقـات،

ومن مخزون حب بانتفاء التفاعل والتكامل بين الاثنين في حب وتعاون، تنحدر الرعية الى الرتابة، وتتجمد في ممارسات تقليدية جدباء في نطاق أكليروسية جافة الكنيسة، كما يحياها فيليبوس، هي ورشة عمل دائمة، دافقة بالنعمة، شبيهة بقفير النحل، حيث لكل مؤمن دور، ومكانة، ومساهمة فـي نـشاطات رعويـة جديـة، مدروسة، ملهمة بهذا المفهوم الدينميكي من التفاعل الخلاق، تصبح الرعية وحدة الجماعة العاملة الحيّة، تحيا المسيح في تخصيب امكانيات البشر والأرض، خدمة للانسان، وحبا لله

في سبيل ايصال الرعية، عمليا، الى هذا المستوى من التفاعل البنّاء، جهد فيليبوس، طوال حبريتـه، في بناء الرعايا، عددا ورسالة في العمق، بحسب التزام الفرقاء بمفاهيم الشراكة البناءة فاذا بعددها يتضاعف أربع مرات في أربع عقود، ليجمع فراخ أنطاكية على كامل مساحة أميركا الـشمالية واذا بـالراعي الكبيـر ينشيء القرية الأنطاكية ، ويقيم المدراس والمعاهد الأكليريكية، ويمد الرعايا برعاة يتمتعون بعلـم، وثقافة دينية روحية عالية، ومنعة في الأخلاق، أن يلعبوا بنجاح دور الشريك المطلوب للعلماني في حياة ومسيرة هذه الرعايا وتطويرها

على أن بناء الرعايا وتجهيزها بشرا وحجرا يأخذ كل بعده الروحي، عندما نعي أن الغاية الكبرى منه هي الوصول الى تحقيق مبدأ **الكنيسة الخادمة** والتحقيق يكون بالأفعال للانسان ليس من قال ربي ربي بل من **فعل** مشيئة أبي وقد ساوى المخلص بين حب لله، والالتزام بخدمة الانسان الآخر، وبهـاتين الوصيتين يتعلق الناموس كله والأنبياء متى 22:40 ، وحدد بوضوح كلي ماهية الأفعال كنت جائعا وعريانا ومريضا وسجينا وغريبا فأتيتم الي

هذه الكلمات المقدسة هي دائما على لسان فيليبوس، وهي شعاره، وأساس تحقيقات حبريتـه المتعـددة الاجتماعية والروحية والثقافية في كامل نطاق أبرشيته، والتي امتدت الى انطاكية الأم، فإلى بلـدان وشـعوب عدة، تعاني من فقر وتخلف، والى أصقاع، حيثما كانت، عندما تبلى بكوارث طبيعية حادة

قدرة فيليبوس في ربط الكرازة بالتحقيق الفعلي، العملي، جمعت اليه قلوبا وبـشرا فـاذا ب جمعيـة القديس أغناطيوس الإنطاكي التي أنشأها يزيد أعضاؤها عن الألفين، يسيرون ويعملون بخطـاه، ويحققون

برعايته، واذا بـ رابطة الأرثوذكسيات الأنطاكيات في شمال أميركا تنشط وتقوم بتمويل مشاريع خدمات حية في أميركا اللاتينية وبلدان الشرق الأوسط

بإنجازاته وأفعاله الحيّة الملموسة، بعث فيليبوس بكنيستنا الأنطاكية من جديد، وربطها بتراث ماضيها العريق في الخدمة فمن تراث كنيستنا الالتزام بقضايا الانسان المعذب ولقد أقام باسيليوس المراكز الصحية في كل كبادوكيا، حيث عرفت بالباسيليات، وتبعه الذهبي الفم الى تحقيقات مماثلة في القسطنطينية واستوحى عملهما فيما بعد كل من الشرق المحمدي، وأوروبا اللاتينية في قرونها الوسطى

وقد تجلى عمق و نضوج فيليبوس في ارتباطه بالتراث الأنطاكي بانفتاحه على الارثوذكسية ككل، وعلى كل من رأى في المسيح الخلاص ليضمه الى صدر الكنيسة فكان من الطبيعي من هذا الراعي البعيد النظر والكبير في الإيمان ان يدعو ويساهم في تأسيس رابطة الاساقفة الارثوذكس في امريكا الشمالية (SCOBA)، حيث لكل واحد من الاربعة عشر اسقفا أبرشية مستقلة عن الاخرى على أساس البلدان الاولى التي انتجتها بمساعيه الخيرة في هذا الاتجاه المبارك، نرى فيلبوس يعمل لأرثوذكسية رسولية حقا، واحدة في الجوهر، مترابطة كنائسها في حب جامع، قائم على التكامل والاحترام المتبادل بين الاعضاء، في بنيوية خالصة، ضمن مبدأ احترام خصائص وفرادات وليتورجية كل كنيسية، بدلا من أن تكون أرثوذكسيات كما يسميها اللاهوتي الفرنسي (OLIVIER CLEMENT)، متناحرة ومتباعدة، لا بل ومتخاصمة

إن النشاطات الدينية والاجتماعية والثقافية المتعددة التي تطورت وتكثفت خلال العقود الاربعة الاخيرة من حبرية فيليبوس، تعطي المؤمن الانطاكي، أينما كان، شعورا عميقا ولا اعذب بالإنتماء الى كنيسة عريقة، وأملا كبيرا مقرونا بدعاء، أن تعم النهضة كافة رعايا أنطاكية لتكون بمستوى التحدي التي تفرضها هذه العراقة، بعد ان رأينا ما تحقق من مثال لها في بيتها الامريكي ثم عبر مساعي فيلبوس المسكونية الحميدة وصولا الى بناء الجسور وتقويتها مع الكنيسة الام في القسطنطينية، يتضاعف شعور الارثوذكسي الانطاكي

بالانتماء الى العالم الارثوذكسي الاكبر، مما يعمق الشخصية الارثوذكسية ويزيدها غنى وعمقا وتألقا في الاصالة

لا أبالغ ان قلت ان التاريخ الكنسي سيعطي اسم فيلبوس لهذه الحقبة من مسيرة كنيسة انطاكية فقد كان الرائد في صفوة نخبة عملت وتعمل على إيقاظها من سبات امتد على مسافة قرون عدة، وبعثها كنيسة خدمة وفعل في الكوكبة الارثوذكسية، وربطها بالتراث الانطاكي المجيد في مسيرتها نحو الاب

PART 4

IN THE VIEW OF

✦ Family, Friends, Priests
   and Church Administrators

IN THE VIEW OF

Dr. Najib Saliba
Metropolitan Philip's Brother

Metropolitan Philip: Family Reflections

Born as Abdallah, "the servant of God," June 10, 1931, Metropolitan Philip has been a success story. Little did my father know that the little boy he led by the hand and offered to Patriarch Alexander Tahhan in July of 1945 at St. Elias Monastery would grow up to become the Metropolitan Archbishop of New York and All North America. The name "Abdallah" was probably a good omen for things to come. Abdallah was the fourth child born to my parents, Elias and Salimeh Saliba, after Nasif, Shahid and a daughter, Nazira. I, Najib, the author of this article, was the fifth and last, born some four years after Abdallah. We were all born and grew up in Abou Mizan, a humble village in Mount Lebanon. Larger towns nearby included Bikfayya, Shweir and Btighrine, the capital of the Saliba clan. I remember we used to walk to all these towns to shop, work or break the monotony of life in Abou Mizan.

Early Recollections

I actually didn't get to know my brother well when he was in Lebanon since he left home at an early age and joined the church, assuming the name "Philip." After that he occasionally came home but only for a short stay. However, I do recall some fond memories of that short period in our lives. Since we were the youngest in the family we were close to each other and he often used to tease me. Being older and more experienced, I looked up to him and considered him a role model, especially after he left the limited environment of Abou Mizan for a wider world.

Since Abou Mizan was a small village with little to do beyond the house and the farm, the church and religious holidays became the center of attention. Church festivals filled a void in people's lives. Of all the church holidays, Good Friday, Easter and Christmas were the most important. Good Friday, for example, provided a good occasion for the children of the village to show teamwork. My brother and I, along with the other children, used to spend the whole day collecting wild flowers from the fields to decorate the bier of Jesus. We used to walk a long distance to fetch the sweet smelling laurel leaves for the occasion. This was annually the most anticipated event of the spring. Nature was waking up after a long winter. The weather was warm, sunny and beautiful. Things just looked right for the Resurrection.

Abou Mizan did not have the regular services of a fulltime priest. It was dependent on St. Elias Monastery for services, and at times no priest was available. On such occasions, especially on Easter and Christmas, my brother and I would awaken at about two o'clock in the morning and walk the distance in the dark, up the mountain to Shreen in order to attend services. An elderly priest from Btighrine, who never missed a service, serviced the church in Shreen. The church was cold with no heat and no seats. Given the conditions, the service seemed endless. But there was always something to sweeten the occasion. After the liturgy, we of course visited Aunt Zainy who lived near the church, in order to warm up and wish her a happy *eid*, "feast". This was the highlight of the day. Aunt Zainy had no children of her own, so she always welcomed us. She was known for her generosity, and she always prepared special foods and sweets for the occasion, which we always enjoyed. My brother has a sweet tooth and used to enjoy Aunt Zainy's *tein*, "cooked figs," especially when cooked with walnuts, among other ingredients. This was certainly a special treat that no one wanted to miss. May God bless her soul!

Coming to America

It was here in America that I got to spend more time with my brother, getting to know him better. He came to the United States early in 1956 and I followed some five years later. By the time I came in September 1961, he had already been ordained a priest and was serving the parish of St. George in Cleveland, Ohio. I remember I sent him a note informing him of my arrival time to New York City, and that I would be attending Miami University in Oxford, Ohio. When my plane landed and I cleared customs together with a couple of friends, I had the greatest surprise of my life: I found my brother, Father Philip, our friend Father Antoun Khouri (whom I knew from Lebanon), and my brother's friend Edward Khouri from Cleveland all waiting for me outside. When I heard my name being called, worlds away from Abou Mizan, I just could not believe it! I had no idea that anybody would be waiting for me at one of the largest airports in the world. That is indelibly etched in my memory. We drove to Philadelphia that evening where we spent the night in the hospitality of Father Antoun, later Bishop Antoun, then serving the Philadelphia parish.

After a good night's sleep we woke up refreshed and ready to drive the distance to Cleveland. This was my first full day in America. I was so impressed by the scenery, by the weather and by the size of America. I could never imagine that Cleveland was so far away. In Lebanon distances are so short. In a couple of hours one crosses Lebanon from north to south and east to west. Finally, after what seemed to me an endless drive we arrived at my brother's residence in Cleveland, where I rested for about a week before we took to the road again, this time to Miami University in southern Ohio.

Throughout my undergraduate work at Miami University I spent my summers and Christmas vacations with my brother in Cleveland, doing odd jobs. During this time I came to realize what priests endure in America. Not only do they minister to their parishioners spiritually, but also they serve as administrators, educators, psychologists, marriage counselors, missionaries, fund-raisers and public relations experts. My brother did all that. He was on the job twenty-four hours a day. The telephone rang constantly. Sometimes I had the unpleasant duty to answer the phone when he was not at home.

Following my graduation from Miami University in the spring of 1965, I transferred to the University of Michigan at Ann Arbor for graduate work. This practically ended the Cleveland period, with all its memories for both of us. As to my brother, he took a leave of absence from parish duties in 1964 to finish a degree in theology at St. Vladimir's Orthodox Seminary. Then, in 1966, he was nominated, elected and consecrated Metropolitan Archbishop of New York and All North America, succeeding the late Metropolitan Antony Bashir. Shortly after, he moved the archdiocesan headquarters from Brooklyn, New York, to Englewood, New Jersey. In the meantime, and before I finished my doctoral work in 1971, I married Elaine Abodeely of Worcester, Massachusetts, in 1969. Our first child, Philip, was born in August 1971, and was followed by our daughter, Leslie, a few years later. In addition, chance had it that I was offered and accepted a teaching position at Worcester State College, Worcester, Massachusetts, a three hour drive from Englewood, my brother's residence.

Staying Close

Although each one of us has his concerns and responsibilities in our new roles, we remain close and constantly in touch. My brother has insisted that we spend major holidays such as Thanksgiving, Christmas and Easter together at his headquarters in Englewood. This we have done faithfully since 1971, with little exception. It has become a tradition, a family get-together that we—especially the children—look forward to from year to year. To listen to the service on Good Friday, Easter and Christmas, much of it chanted in Arabic, is an inspiring and spiritually uplifting experience to me personally. Somehow, Arabic moves me in a way English never does. Besides attending the religious services, we use the time to discuss family issues, work, religion, politics, Lebanon, the Arab-Israeli conflict and Iraq. Or we reminisce about Abou Mizan, childhood days, St. Elias Monastery, Balamand, etc. In this regard, His Grace Bishop Antoun is invaluable, since my brother and Bishop Antoun are school friends and have shared many experiences together. These family meetings have strengthened our bonds and built special relationships between my children and their uncle, my brother.

The Magnitude of His Leadership

Although certain aspects of my brother's leadership qualities came to light early, when he was in Lebanon as well as the United States, the full weight and magnitude of his leadership became apparent only after his elevation to the rank of Metropolitan. Metropolitan Philip provided not only the Antiochian Orthodox but also Orthodoxy in America with a dynamic, charismatic and selfless leadership unprecedented in the history of Orthodoxy in this land. He never played the role of a *charge'd'affaires*. He was and is an enemy of the status quo. He never lets events take their course; he shapes events. When he assumed his responsibilities as Metropolitan, the Antiochian Archdiocese in North America was divided into two rival and competitive jurisdictions. He immediately contacted the late Archbishop Michael, appointed committees and began the work to heal the split. Archbishop Michael, to his credit, responded positively, and by the summer of 1975, unity papers were signed and the split became history, all with the blessings of the Holy Synod of Antioch.

Not only did Metropolitan Philip work for Antiochian Orthodox unity in North America, he also worked for the unity of all Orthodox Christians in North America. It pains him tremendously to see Orthodox Christians divided into several jurisdictions based on national lines. Although efforts in this regard have so far been unsuccessful, work continues and Metropolitan Philip is in the forefront of this effort.

On the Antiochian level, since Metropolitan Philip assumed the leadership of the archdiocese, the number of parishes and missions has increased substantially, perhaps quadrupled. Being a firm believer in the universality of the Orthodox Church, he opened his jurisdiction to all those who wanted to become Orthodox and who agreed to abide by the rules of the Church, regardless of national or ethnic background. On this basis, in 1987 he welcomed the Evangelicals who wanted to become Orthodox. Having come to the conclusion that being administratively dependent on the Holy Synod of Antioch impeded the growth of the archdiocese, he worked diligently for self-rule, which has already been achieved. His achievements also include the organization of the Antiochian Orthodox Christian Women of North America (1973), the establishment of The Order of St. Ignatius (1975), and the purchase of the Antiochian Village (1978).

Metropolitan Philip's leadership has not been limited to church affairs only. He has been an active leader for peace and justice in the Middle East, both between Israel and the Palestinians, and between Israel and the Arab states. When the Lebanese civil war broke out in 1975, he worked tirelessly to stop it and to effect reconciliation among the Lebanese. He worked in harmony with other Lebanese religious leaders, Christians, Muslims and Druzes to achieve that objective. He has always been a voice of sanity and moderation in Lebanon and the Middle East.

In conclusion, Metropolitan Philip is action-oriented, an achiever; he is never satisfied with what there is, he is always striving for the better. He has been and continues to be a source of inspiration to me personally. My family and I, here and abroad, are proud of the creative, forceful and decisive leadership he continues to provide for the Antiochian Orthodox Church of North America, and for Orthodoxy in general. May God grant him "Many Years!"

IN THE VIEW OF

THE VERY REV. PAUL DOYLE
PROTOSYNGELLOS OF THE ARCHDIOCESE

Philip, the Dynamic Leader

IT IS AN HONOR AND A PRIVILEGE FOR ME TO CONTRIBUTE THIS MESSAGE in honor of the fortieth anniversary of the ordination of His Eminence Metropolitan Philip to the rank of Metropolitan and Archbishop of our God-protected archdiocese.

My Early Years and My Discovery

No doubt, I am not the only convert to contribute to this book. Towards the end of 1971, after serving about ten years as an episcopal priest, I realized, quite frankly, that I was simply not in the Church that Our Lord Jesus Christ had established. May I say, somewhat parenthetically, that I am not suggesting that there is no salvation outside the formal boundaries of Orthodoxy, but I needed to have my membership in the Holy Orthodox Church. There were numerous jurisdictions. Which one was I to choose?

From a friend I heard about the Antiochian Orthodox Archdiocese led by the dynamic and forward-looking Metropolitan Archbishop Philip. The English language was widely used and converts were welcomed. The fact that they had a Western Rite interested me. My first step was to contact

Father Antony Gabriel, who was pastor of a multi-ethnic, English speaking parish located at that time in Oak Park, Illinois. Under the direction of Fr. Antony, I studied about the Orthodox Faith, and I was chrismated in 1973. I met His Eminence at St. George during Lent that year. I had an opportunity to take an extensive trip to the Middle East. When I returned by way of New York His Eminence invited me to have lunch with him at the headquarters in Englewood, New Jersey. He was most gracious and kind, and encouraged me in my study about Orthodoxy. Subsequently, I was ordained to the Holy Diaconate in 1974. Metropolitan Philip permitted me to attend one year at St. Vladimir Seminary with an unexpected gift of a full scholarship for the academic year 1974-75.

On Marcy 16, 1975, His Eminence ordained me to the Holy priesthood. In order to enable members of my family to be present, Metropolitan Philip decided to ordain me at St. Nicholas, San Francisco, California. My first assignment as a parish priest was to St. Elias in Atlanta, Georgia. After two years ministering to the wonderful people of Atlanta, His Eminence assigned me to Portland, Oregon. I learned the very important lesson that a priest obediently goes where he is assigned. Metropolitan Philip continued to give me his pastoral guidance, love and support. In March, 1980, during his visitation to St. George in Portland, Oregon, he elevated me to the rank of archimandrite. This honor was completely unexpected.

A Concerned Overseer

St. George in Portland, Oregon, was a very vibrant parish, and being there certainly enriched my ministry. However, it was with sadness and regret that I asked Saidna about transferring to a parish located in a warmer climate. He was concerned about my health and decided to send me to a new mission station in the South Bay area of Los Angeles County. In 1984, His Grace Bishop Antoun named the mission, "St. Matthew," and I was the first pastor until the summer of 1999. In 1990, I was diagnosed with angina and, subsequently, had open-heart surgery. The members of the parish were very supportive. Again Metropolitan Philip showed his thoughtfulness and loving care by writing to me with regard to my treatment, urging me to have open-heart surgery. My cardiologist agreed and this was performed in July, 1990. His Eminence kept close tabs on me throughout my surgery and recuperation.

In 1991, our archdiocese had a convention in Washington, D.C. At the end of the assembly meeting, His Eminence called upon me to come to the podium. I had no clue as to the reason why I was summoned. To my great surprise, he announced that he was appointing me to the position of Protosyngellos of the archdiocese. Needless to say, I was overwhelmed!

His Eminence had previously appointed me Mission Coordinator of the Western Region, and I made monthly reports to His Grace Bishop Antoun. He later appointed me Dean of the Southern California Deanery, and I made regular reports about our Deanery activities. He always encouraged and supported me in these endeavors.

As I reflect upon my years of ministry in this archdiocese, I am so very grateful that the Holy Spirit directed me to the Antiochian Archdiocese. These past thirty-three years have shown me that I definitely became a member of a vibrant archdiocese under a most dynamic Hierarch. Metropolitan Philip has always had a great vision for the Orthodox, especially in America. He has continually fought for a united Orthodox Church, and no obstacles have dimmed that vision.

He has never ceased to promote jurisdictional unity by reminding us all that Orthodoxy should not be a best-kept secret. Within the archdiocese, he has promoted the entrance of converts to the Church. He dramatically welcomed the Evangelical Orthodox Church to the Antiochian Archdiocese with the approval and consent of Patriarch Ignatius IV and the Holy Synod of Antioch.

I join all the members of our God-protected, self-ruled archdiocese in giving thanks for Metropolitan Philip's leadership. May Our Blessed Lord protect him, and grant that he will continue to press forward with his vision of a united Orthodoxy. God grant "Many Years!" to our chief shepherd, His Eminence, Metropolitan Philip!

—The Rt. Rev. Paul Doyle

 **IN THE VIEW OF**

THE VERY REV. ELIAS BITAR
VICAR-GENERAL, ANTIOCHIAN ARCHDIOCESE

Forty Years Ago I Heard His Voice

Our First Meeting

IT WAS A FALL AFTERNOON, NOVEMBER 1968, when I, a seminarian serving at the archdiocese headquarters in Tripoli, Lebanon, heard that the Metropolitan of New York and All North American was coming for a visit; my heart rejoiced!

I finished the Balamand Seminary in 1967 and was chanting at the St. George Cathedral of Tripoli, Lebanon. I was excited to meet this famous bishop who greatly loved his clergy and his faithful. I had heard about him and seen him two years before at his consecration at the St. Elias Monastery in Dhour Shweir, Lebanon, where the Balamand choir of which I was a member chanted the Liturgy.

After lunch, His Eminence asked me to chant something. I got my music book and chanted the ninth Ode of *Pasch*, "The Angel," in Arabic, from the *Mitry Murr* book (*Alkithara Alrouhia*). He smiled and said: "Do you want to come to America?" *Iza Alla Raad*, "If God wills," I responded.

Those years, people just dreamed of going to America.

From Thessalonica to Little Falls

In 1971 I left the University of Thessalonica, Greece, and came to New York, where Father Elias Audi of Yonkers (now Metropolitan of Beirut), picked me up and brought me to his parish. After one year of intensive English, three years of St. Vladimir's and thirty-one years in the priesthood, I believe that God had a plan and Saidna Philip executed it. He saw in me what I could not see in myself. Sometimes parents with real vision are able to see in the lives of their children a future beyond the child's own imagination. Saidna Philip had that ability. He, in reality, adopted me as one of his clergy and spiritual children. When I was in California the first ten years, he made sure I received the proper training under Father Paul Romley, my friend and best man. Father Paul requested that after seminary Saidna would assign me to assist him in Los Angeles.

Then, five years later, during a pastoral visit to Los Angeles, Saidna Philip, once again issued the next call. "It's time to be on your own." From Los Angeles to Northern California I went. Five years later, a call from Saidna Antoun initiated my transfer to Little Falls, New Jersey, ten miles from the archdiocese headquarters and eight miles from Father Joseph Allen. At St. Vladimir's Seminary, I took over Bishop Basil's place in teaching Byzantine chant and music, with the blessings of Saidna Philip, in addition to teaching the Arabic language.

A Step Further

Since I was eleven years old I lived among priests and bishops and everything in between, but Saidna Philip stands a mile above all the rest. What he saw in me brought me to these shores of the United States to serve Antioch in America. What I see in him now, and saw in him then, is the image of the good shepherd. Every priest leaves father, mother and family to serve the Church, but Saidna Philip takes shepherding a step further.

First, he listens to the voices of his priests. A metropolitan with all sorts of administrative situations and challenges, he still finds time to actually listen to the concerns of his priests. He listens not only as a priest, but also as a father and a concerned friend. Then he *does* something about that. Whether the concerns are legitimate or not, Saidna comforts, consoles, encourages, realigns and assures his love. Like a doctor, sometimes he needs to perform surgery, sometimes even a radical operation! As painful as something like this might be, he makes the healing process easier to accept, tolerate and bear.

Secondly, Saidna Philip never leaves his priests destitute, even when they leave him. His love overshadows even those whose mistakes led them out from beneath his *omophorion*. His compassion has no end or boundaries. Isn't that the same with our Lord? The priest's *family* is as special as the priest himself to Saidna Philip. He receives letters and calls from priest wives and children, which he answers patently and compassionately. Not too many people are willing to do that!

His Home is Our Home

First, as his neighbor I am always overwhelmed by his hospitality and kindness. I am always treated with utmost respect. He greets everyone as if he was extremely special. He makes his guests feel welcomed and loved.

For a long time, as I went through school, I saw that bishops don't dine with priests. This bishop dines even with seminarians more than once a year. When I attended St. Vladimir's I was invited to the headquarters for dinner with the seminarians. Even until this day the tradition continues.

His modesty brings him closer to our hearts. Not only do we have great love for him, but we also know that he loved us first with the love of God. Every time I happen to visit his home, I can't leave without having lunch. His home is always open to everyone—"but please call first so Almaza may have enough plates on the table."

I traveled with him on a few occasions. I have never sat next to a Metropolitan to receive confession, never stayed in a room next to his on a trip or had to call room service to bring breakfast. Who am I? He made me feel good as an individual and I thanked God that Saidna Philip is my metropolitan. I am proud to be associated with him.

For What He Sees in Me

Music has been my life and serving him was, is and always will be, an absolute honor. Then he appointed me his Vicar General. Unworthy as I am, I have his love and trust. For that I am grateful. There is a song by Kenny Rogers entitled: "For what he sees in me." Thank you Saidna for what you saw and still see in me. Looking back at these forty years, I see not only hundreds of accomplishments which are a result of a deeper, and a more special you; I also see a heart which has once been opened by doctors, and thousands of times by your children, seeking your love and friendship. You kept your heart open all your life. You have taken the Church from glory to glory because you are driven by faith, determination and conviction.

God has carried you across stony and thorny terrains. He has led you over mountains of illness and valleys of challenges. You have gone through everything to see your dreams come true. But those dreams were the Church's promised land. You took all of us by the hand. You did not split the Red Sea or cause water to gush forth from the rock. You did not bring down manna from heaven or talk to the burning bush. But to *us* you are the Moses whom we know and love. With you we laugh and cry, we stumble and rise. In you we find consolation in times of sorrow, and hope in times of despair. Progress with you has been a joyful journey. You have been a good captain and a shepherd. You have gone after many lost sheep and brought them home. You have taken us to war over apathy, regression and stagnation, and we can feel confident and victorious.

You kept us deeply rooted in Antioch and kept our arms open for America. You have made the Antioch of North America as the promised land of Orthodoxy, due to your faith and leadership. Your leadership is an everlasting journey with us. When we are not led by your word, we are driven by your love.

Many Years, Saidna! Thank you for the precious gift you continue to give to us: your life. May God grant you good health to continue the journey, so that we may continue to be led by you!

—Father Elias Bitar, Vicar General

IN THE VIEW OF

GEORGE J. FARHA, M.D.
VICE CHAIRMAN, ARCHDIOCESE BOARD OF TRUSTEES

IT IS INDEED A PRIVILEGE AND A BLESSING to be provided with the opportunity to celebrate your fortieth anniversary as our Metropolitan Archbishop. I am cognizant of the fact that your burden has been very heavy, but, hopefully, it was made lighter by your faith in our holy Church, your determination to propel us forward and your strong belief that "faith without works is dead."

Thank You! Thank You!

Thank you for being our spiritual father for forty years. Thank you for being a true leader, a great visionary and a courageous soldier who throughout his life has defended the principles of our Holy Church, on this continent and in other parts of the world. Thank you for consistently helping the needy, the oppressed, the orphans, the sinners and the despised. Thank you for being the magnificent communicator and the brilliant debater that you are.

August 14, 1966, the day you were consecrated as Metropolitan Archbishop of North America at St. Elias Monastery in Lebanon by Patriarch Theodosius VI, will be remembered as the most significant date in the life of this archdiocese. We are the recipients of all your accomplishments and we will always remember that! Thank you for founding The Order of St. Ignatius of Antioch, which has become the financial backbone of this archdiocese. Thank you for purchasing the Antiochian Village property, which has become a symbol of our heritage and the glue that holds our children together. Thank you for founding the Antiochian Orthodox Christian Women of North America, which has become a major player in the life of this archdiocese. Thank you for merging both Antiochian Archdioceses into one. Thank you for accepting into Orthodoxy the Antiochian Evangelical Mission. These are but a few of the many accomplishments that you, Saidna, have given us.

Our Travels Together

On a more personal note, thank you for allowing me to travel with you to Moscow, where we visited His Beatitude Patriarch Alexis II, and witnessed the remarkable strength of the Orthodox Church in that country. Thank you for the opportunity to travel with you to the Middle East on three different occasions (2001, 2002 and 2003), where you so brilliantly convinced members of the Holy Synod of Antioch of the necessity of the North American Archdiocese becoming a self-ruled entity, which it is now. Thank you for the many nights in your suite in Damascus where, in the presence of several Metropolitan Archbishops, the Holy Synod agenda as it pertains to North America was discussed and defended so logically by you. Thank you for lifting me up in a moment of frustration and doubt, saying: "George, don't let what you hear or see weaken your faith."

Finally, thank you for your friendship and the many lessons I learned from you, including humility, tolerance and love.

Saidna, we love you! May God grant you many more anniversaries!!

Yours in Christ,

—George J. Farha, M.D.

 **IN THE VIEW OF**

THE VERY REV. PAUL SCHNEIRLA
VICAR GENERAL, WESTERN RITE

Metropolitan Philip and My Journey to Orthodoxy

LET ME BEGIN MY EARLIEST REMEMBRANCE OF METROPOLITAN PHILIP by stepping far back in time. After my ordination in the early 1940s, and following some dozen years as pastor of two Lebanese parishes in northern Michigan—a Syrian community in Allentown, Pennsylvania, and nine months as the first pastor of St. Mary's, a newly founded parish in Brooklyn, New York—I decided to check the background of my chosen church. As a convert to Orthodoxy, I felt my calling and faith could only benefit from a journey to Antioch and the centers of Near Eastern Christianity.

And so in 1952, with my wife, Shirley, and eight year old daughter, Dorothy, I headed *ad Limina Apostolorum* to the Pentarchy including the fallen see. The only patriarch of the five I knew personally was Athenagoras of Constantinople, who had lived in the United States as the Archbishop of America.

Our Trip to Antioch and Meeting Saidna
For me, the most significant event of our trip to the Levant occurred in the courtyard of the Antiochian

Patriarchate in Damascus. Having arrived on a day the Holy Synod was meeting, we were invited for lunch with the assembled group. We were standing in the courtyard waiting for the call to lunch with the lay scholar George Khodre, present Metropolitan of Mt. Lebanon, and perhaps a dozen deacons in Middle Eastern clergy street dress. Embarrassed to be in my Western clericals, I mentioned this to the deacons. Immediately, one of them with a small beard replied in perfect English: "On the contrary, we are behind the times dressed as we are. We should be wearing clothes like yours." *Ah ha*, I thought, *this young man has a spirit like our Metropolitan Antony, and if given the chance, he could drag our Church, no doubt kicking and screaming, in to the 19th, or at least the 18th, century.* That was my very first meeting with Philip Saliba. He was later to become a student of mine at St. Vladimir's, where my early, positive remembrance of him was reinforced by his intelligence and scholarly mind.

Our pilgrimage to the roots of Orthodoxy was memorable for all of us. A decade later, Dorothy chose to spend a summer vacation from college at the Russian convents of Gethsemane and Bethany, whose superiors were the former Anglican nuns, Mothers Mary and Martha. Following our initial trip to Jordan in 1952, dedicated as the good Abbesses were to pray for an addition to our family, our son, Peter, was born and greeted with joy by our new acquaintances in the Near East.

When Philip Saliba moved to the United States to follow an academic career at Holy Cross Seminary in Boston, Massachusetts, he also studied at Wayne State University in Detroit, Michigan, and served parishes in Detroit and Cleveland. As expected, he associated with younger clergy in these years but his bilingual skill, keen mind and talent for communication confirmed early on that he was indeed the ideal candidate for promotion should the need arise.

Being Elected as Metropolitan

At the untimely passing of Metropolitan Antony Bashir in 1966, I was Corporate Secretary of the archdiocese, Secretary of the Archdiocese Board of Trustees, and Secretary of the Faculty at St. Vladimir's Seminary, with an extensive network of friends in our community. I assumed that my preference for

Father Saliba as successor to Metropolitan Antony, with whom I had been very close, required a strong supportive stance within the archdiocese. A neighboring pastor and colleague had in fact established his own network of friends and supporters who regarded him as the ideal successor to Metropolitan Antony. Faced with the delicate situation of Father Saliba actively expressing his appreciation for his rival, I attempted to assure my neighbor that there was nothing personal in my campaign as I made every effort to offset his own plans and promote the election of Father Saliba. I am unashamed to be highly gratified by the results of the successful election of Father Saliba to Metropolitan of the Antiochian Orthodox Church in North America.

In my review of Saidna Philip's accomplishments, there is no question his openness to adapt to life in the "new world" is of special significance and importance. The Western Rite Vicariate, originally endorsed by his predecessor, was fostered and supported by the new metropolitan, who has unceasingly championed its relevance to American Orthodoxy. This would not have been the case with a less visionary leader. I am most grateful that Deacon Saliba, who so graciously made me feel at home in Damascus in the 1950s, was destined to come to the West, adopt our clerical code of dress and embrace the culture in which he found himself.

There is no need for me to recount once again, as I know my colleagues will do, the details of the enormous growth and extensive development of the archdiocese in the last forty years. It has been an amazingly productive era, in which the progress has been upward and onward—an inspiring time for which we may gratefully thank the Almighty God whose inspiration led us into this leadership. Metropolitan Philip's warmth and encouragement has remained a constant source of strength and spiritual enrichment for the clergy and laity of the Antiochian Orthodox Church in America.

Thank you, Saidna, and "Many Years!"

—Father Paul, Shirley, Dorothy and Peter Schneirla

IN THE VIEW OF

ROBERT H. LAHAM
TREASURER, ARCHDIOCESE BOARD OF TRUSTEES

Fifty and Counting

MY RELATIONSHIP WITH METROPOLITAN PHILIP GOES BACK FIFTY YEARS. We met in 1956 during his first trip to Boston; he was here as a chanter and deacon at Saint Mary's in Cambridge, Massachusetts, while attending Holy Cross Seminary. I have known him from his priesthood to his elevation as Metropolitan of North America. It has been a journey I have been proud to witness.

A Familial Friendship

My father, Monsour Laham, was lay chairman of the Archdiocese Board of Trustees and Ted Mackoul was the treasurer at the time of Metropolitan Philip's installation as Metropolitan. They worked well together as Saidna transitioned into his new position and established himself as spiritual leader of our archdiocese. Thus began a familial friendship and so much more.

When Metropolitan Philip became Primate of North America in 1966 we had sixty-six churches. Today, forty years later, we have over 250 churches. Many organizations have been established and have indeed flourished under the leadership and tutelage of Saidna. It has been gratifying to see that the Metropolitan recognized that for us to become more than just churches in America, we needed the model church to grow. These changes include: Teen SOYO, providing a structured foundation for our future leaders; the Antiochian Women of North America, giving voice to the backbone of our church; and The Order of St. Ignatius of Antioch, enabling us to fulfill Saidna's dream of spreading Orthodoxy to this great nation. The largest project undertaken by the Metropolitan has been the Antiochian Village and Camp. Additionally, seven satellite camps have now been established throughout the United States. Over 2,000 children attend these camps each year, enjoying sports and companionship and having fun, while learning about their faith. Many establish lifelong friendships. Through his foresight and vision our archdiocese has grown to what it is today: a leading voice of Orthodoxy in America. His is a legacy of building up our Church, reaching out to our youth and encouraging all of us to answer our own calls to Orthodoxy.

A Careful Listener and Diplomat

As treasurer for the archdiocese I have had the pleasure of working with the Metropolitan on many projects for thirty-five years. He is a man open to ideas—a careful listener. He values loyalty and is loyal in return. He is a champion fundraiser. Metropolitan Philip has a way of getting people to work with him, and to work for him. He is a charismatic man and leader.

I have had the real pleasure of traveling extensively with Metropolitan Philip. Together we went to Russia for the 850th anniversary of Moscow and the consecration of the cathedral there. We have traveled to Lebanon and Syria. In fact, during the Iran hostage crisis, the Metropolitan, who is held in high esteem in Syria, was called to meet with President Assad. As treasurer of the archdiocese and an Arab American businessman, I was one of several who were asked to accompany Saidna. President Assad was eager to hear the opinions of Arab Americans, and mostly to listen to Metropolitan Philip. We flew by military plane and then by Russian helicopter to President Assad's summer home. For over four hours we met and discussed many topics, including the hostage situation. At the close of our meeting, President Assad, clearly impressed with Saidna, promised to do all he could to secure the release of the hostages—although he conceded it was not in his sole control. The hostages were released two weeks later.

Metropolitan Philip Saliba is a man of principle. He is well read and knowledgeable, a man of keen intellect, a deep thinker. He has varied interests and a wonderful sense of humor. He is a man of dignity who has brought honor to his role as Primate of our archdiocese. It is an honor to work with Saidna Philip and to consider him to be a good and trusted friend.

IN THE VIEW OF

CHARLES AJALAT
CHANCELLOR, ANTIOCHIAN ARCHDIOCESE

Saidna Philip, A Man of Unity

SAIDNA PHILIP HAS WORKED EXTENSIVELY WITH ME as Chancellor, both with regard to legal affairs and with regard to the external relations of the archdiocese. It has been a privilege to work with him during the years I have served. He has been a mentor, a teacher and, most importantly, a friend.

"That they all may be one" (John 17:21). The essence of Metropolitan Philip Saliba is that he is a man of *unity*. This unity is made real by three other words: vision, courage and leadership.

Vision and Courage in Leadership

"A people without vision perishes" (Proverbs 29:18). Metropolitan Philip's vision is the vision of Christ— a *united* body righteously and justly transforming our own souls and the cultures in which we live. Here are ten examples of Saidna Philip's ministry of unity with vision, courage and action, a number of which I had the privilege to work on with him:

1. He had the courage to *unify* the two Antiochian Archdiocese when the Mother Church simply would not act.
2. He had the courage to *unify* the Evangelical Orthodox into the canonical Orthodox Church when everyone else refused or delayed.
3. He has the courage to repeatedly exhort the Arab world and all Arab religious leaders, who respect him so much, to be *unified* in the search for peace and justice.
4. He had the courage, against nay saying, to building the Antiochian Village and national camping programs where many of our youth have become *unified* into the body of Christ.
5. He had the courage, against nay saying, to build The Order of St. Ignatius, so that we might have the resources to make *unity* meaningful.
6. He had the courage to *unify* the women of the archdiocese through the Antiochian Orthodox Christian Women, and the youth of our archdiocese through the Youth Department, the Fellowship and Teen SOYO.
7. He had the courage to preserve the *unity* of the Church around the episcopacy, rather than to allow schism and Protestant-type disunity, as in the painful Ben Lomond situation.
8. He had the courage to *unify* all of the Orthodox bishops in North America for the first time in history in the beautiful place in the mountains, which his vision created—the Antiochian Village.
9. He had the courage to lead the Standing Conference of Canonical Orthodox Bishops in the Americas into a *unified* ministry to the poor through International Orthodox Christian Charities.
10. He had the courage to achieve self-rule for our archdiocese, and to lay the groundwork for a stable, continued, flourishing and *unified* archdiocese—and a future *unified* Church—on this continent.

In His Own Words

To feel Metropolitan Philip's spirit of unity let us listen to his own words in just two of these areas:

First is the Toledo-New York split. Years ago, the Antiochian Church in America unfortunately became divided into two archdioceses, and then through the vision, courage and leadership of Metropolitan Philip, became united again in the early 1970s. Listen to his historic words to the people in Charleston, West Virginia, in 1973:

> In the past, we have had some encounters to find a solution to our North American problem. Regretfully, these encounters have failed because both of us, deep in our hearts, were relying on the Holy Synod of Antioch, which is 7,000 miles away from us, to resolve our problem and bring unity to our divided people in North America.
>
> How can we dream of a united Arab world, or how can we dream of a united Orthodox Church in North America, if our own family is divided.

And Metropolitan Philip proceeded to lead the two archdioceses into the full unity of the one strong archdiocese we have now.

The second example of his love for unity has been his leading the Orthodox Church on this continent toward a unified witness. Why Orthodox administrative unity? So that Christ and His Church—the Orthodox Church—might accomplish its mission and that the proclamation of the true Good News of Christ might be more visible and available to all North Americans. An Orthodox Church in North America, kept fragmented by the Mother Churches, is hampered in truly witnessing to Christ on this continent, and in transforming its culture, its peoples and its policies. As Metropolitan Philip says:

> When the American media refer to the main religions in this country, it always mentions Protestantism, Roman Catholicism and Judaism. Can we blame America for its

ignorance of Orthodoxy? I think not. It is we Orthodox who are to blame. . . . This Church, which was established by Christ Himself through the power of the Holy Spirit, cannot be limited by geography or culture.

Where is our influence on our national and local politics? Where is our common position vis-à-vis abortion, euthanasia, homosexuality, social injustice and world hunger? . . . The only way we can respond effectively to this challenge is through Orthodox unity . . . I strongly believe that Orthodox unity is inevitable because the All-Holy Spirit continues to work in the Church.

From Vision to Action

Our Metropolitan puts his vision into action. He was instrumental in forming International Orthodox Christian Charities (IOCC) as a united North American Orthodox witness. From 1992 to 2005 IOCC has distributed over $225,000,000.00 through thirty countries in short-term and long-term assistance to those in need. This includes millions of dollars of aid to school children in Lebanon, which will impact an entire generation of Lebanese children.

In 1994, Saidna Philip hosted the historic First Conference of Bishops at the Antiochian Village, an event which was a turning point for the entire Orthodox Church in North America and for the Orthodox Churches of the world. Listen to Saidna's words:

> Ninety-five percent of my priests were born in this country. Therefore this is their burning desire, their constant dream—to see Orthodoxy united in this country. This does not mean that we sever relations with the Mother Churches. On the contrary. . . . We want to be more effective in our helping the Mother Churches. I am sure that the Mother Churches will benefit from a strong united Orthodox Church more than they can benefit from a fragmented Orthodox Church in North America.

As he gave the final homily to all the Orthodox bishops in North America—gathered for the first time in history—they hung, literally hung, on his every word, it was so quiet that truly one could hear a pin drop. Our Metropolitan, concluding that brilliant homily, said:

> The two past days which we have spent here prove to me beyond doubt that an old era has passed and a new era has begun and a new day has dawned on us in inter-orthodox relations.
>
> Yes, the grace of the Holy Spirit has gathered us from throughout this continent to witness to Holy Orthodoxy, to say that we are one; to tell the world that the Orthodox Church on this continent has a dynamism which you cannot find in any place in this world.
>
> Therefore, the future is ours: the future belongs to our children, our clergy and our faithful.

In both the Toledo-New York situation and administrative unity on this continent, we see three characteristics of our Metropolitan that have infused his ministry of unification. They are his *vision* for unity, his *courage* to move the Church toward unity and his *leadership* to consummate actions of unity.

Metropolitan Philip, in his very essence, is a man of unity.

May the Father, Son and Holy Spirit, one God, who loves unity, continue to honor and keep safe this man of unity, our beloved Metropolitan Philip. Saidna, may God grant you "Many Years!"

—Charles R. Ajalat,

Chancellor, The Self-Ruled Antiochian Orthodox Christian Archdiocese of North America

 **IN THE VIEW OF**

ROBERT A. KOORY
CHANCELLOR, ANTIOCHIAN ARCHDIOCESE

Saidna Philip from a Chancellor's View

THE CHANCELLORS IN OUR ARCHDIOCESE ARE LAWYERS who are appointed by the Metropolitan Primate with the consent of the Board of Trustees. They are officers of the archdiocese whose function are to be the legal advisers to the Metropolitan and to the Board of Trustees. They serve at the pleasure of the Metropolitan.

Working with Saidna Philip, Seeing His Compassion

When I was first appointed to this position in 1989, to replace the retiring George Elias Jr., I found the position to be largely a position of honor without any substantial responsibility. Certainly there were the rare occasions in which legal advice was required, but for the most part those consisted of questions involving corporate law or liability avoidance issues. Some issues would involve the referral of parish questions often pertaining to the parish constitution, the incorporation of a local community, or the role of the priest or parish council. Drafting the resolutions presented at the Archdiocese Convention was a significant portion of the job.

The tranquil life of the chancellor changed almost overnight. Suddenly, as a result of claims of inappropriate actions by certain individuals, as the senior chancellor, and being experienced in civil trial work, I was asked to investigate these allegations and advise the Metropolitan as to the possible responses. On some occasions, if the matter proceeded to court, I would monitor the proceedings. At all times, the Metropolitan would be apprised of any significant developments.

Needless to say, because of the nature of these claims and the privileged relationship that a lawyer maintains when giving advice, it is not possible to divulge any details of these matters. But by merely observing that a lawyer was involved with possible court proceedings, it could be fairly concluded that there were allegations of inappropriate conduct of some kind.

It is through the discussions with Metropolitan Philip pertaining to these matters that I gleamed a side of him many individuals may not appreciate. To me, Metropolitan Philip's response was one of true Christian love. At the same time, when others may have been repulsed, he would show true compassion for the fallen nature of man.

While I know that Saidna Philip understands human nature much more deeply than I ever will, he always seemed amazed, regardless of the nature of the allegations, that an individual, especially the one involved, would behave in the manner claimed. Perhaps as a lawyer for over thirty-five years and having seen and read cases involving the most bizarre of human behavior, I have become cynical. When it comes to man's self interests, I have come to believe that almost any conduct, no matter how deviant, is within the realm of possibility. Men and women will seemingly stop at nothing when motivated by their own greed or pride; and it matters little from where they came or what their walk of life is.

Yet, while I looked at a person's actions and expected the worst, Metropolitan Philip reacted just the opposite. He would see the great potential for an individual to be Christ-like, and see the inability to live up to that potential as a great tragedy. When he would ask me rhetorically, "How could he have done such a thing?", he meant more than how could the person have so acted. He meant how could that individual who had such Christ-like qualities have thrown it all away for a relative moment of pleasure.

It was to him always "tragic"; it mattered not whether the individual was a man or a woman, a member of the laity or of the clergy. All situations were ones of personal and individual fallings for which Saidna always showed the greatest compassion.

When I would vent my righteous indignation and state a diatribe against the person, Saidna Philip would sigh and say: "Bob, we must hate the sin, but we must love the sinner." Saidna follows in the tradition of the Fathers who also teach us to love the sinner but hate the devil who caused him to sin.

His Healing Forgiveness

I would see this ability to love the sinner in his readiness to forgive those who had committed the transgression. Although it pained him personally that some would act the way they would, especially if the actions were against him or this God-protected archdiocese, he remained willing to heal the rift caused by the person's actions and to forgive. At the same time, he well understands that for the protection of the Church and laity, and for the sanctity of the holy priesthood, there are times that forgiveness does not mean restoration to one's prior position. True Christian love sometimes means strict Christian discipline.

One story stands out in my mind as a pristine example of the fatherly love that Saidna Philip has for all of his sheep. One of the priests, who had a terminal illness, because of a bitter disagreement with Metropolitan Philip sought Saidna's permission to be released to the Orthodox Church in America. Metropolitan Philip knew of the priest's illness and also knew if he released him to the OCA that, when the man died, his widow would not receive any benefits from the OCA, and would no longer be eligible for benefits from the Antiochian Archdiocese.

While lesser men would have been happy to see the man leave and would have considered the impending misfortune that would befall the widow as the man's own doing, Metropolitan Philip showed true love for the priest who was at enmity with him, and begged him to stay in the archdiocese. He advised the priest that if he insisted, that he would release him to the OCA. But he asked him to stay, and to think of his wife who would receive nothing when the priest died if he moved to the OCA. The priest heeded the Metropolitan's advice and stayed. He died shortly thereafter and his widow received the housing allowance paid to the widows of priests in our archdiocese.

We hear so often of what true Christian love should be. Through my work as Chancellor, I have been blessed to witness in our beloved Saidna Philip the personification of that love. "Many Years" to our chief shepherd!

—Robert A Koory, Chancellor

# IN THE VIEW OF

Dr. John D. Dalack
Secretary, Archdiocese Board of Trustees,
Co-Chairman, Department of Lay Ministries

A True Father

Forty years ago, the Rt. Rev. Archimandrite Philip Saliba was chosen by God to be the Metropolitan Archbishop of our North American Archdiocese. As he prayed before the altar of the Patriarchal Cathedral, the Holy Spirit descended upon him and consecrated him, and elevated him to be our spiritual father. And *father* is exactly the word that fits. As I see him, and as I have experienced him, the manner in which Metropolitan Philip has fulfilled, and continues to fulfill, the calling of his Episcopacy has transformed our archdiocese into nothing less than an *extended family*.

It was within the context of family that the man, Philip Saliba, first became a presence in my life. He was one of the many seminarians who graced the table of my parents' home in Brooklyn, New York. For the Very Rev. Wakeen Dalack and his Khouria, Alice Kerbawy Dalack, the feeding of future priests was an ongoing ministry of love.

In 1966, when the falling asleep of Metropolitan Antony set in motion the established process of selecting a new Metropolitan, the name of Archimandrite Philip Saliba was again on the lips of people who cared about our archdiocese. It was my father who told me, and anyone else who was able to hear, that "there is no one else—Father Philip and Father Philip alone—who is worthy of leading, and who is capable of leading, this archdiocese into the future." And that conviction turned out to be God's will as well.

Showing His Care

With the passage of time, it has become impossible for me to think or talk about Metropolitan Philip without also being reminded of a loving father who cares for everyone in his family. In 1970, it was my honor to be elected to the Board of Trustees of the archdiocese, and I have been a member of the Board ever since. Likewise, in 1974, it was my honor to be elected Secretary of this Board, and I have held that office ever since.

In each instance, His Eminence let me know in a very gentle and loving way that his expectations were simply that I use the abilities and the means that God has given me to do the best that I can for the Board and for our archdiocese. If I needed help, I had only to ask; Metropolitan Philip has been true to his word. When I needed help, I asked, and I received. For the most part, however, he has had the trust and respect to allow me to carry out my duties and assignments in accordance with my abilities and my means.

Respect and trust of this kind are all that any son, spiritual or otherwise, needs from a father. In turn, I express my thanks and appreciation to Metropolitan Philip, because the way he has always treated me has encouraged me to work even more diligently to live up to his respect and his trust.

Likewise, his loving trust and respect were again made manifest in the early 1980s, when he established the Department of Lay Ministries and appointed Dr. Anthony S. Bashir and me as co-chairmen. He has always afforded us an essentially free hand in developing and carrying out our programs. His unquestioning faith in us has prompted us, in turn, to give of ourselves in every way possible.

Once again, in the early 1990s, when I served as President of what was then the Eastern Region of the Fellowship of St. John the Divine, I asked and received the help of His Eminence on many occasions. The only thing he ever wanted to know was whether or not I needed any more help!

Continuing with the theme of family, I also feel moved to point out that Metropolitan Philip has given every one of us a visible and tangible expression of the love and concern he has for all the children and families of our archdiocese. The Antiochian Village, with its Camp and its Heritage and Learning Center, is the crowning jewel of his episcopacy. By virtue of his God-inspired vision and foresight, this "Holy Mountain" has become his gift to us and every generation to come. It is on this mountain that all of us, adults and children alike, have increased our knowledge of our Faith, and have increased the size of our extended family.

Because of the way he has arranged for our Archdiocese Conventions, Parish Life Conferences and Board of Trustees meetings to take place throughout our North American Archdiocese, I, along with so many others, have close friends and loving friends in every corner of the archdiocese. In truth, I can say that I am with this extended family wherever I go. And I have Metropolitan Philip to thank for making it possible.

On a more personal note, I also want to say how thankful I am for the many ways that Metropolitan Philip has been a source of inspiration to every member of my family. When he first established the Antiochian Orthodox Christian Women of North America, he appointed my wife, Shamseh, to be its first Vice President. He treated her with the same trust and respect that he treats everyone he loves, and she has made it her life's ministry to live up to his trust and respect by laboring diligently in the many vineyards that are nourished by our archdiocese.

More recently, she has endured illness and surgery. Metropolitan Philip responded as the concerned and loving Father in Christ that he is. His prayers and phone calls have helped her to cope with the pain and the fear that illness and surgery leave behind. We are most grateful, and even a bit in awe, that, despite his many responsibilities and his own recent medical history, he took the time to express concern and encouragement. Yet, knowing the kind of caring, generous, hospitable, and sharing Spiritual Father he is, we were not surprised.

I am also very grateful for the influence His Eminence has had on the lives of my children. Inspired by his example and by her experiences as a counselor at the Antiochian Village Camp, which he made a reality, my daughter, Lalia, is now a Khouria. With her husband, the Very Rev. Michael Ellias, she serves the Church as a spiritual daughter of Metropolitan Philip.

My son, Gregory, and his wife, Amal, have been no less inspired. They have committed themselves to the monumental task of establishing and nurturing the Mission of St. Catherine in their home community. The challenge is not easy. It makes many demands on their energies and their resources. Nevertheless, they persevere, because Metropolitan Philip is, and has long been, a very vital and very powerful motivating force in their lives. For this also, I am grateful and appreciative.

Thus, it can be seen that, for most of the past forty years Metropolitan Philip has been a vital presence, a powerful example and a guiding influence on my family and on me. He has made it possible for me and my family to form a loving relationship with a great many brothers and sisters in Christ in every corner of our God-protected, self-ruled Antiochian Archdiocese. For this also, I am grateful and appreciative.

In a very real sense, our father in Christ, His Eminence Metropolitan Philip has been a member of my family for many years, and I pray that God will continue to grant him "Many, Many Years!"

Respectfully,

—John D. Dalack, Ph.D.

The Very Rev. Thomas Hopko
Dean Emeritus, St. Vladimir's Seminary, Crestwood, New York

Three Marvelous Achievements

FORTY IS A SYMBOLIC NUMBER FOR ORTHODOX CHRISTIANS. It signifies an accomplished event, a completed action, a fulfilled achievement. Thus the completion of forty years of episcopal service is a most fitting moment to contemplate Metropolitan Philip's archpastoral ministry, and to acknowledge with gratitude what, by God's grace, he has thus far accomplished for us.

I never worked closely with Metropolitan Philip. I met only twice in my life with him at his residence in Englewood. The first time was in 1986 when he called me to speak with him after I wrote a report for him (and two other bishops) about my five-day meeting with the leaders of the Evangelical Orthodox Church concerning their entry into Orthodoxy. The second time was in the late 1990s when I was serving as dean of St. Vladimir's Orthodox Theological Seminary, where the metropolitan had students from his archdiocese. I did, however, like countless church workers, closely observe Metropolitan Philip's many activities and directly participate in many of his ministries.

Three marvelous achievements stand out in my mind when I think of Metropolitan Philip's forty years of archpastoral service.

His Commitment to Theological Education

The first is the Metropolitan's unwavering commitment to education in the Church. Metropolitan Philip insisted from the beginning of his episcopal ministry that all Orthodox people, especially the clergy, be thoroughly and properly instructed and trained in the Orthodox Faith. He consistently supported the work of all Orthodox theological schools, beginning with his alma mater, St. Vladimir's Seminary, where he continues to hold the office of Vice-President of the Board of Trustees. The spacious auditorium in the seminary's new library and administration building is named in the Metropolitan's honor.

In addition to his unwavering support for graduate theological education, especially at St. Vladimir's Seminary, Metropolitan Philip also implemented a Doctor of Ministry Program in conjunction with Pittsburgh Theological Seminary. He also established the St. Stephen's Course of Studies, a correspondence course in theological education for those unable to attend seminary in a full-time program. He also consistently supported the work of the Orthodox Christian Education Commission under the Standing Conference of Orthodox Bishops in the Americas. In a word, the Metropolitan has been an extraordinary supporter of education on every level of church life during his entire service as Archbishop of the Antiochian Orthodox Archdiocese in America.

The Creation of the Antiochian Village

Another spectacular achievement of Metropolitan Philip, which goes together with his unwavering support for theological, pastoral and catechetical education on all levels of church life, is the establishment and ceaseless development of the Antiochian Village in Legonier, Pennsylvania. It is literally impossible to assess the manifold fruits of the countless events, conferences, retreats and camping programs conducted at this excellent facility. Orthodox Christian homes, churches, schools, monasteries, missions and philanthropic organizations in all Orthodox dioceses in the United States and Canada are filled with people who have been instructed, inspired and shaped by programs and events held at "the Village." For this, we give glory to God, and to Metropolitan Philip.

Transforming Orthodoxy in North America

A third achievement of Metropolitan Philip that has literally transfigured North American Orthodoxy in our time is his reception of the Evangelical Orthodox Church, together with countless other converts to Orthodoxy, during his forty years of archpastoral service. It is impossible to imagine what our Orthodox Church, and all of our Orthodox churches and institutions in all jurisdictions, would be like today without the impact of this momentous event that Metropolitan Philip made happen. For this alone, I am convinced, had he done nothing else, he would deserve our deepest admiration and most heartfelt gratitude.

Metropolitan Philip is known for saying that "nothing happens unless we make it happen." During his forty years of hierarchal service he has made many marvelous things happen for us. May our Lord grant that still many more wonderful things will come to pass through his ministry in years to come. *Eis polla eti, Despota!*

—Protopresbyter Thomas Hopko

 **IN THE VIEW OF**

The Very Rev. Nicholas Triantafilou
President, Hellenic College and Holy Cross Greek Orthodox School of Theology

Saidna Philip and His *Diakonia*

The Gospel of St. John clearly records the tenets that render each Christian's life journey a holy pilgrimage. Prayerfully reflecting upon the episcopal journey of His Eminence Metropolitan Philip, each of us privileged to know him and to experience a small or major portion of his *diakonia*, recognizes the singular blessings God has granted us in observing Saidna's archpastoral pilgrimage. I am indebted to the co-editors, the Very Rev. Dr. Joseph Allen and the Very Rev. Joseph Antypas, for inviting me to share in such a correct and well-deserved tribute. I say well deserved by Metropolitan Philip, by his personal family and by his family of Antiochian Orthodox Christians in America. Together, His Eminence and the archdiocesan faithful forged, over these forty years, a historically significant worship and service dynamic. This dynamic has served our Orthodox people well. It has presented the Gospel of our Lord in a most creative manner. This dynamic has witnessed humbly to the proclamation of our Pre-Sanctified Divine Liturgy's salvific verification: "The Light of Christ Illumines All."

Personal Remembrances

My personal reflection of these forty years commences in the late 60s (1968-69) when Saidna visited St. George Parish, Houston, Texas. Fr. Thomas Skaff and his family warmly welcomed my Presbytera, Diane, our family and me in 1968 when we commenced our assignment at the Annunciation Greek Orthodox Cathedral. Starting with Saidna's first visit to Houston after his elevation, Frs. Thomas Skaff, John Namie, Anthony Sabbagh and Joseph Shahda included our Annunciation parish and me personally in each of His Eminence's visits. I vividly recall how the children always gathered around Saidna, with his loving arms stretched out to them. Our entire Orthodox community of the greater Houston area was always elevated by his frequent visits.

My privileged witness to His Eminence Metropolitan Philip's archpastoral *diakonia* centered on archdiocesan activities involving both our jurisdictions, the Antiochian and Greek Archdiocese. As Administrative Assistant, Vicar General and then Chancellor to the late beloved Archbishop Iakovos, I again came into the environs of Saidna's far-reaching activities. His candor is couched in a vibrant faith and a passionate spirit for all that is good and beneficial to his people. His visionary thoughts for the development of our church in America are borne out of an inner cry for a united proclamation of the gospel in the rich beliefs and practices of Orthodox Christianity.

His Love for the Church

These past six years have offered me underserved and privileged first-hand witness of Saidna's love for Christ's Church. This witness includes his archpastoral care for the priests, parishes and people of his archdiocese. My position these years as President of Hellenic College and Holy Cross Greek Orthodox School of Theology allows me to share in prayer, ministry and study with young men and women from the Antiochian Archdiocese who matriculate here at our dear School. Some are preparing for ordination to the Holy Diaconate and Priesthood, while others are people preparing for lay ministry in the Church. These young men and women have edified our entire community of Board of Trustees, deans, faculty, students and staff. They form a group of respectful and aspiring pilgrims of Christian Orthodox Faith. All of us here are indebted to His Eminence Metropolitan Philip and to His Grace Bishop Antoun for sharing these young people with us. It is especially nostalgic for me to welcome young people from Houston who are among the numbers of Antiochian students studying with us.

Therefore, on behalf of our entire Hellenic College and Holy Cross family, I express deepest appreciation to His Eminence Metropolitan Philip for these forty years of archpastoral embrace. We pray that God grant him health and "Many Years!"

Respectfully,

 —Rev. Nicholas C. Triantafilou, President

 Hellenic College and Holy Cross Greek Orthodox School of Theology

IN THE VIEW OF

The Rev. John Erickson
Dean, St. Vladimir's Seminary, Crestwood, New York

Saidna Philip and the Legacy of St. Vladimir's Seminary

Alumni of St. Vladimir's Seminary now number over 1,300. Among them are distinguished church-men and theologians from around the world, including over thirty bishops. In my estimation, none of our alumni has embodied more fully what the seminary stands for, none has affirmed its core values and vision more insistently, than His Eminence Metropolitan Philip. Throughout his forty years of archpastoral ministry, he has been a tireless proponent of Orthodox unity, of mission and of cultural engagement. In the process, he has transformed the face of Orthodoxy in America.

Personal Remembrances
My own acquaintance with Saidna Philip goes back to 1964-65, when he was a student at St. Vladimir's and I was a young convert who visited the seminary as frequently as my college schedule allowed. Saidna was at the seminary to complete his M.Div. degree, though by that point he already had an extensive education in theology as well as in literature and other disciplines, along with many years of

pastoral experience. A year later he would be the successor to Metropolitan Anthony Bashir as Metropolitan of New York and North America. But as students and faculty from that period recall, Saidna Philip did not expect or get much in the way of special treatment during his time at the seminary. He occupied a standard seminary dorm room—hardly luxurious. He participated in chapel services on a regular basis, alongside the other students and visitors like me. He attended a full range of classes. But perhaps more than most students, he enjoyed the company of Fr. Alexander Schmemann, dean of the seminary, with whom he shared an interest in literature and current events, as well as a conviction that the mark of authentic Orthodox theology is its pastoral power.

It sometimes is said, he who knows but one language knows none. In other words, to really understand and appreciate a given language or culture, even your own, you have to be, in effect, multilingual and multicultural. Like his professors at St. Vladimir's, and like so many other notable leaders in the Church of Antioch, Saidna Philip is just that—a master of many languages and at home in many cultures. He is as likely to quote Dostoevsky or one of the English Romantic poets, as he is Khalil Gibran or a medieval Arabic lyric. Saidna Philip not only speaks, and speaks eloquently, in many languages, he also understands the transformative power of the word. When he speaks, whether in a formal address or in casual conversation, he communicates. He evokes a response. After he speaks, the room is never the same.

Cultural Awareness

Behind Saidna Philip's gift for words lies his awareness of the significance of cultural context. The Word proclaimed in Damascus or in some other bastion of Old World Orthodoxy may be the same Word proclaimed throughout the centuries, all the way back to the first days of the Church. But to be truly powerful and life giving this Word must be articulated in new ways in each new age, in response to new circumstances and new needs. Our goal therefore should not be the repetition of the same age-old formulas. Our goal must be the one Kingdom, which we anticipate and celebrate when we gather together as one body of Christ in the one Eucharist. This has been the message of St. Vladimir's Seminary. This has been the message of Metropolitan Philip.

In season and out, Saidna Philip has proclaimed the need for Orthodox unity in America. This has not made him popular in some quarters—particularly in Old World churches that tend to treat their overseas dioceses as pawns in a global chess game. The 1994 Conference of Orthodox Bishops at Ligonier, Pennsylvania, which Saidna hosted, drew attention to the importance of unity, but also to the intimate link between unity and mission. Unity is necessary not simply because it is mandated by the canons. Unity is necessary for the sake of effective and credible mission. If we are to fulfill our calling—to make disciples of all nations—we cannot continue to present Orthodoxy as an exotic smorgasbord of Eastern foods and folkways. We must demonstrate our unity in Christ in tangible ways. We must show that this unity is meant not just for ethnics of the so-called "Diaspora," but also for all who thirst for salvation. Unfortunately, the vision of unity and mission set forth at Ligonier still has not been achieved—but this has not been for want of trying on the part of Saidna Philip!

Unity, Mission and Evangelization

Concern for unity, mission and evangelization in our North American cultural setting has been one of the hallmarks of Saidna Philip's archpastoral ministry. The same concern has characterized the approach to theological education at St. Vladimir's Seminary. Throughout its history St. Vladimir's has been intentionally pan-Orthodox—in its student body, in its faculty and in its Board of Trustees, on which Saidna serves as Vice-President. It has fostered ways of more effectively presenting the Orthodox Faith to America, whether through its classes or through the work of SVS Press. It has welcomed a growing number of converts. Saidna Philip has supported the seminary's work in many ways. Most tangibly, this has been through the full scholarship assistance that the archdiocese gives to all its qualifying seminarians. This is unique in North American Orthodoxy. Saidna's generous support for theological education may help explain why priests of the Antiochian Archdiocese have been relatively free from the cynicism and burnout that so often afflict Orthodox clergy in America. But Saidna's support for his students goes beyond monetary assistance. He is deeply concerned about them as human beings, and he responds generously to their immediate human needs. Around the seminary, the story is still told of one young student who, far from the warmth of his home state, was shivering through a New York winter with only a light jacket. Saidna Philip spontaneously gave him his own overcoat—and a very fine overcoat it was!

According to the English writer Jonathan Swift: "Vision is the art of seeing things invisible." Certainly Saidna Philip has been a man of vision. Where disunity seems to be the order of the day, Saidna Philip sees the unity to which our churches are summoned. In a world where Orthodoxy seems in danger of succumbing to sectarianism or retreating to an ethnic ghetto, Saidna Philip sees a united church in which it is possible to be both truly Orthodox and truly American. May he keep this vision before us during many more years of archpastoral ministry!

—Fr. John H. Erickson, Dean

St. Vladimir's Orthodox Theological Seminary

 **IN THE VIEW OF**

THE VERY REV. MICHAEL DAHULICH
DEAN, ST. TIKHON'S SEMINARY, SOUTH CANAAN, PENNSYLVANIA

Metropolitan Philip and Theological Education

SIXTEEN CENTURIES AGO, ST. GREGORY THE THEOLOGIAN WROTE: "One must be purified before purifying others, be instructed before instructing, become light in order to enlighten, draw near to God before approaching others, be sanctified in order to sanctify" (Oration 2, 71). These words make very clear to us that seminary training for future priests is absolutely essential. And that such training must continue beyond ordination is equally necessary. Saint Gregory explains that the growth of the shepherd never stops; even after his initial training he is to grow steadily and continually, like "the common sailor grows to be the helmsman," or like "the brave soldier grows to be the general."

Preparing Pastors for Today and Tomorrow
Throughout the forty years of his distinguished episcopacy, His Eminence Metropolitan Philip has time and time again demonstrated that he fully understands the meaning of these words taught by the

Revered Archbishop of Constantinople. He has done this through his unwavering commitment to preparing men for holy orders through theological education and priestly formation. And he is likewise well aware that our theological schools must prepare seminarians to be more than just theologians. In today's world, pastors need to be computer savvy; they need to have a good background in finance; they need to be able to counsel marriages, troubled teens, confused souls and lonely individuals in the face of such crises as disease and death, divorce and depression. His Eminence knows well that clergy in the twenty-first century need to possess leadership qualities and organizational skills that can be suited for various circumstances—whether it be a large or small congregation, a long-established parish or a newly-formed mission, a community with an elderly population or one with many young families, one that is composed primarily of converts or one that is a home for a growing number of new immigrants.

On the other hand, as the saying goes, the more things change, the more they remain the same. The Gospel of John records Our Lord saying to His Church's leaders: "Ye have not chosen Me, but I have chosen you, and ordained you, that ye should go and bear fruit" (John 15:16). For Metropolitan Philip, as for every Orthodox hierarch, this means that future priests must be taught to speak Christ's words—the words of His Church—not their own words. They are to proclaim His Gospel—the Gospel of His Church—not their own. They must learn to accept, not speculate; preserve, not innovate; defend, not attack; uphold, not tear down our Tradition that is "the life of the Holy Spirit in the church," in the words of Vladimir Lossky. This means that they need to have the mind, the *ethos*, the *phronema* of the Church. This means that they must understand that they have been chosen and ordained to be part of the continuum of truth-bearers that spans the history of Christ's Church. They must be one with the Holy Fathers of the Faith—"the Faith which was once delivered unto the saints" (Jude 3). Thus, the Church will have but a single voice amid today's cacophonies, and a single mind—that of her Head: "For who has known the mind of the Lord that he may instruct him? But we have the mind of Christ" (I Corinthians 2:16).

His Giant Steps in Education

To insure that this vision of ministry be actualized in the Antiochian Orthodox Archdiocese of North America, Metropolitan Philip has undertaken in his episcopacy several giant steps and created a number of innovative programs under his *omophorion*. First and foremost, he confirms the necessity of theological education and spiritual formation for his deacons and priests. In most cases, men seeking ordination spend three years in seminary for a Master of Divinity degree at one of the three existing accredited Orthodox graduate schools of theology in this country: Holy Cross, St. Vladimir's or St. Tikhon's. His Eminence serves on the Board of Trustees of St. Vladimir's Seminary, and the archdiocese financially assists all three theological schools. During his reign as Primate, Metropolitan Philip has established a full scholarship program that aids every archdiocesan student who maintains an acceptable academic record during the years of his priestly preparation at one of the three seminaries.

In addition, to produce the highest caliber of clergy and lay workers for his rapidly growing and vast expanse of an archdiocese, His Eminence has created the Antiochian House of Studies, an educational program for "applied theology." It provides an ongoing forum for all theological and pastoral education activities within the archdiocese itself. This very successful program has a number of individual components, tailor-made for the various needs of the archdiocese and for the special circumstances in which practicing and future clergy and Church workers find themselves.

One of the components of the Antiochian House of Studies is the Residency Program—an intensive two-week program, based at the Antiochian Village, aimed at practical issues within the theological training received by all the students studying at seminary and others who are unable to attend an Orthodox theological school. Its goals are: 1) to orient students to the application of theological study; 2) to emphasize contemporary programs and issues within the ministry of the Church; 3) to create an arena where seminarians and other students can dialogue about the future of their Church; and 4) to provide for seminars which are rooted in the spirit of Orthodox Antioch.

His Eminence boldly entered into partnership with Pittsburgh Theological Seminary to formulate the Doctor of Ministry Program, which is available to those who have acquired a Master of Divinity degree and have served in full time ministry for at least three years following graduation from seminary. This program leads to an accredited Doctor of Ministry degree. Its purpose is to deepen and enhance the priest's ministry through systematic study and reflection. Participants remain in their assignments of ministry during the program and attend classes four weeks a year. Emphasis is placed on the integration of the theological disciplines with Church leadership. In addition to attending seminars on the theology of ministry, ecclesiology, canon law, homiletics, spiritual pastoral care, education, ethics and community service, taught by a combined faculty of Pittsburgh Seminary and recognized Orthodox scholars, students also select a specific area for further study and design a doctoral project in that area of interest. A colloquium, a Biblical seminar and two electives help to prepare for the implementation of the project and the writing of the doctoral paper. This program has been hailed by the students and their hierarchs as well.

Another achievement of the Metropolitan's episcopacy has been the St. Stephen's Course in Orthodox Theology—a distance education-based, non-degree program designed for the following: anyone unable to attend an Orthodox seminary; clergy converting to Orthodoxy and intending to seek ordination, who have earned an Masters of Divinity Degree from a non-Orthodox seminary; those seeking advanced training in Christian Education or Youth Ministry; and those who are permitted by their bishops to prepare for the diaconate through this program. It is aimed at introducing practicing and future Church workers to the richness of Orthodox theology. Reading courses are mentored by mail, while local clergy provide the student with auxiliary support and *praxis*.

His Eminence has also established the Master's Degree in Applied Orthodox Theology, a formal degree program, in cooperation with the St. John of Damascus School of Theology of the University of Balamand. This degree is awarded by the University of Balamand and is accredited by the Government of Lebanon. It requires the St. Stephen's Diploma, the completion of a master's thesis and one additional pastoral project. Again, it is designed for those wishing to pursue graduate study in

Orthodox theology but who are unable to attend an Orthodox seminary. A new concentration in Youth Ministry has been recently offered, in order to train and prepare people for full-time youth ministry work in an Orthodox Christian setting.

Metropolitan Philip insists that all the archdiocesan priests and deacons attend the Clergy Symposium that he initiated. It is a biennial conference that: 1) provides information relative to the theory and practice of the Orthodox ordained ministry; 2) imparts through guest lectures knowledge of issues and problems crucial to the clergyman in today's culture; 3) creates a forum for common discussion regarding ministerial challenges; and 4) teaches on a continuing basis the spiritual and historical roots of the Church and her theology.

Finally, the Metropolitan oversees the St. Athanasius Academy of Orthodox Theology, which was founded in 1976 as an arm of the Evangelical Orthodox Church and entered canonical Orthodoxy when that body was brought into the archdiocese. Its mission is to prepare and communicate materials on the Orthodox Christian Faith in English for both Orthodox and non-Orthodox people, especially the laity. Its goals are three-fold: 1) to be a valuable and helpful teaching ministry of the archdiocese and a service to all; 2) to help all Christians learn more about the history, teachings and practice of the Orthodox Church; and 3) to help spread the spirit of Orthodox Christianity to all Americans.

From the very beginning of his episcopacy, His Eminence has always been a champion of Orthodox cooperation and unity in this country. In this spirit, he has made all of these wonderful programs open to clergy of all jurisdictions—for the good of the One Holy Catholic and Apostolic Church that dwells in North America. In this regard, his visionary leadership blesses all of us.

What the Priest Must Be and His Example

Besides all these programs, and perhaps even more importantly, His Eminence has impacted theological education by his example. He lives the essential things that a priest should be in his ministry. First and foremost, the priest must be a man of prayer. We know this because Our Lord, the High Priest, is found to be at prayer to His Father before the most important events in His earthly life, as recorded in the Gospel of Luke. The priest must be, in the words of St. Gregory, a good "model!" for the flock—as Metropolitan Philip has certainly been for the archdiocese. Is this something to be learned in the formative years of seminary training? Absolutely! In the words of Evagrius of Ponticus: "He who prays is a theologian; and he who is a true theologian, truly prays!" Theological education may be a host of academic courses; but it certainly must also be a chorus of prayer—corporate and private, liturgical and personal. The Antiochian Village, where the House of Studies is located, incarnates this essential aspect of priestly formation—prayer.

A priest must also be mindful that he is still a deacon, in the sense that he is and always will be a servant. Everyday, in countless ways, the priest serves Christ and he serves His people. Such is his privilege, to stand at the altar and serve the Liturgy, and to stand in the soup kitchen and serve "the least of the brethren." The words of Our Lord ring across the centuries: "The Son of Man came not be served but to serve and to give His life as a ransom for many" (Mark 10:45), and "No servant is greater than his Master" (John 15:20). A distinguished career of such service is that of Metropolitan Philip.

All of this is so unlike the modern world in which we live; but then, the devil would not have it any other way. The key to overcoming this tension between the Way of the Lord and the ways of the world is a certain quality that a priest must acquire and consider a cherished possession—humility. St. Basil calls humility "the virtue of virtues"—the means by which we acquire divine grace and a host of other virtues as well. The Psalmist David understood this well; in having been humbled, he tells us in the Psalms: "A heart that is broken and humble God will not despise" (Psalm 50:17). For forty years God has loved the humble heart of His Eminence and blessed him and the archdiocese richly for it.

This leads to the final point of priestly formation. Our clergy must know how to love their people. This is what the New Testament tells us the Christian life is all about: "God is Love," writes St. John. "A new commandment I give to you; that you love one another as I have loved you," Jesus teaches. "Love your enemies" is perhaps the greatest challenge of all to come from Our Lord's lips. If Christ so commands all His followers, should not our faithful rightfully expect their priests and bishops to be loving spiritual fathers? Clergy have often complained that their parishioners treat them as employees. I believe the solution is for priests to be what Christ taught Andrew, Peter, James and John so long ago—to be loving spiritual fathers to His flock. If priests love and serve their parishes as spiritual fathers, this will not guarantee that people will never disagree with them; however, it will ensure that the love that Christ taught, and that laypeople want, will come to pass in His church…as it has so brilliantly in the episcopacy of Metropolitan Philip.

Saidna: For all you have done for Orthodox theological education and priestly formation in America, for the shining example you have been to priests everywhere, and for the spiritual father you have become to countless souls, may God grant you many more blessed years of outstanding service to Him and to His Church. *Eis polla eti, Despota!*

—The Very Rev. Michael G. Dahulich, Ph.D.

Metropolitan Philip, with his
sister-in-law, Elaine, and brother,
Dr. Najib Saliba.

Metropolitan Philip with nieces
Amal Dalack and Najat Nicola
and brother Dr. Najib Saliba.

Facing page:

Top left:
With Protosyngellos Ellis Khouri.

Top right:
With Father Joseph Allen.

Bottom left:
With Edward Khouri of Cleveland, Ohio.

Bottom right:
With Mr. Edward Kassab and Metropolitan Elia of Hama.

This page:

Top:
Chairing the Finance Committee meeting at the Archdiocese headquarters.

Far left:
With Dr. Eugene J. Sayfie, Saidna's physician since 1968.

Top right:
With Dr. George Farha, Vice-Chair of the Archdiocese Board of Trustees.

Bottom right:
Bestowing the Antonian Gold Medal on Chancellor Charles Ajalat.

This page:

Top:
With Sunday school children of St. Anthony Church, Bergenfield, New Jersey.

Bottom left:
With Tom Saba in 1987

Bottom right:
With Dana Bach at a Saint Ignatius dinner.

Facing page:

Top:
With the Church School and Father John Nosal, in Greensburg, Pennsylvania.

Bottom:
Vespers at Antiochian Village Camp.

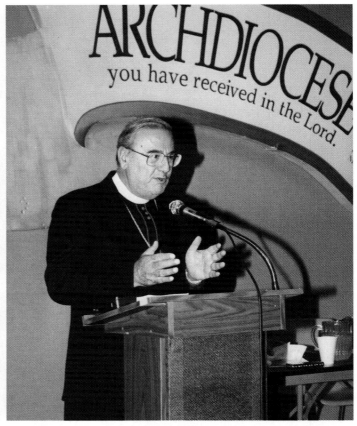

Facing page:

Top left: Blessing "St. Joseph's Garden" at St. George Church in Troy, Michigan.

Top right: Addressing the Task Force to Support Jerusalem; June, 1995.

Bottom left: With Oratorical Contest entrants.

Bottom right: With AOCWNA presidents, Marilyn Robat and Laila Ferris.

This page:

Top left: With Father Paul Schneirla, Vicar General of the Wesern Rite Vicariate.

Left: With the late Professor Edward Said.

Bottom left: With the late Ernest Saykaly, Vice-Chair of the Archdiocese Board of Trustees.

Below: With the co-editors, Fathers Joseph Allen and Joseph Antypas, at the 2006 Clergy Symposium.

Photos from the 2006 Clergy Symposium:

Left: Preaching at the Liturgy on the feast day of Prophet Elias.

Top right: Giving commentary on a lecture by Rev. Dr. John Erickson, Dean of St. Vladimir's Seminary.

Above: Giving commentary on a lecture by Professor Paul Meyendorff of St. Vladimir's Seminary.

 **IN THE VIEW OF**

ARCHDEACON HANS EL HAYEK
MANAGER, PUBLICATIONS DEPARTMENT;
DEACON TO THE METROPOLITAN

A Man of Leadership and Vision

EVER SINCE SAIDNA PHILIP ASSUMED THE LEADERSHIP of the Antiochian Orthodox Christian Archdiocese of All North America he saw very clearly that the archdiocese would not genuinely and practically grow without a very comprehensive plan. It had to be a plan that would encompass all aspects of the growth factor—one which would also impact every organization within the archdiocese and outside it. His Eminence started out by visiting the parishes of the archdiocese, which are geographically spread across the whole North American continent. There is no common denominator which brings all of these parishes together, other than the one Orthodox Faith, from New York to Los Angeles, and from Alaska to Florida. It must also be realized that every parish possesses its own characteristics with respect to its parishioners, its financial situation and even its unique pastor. I have been traveling with him for the past twenty-eight years, and I have watched attentively how he effectively administered all of these parishes—by educating priests, appointing them, transferring them and by listening to the personal challenges and situations in their parishes. With a far-reaching scrutiny and observance, he has been able to assign the right priest to the parish where he can do his best job and be successful in his local ministry.

Saidna's Administrative Strategy

His Eminence's archpastoral strategy focused also on creating healthy, sound and longer lasting lay organizations, so that all of the faithful would be involved in the most basic life of the Church, as they should. The Antiochian Orthodox Christian Women of North America, the Society of Orthodox Youth Organizations (i.e., Teen SOYO, Senior SOYO, and the Fellowship of St. John the Divine) and The Order of St. Ignatius of Antioch were planted in fertile grounds throughout the Archdiocese in North America, so that they would bear fruit abundantly and thereby the spiritual life of the archdiocese would be on course.

Working closely with His Eminence as his archdeacon throughout all these years, I have learned about these various aspects of the Church. My observations, realizations and attendance to all things said, gave me a fuller understanding of the complex nature of the Church. This begins with the diversity of the people, which is something that is certainly more complex than most can imagine. Only with these in mind can an administrator then effectively manage and coordinate the multiple facets within the Church. The individual human person who is placed in a position of responsibility must make it his or her priority to look after all human concerns related to that responsibility, with ultimate seriousness, so that the work of the administrator is not simply a lifelong career, but also a devotion and vocation at the same time. The individual must accept the sacrifices that must be made, while holding fast to true determination, accepting responsibility for his actions. That is the ultimate goal of the administrator.

His Eminence, in the past forty years, has encountered all of the above in various contexts and situations. He is a human being like all of us, subject to error and failure; but unlike all of us (speaking as an Antiochian Orthodox in North America), and due to the huge amount of responsibility laid upon his shoulders, he is bound to focus on achievements and accomplishments. Forty years ago there were two, not one, Antiochian jurisdictions. Perhaps, as history will record, the greatest accomplishment of His Eminence was his studious effort to unite the Antiochian Orthodox name in North America. This will be his legacy. The culmination of his leadership and vision, from the perspective of the Church, is the unity of this archdiocese.

May God grant him "Many Years!"

Respectfully,

—Rev. Archdeacon Hans El Hayek

 **IN THE VIEW OF**

THE VERY REV. PETER E. GILLQUIST
CHAIRMAN, DEPARTMENT OF MISSIONS AND EVANGELISM

The Gift of Administration: Metropolitan Philip

God has appointed these in the church: first apostles, second prophets, third teachers, after that miracles, then gifts of healings, helps, administrations. (1 Corinthians 12:28)

THE FATHERS TEACH THAT THE GIFTS OF APOSTLE AND PROPHET have been incorporated into the office of bishop in the Church. If the bishop is also gifted to administer, all the better—and Metropolitan Philip is gifted in administration. He is the finest leader I have ever known or for whom I have worked. It is a great honor for me to offer tribute to him and his ability to lead on this, the occasion of his fortieth year as our beloved overseer. Three specific attributes of his leadership come to mind.

His Manly Leadership

The first time I met His Eminence was June 1985. Patriarch Ignatius IV was in Los Angeles, California, and I, with some other Evangelical Orthodox clergy, were invited to meet the Patriarch and Metropolitan Philip. We were not yet Orthodox.

We arrived at the Patriarch's suite on the seventh floor of the Sheraton Universal Hotel and knocked on the door. Whoever answered invited us in and said: "Let me introduce you to Metropolitan Philip." He stepped forward, reached out his hand and with a firm grip, looked me right in the eye and said: "It is good to meet you."

My immediate first impression was, *this is a man's man. No plastic piety here.* He then brought us over to where the Patriarch was seated, and we had the high honor of also being introduced to him.

It was on that historic day that we presented the movement of the Evangelical Orthodox Church (EOC) to these hierarchs. At the end of about forty-five minutes, the Patriarch turned to Saidna Philip and said: "I want you to do everything you can to help them." Immediately the Metropolitan asked us to send him specific information about our parishes and a written account of how we came to discover the Orthodox Faith. He is a man of charge. (In the Church, all bishops are given charge; Philip also takes charge!) He is not passive; before we left that day, he told us: "In this archdiocese we make decisions, and we make them quickly."

Closely associated with manliness is courage. God spoke to St. Polycarp at his martyrdom and said: "Be the man"—meaning, be courageous. Metropolitan Philip's courage shone in that, once he made the decision to receive us, it was a father-son relationship all the way. We trusted him and he trusted us, and we knew it. The longer I am Orthodox, the more I realize that had the entrance of our 2,000 people into the archdiocese somehow failed, it would have been a lethal blow to his episcopacy. He had the manly courage to take on this risk.

His Motivational Leadership

Ernest Saykaly, of blessed memory, in speaking of the Metropolitan, told me a decade ago: "He motivates me more than anyone I have ever known."

I thought back to that day in 1987 when I was asked to be the first full-time chairman of the Department of Missions and Evangelism for the archdiocese. I answered: "Saidna, I know how to start

Protestant parishes. I'm not sure I now how to start an Orthodox Church."

His response? "Well you find out and report back to me." Not only was he not taking no for an answer, he was counting on me to produce. That's motivating!

My fear was that the EOC was a one-time phenomenon, which could not be replicated. But what I discovered over and over again was: 1) the Holy Spirit is continuing to call others home to the Church as He called us; and 2) there were still countless non-Orthodox clergy and laity willing to hear that call. To each new mission, Saidna would smile and repeat: "Welcome Home!" He's done that over 100 times since 1987.

His Merciful Leadership

As strong as he is, Saidna Philip is also a man of great mercy.

Very soon after my ordination, we were serving matins before the Hierarchal Liturgy at which the Metropolitan would preside. I was called upon to do the exclamation for the final litany. Saidna was vesting. Immediately after the exclamation, the priest blesses the faithful with the sign of the Cross, chanting: "Peace be to all." I did this, not knowing a priest *never* gives a blessing with the bishop present.

"Father! Father!" I heard my fellow-priests whisper as I stepped back through the royal doors. "You're not to do that with Saidna here." An older priest said: "You're really going to hear about this later."

I never did.

Sometimes converts try to be more Orthodox than heaven. It seems that if the devil cannot get us to compromise the Faith, he tempts us to make Christianity even harder than it is. So here comes our first speed bump as a group of converts. About a year after we became Orthodox, a small handful of our clergy decided the Antiochian Archdiocese was not "hard core" enough for them. (Where were they during Great Lent!) So they walked out and took up with one of those "True Church outside of Orthodoxy" outfits. My heart sank. Here our Primate had put his neck on the line for us, and suddenly he was no longer good enough.

Personally, I probably would have excommunicated them on the spot. Not Saidna Philip. He was patient. A year went by. I had a cordial breakfast with one of the defectors. He was warming up. But what would be the cost of them returning?

About the same time, another of these men wrote a letter of repentance to the Metropolitan, which I never read. But I did read Saidna Philip's reply, and cried through the entire letter. "My son, who was lost, is found!" he proclaimed. These clergy were very mercifully restored, and he never held a grudge.

Saidna Philip, you are a once-in-a-lifetime kind of leader. You didn't have to receive us, but you did. You didn't have to trust us, but you did. And you didn't have to love us, but you do.

I shudder to think where we converts to Orthodoxy in America would be without you. Though others were received in most all the jurisdictions before us, you took the unprecedented step of taking in so many of us at one time. And that move has not only broadened the vision for evangelism in our archdiocese, but for all of Orthodoxy in North America—and likely the world. May we in turn open wide our arms to others as you and the Lord have done for us.

—Archpriest Peter Gillquist

IN THE VIEW OF

The Very Rev. Antony Gabriel
First Chaplain, The Order of St. Ignatius of Antioch

A "Word" about Philip: An Eyewitness Account

I conquer the world with **words,**
conquer the mother tongue,
verbs, nouns, syntax.
I sweep away the beginnings of things
and with a new language
that has the music of water the message of fire
I light the coming age
and stop time in your eyes
and wipe away the line
that separates
time from this single moment.
　　　—Nizar Qabbani

THE SCENE FOR THIS ARTICLE OPENS IN 1966 AT ST. ELIAS MONASTERY IN DHOUR SHWEIR, LEBANON. After an agonizing wait of months for the Holy Synod of Antioch to respond to the overwhelming mandate selecting Philip Saliba as our Metropolitan Primate, the efforts of our North American delegation headed by the late Protosyngelos Ellis Khouri were finally rewarded.

Today's generation of clergy and faithful in this archdiocese have no idea of the pivotal nature of the election of Metropolitan Philip for the history of the Antiochian Patriarchate and our archdiocese. The Cold War of the sixties was a dramatic period in which the East-West tensions were filtered through the Church. Major powers were at play in the attempt to influence the election of the next Metropolitan of North America that would hence affect the patriarchate in important sees, as well as dividing North America.

From the Crowning to a Renaissance

When the late Patriarch Theodosius VI placed the crown on Philip Saliba on August 14, 1966, the conspiratorial dominos began to fall; all the subsequent consecrations that year in the See of Antioch saw the beginning of the liberation of the Church from the claws of insidious forces.

The twenty-first century has little memory of the tensions of those heady days when there was a confrontation, through Antioch, between Western democracies and leftist regimes. Metropolitan Philip believed that the most holy form of theory must pass through the world of action, and so the story unfolded.

The victory that was achieved by Metropolitan Philip's election has reverberated throughout the Church of Antioch; the stage was set for the renaissance of the Patriarchate of Antioch. When the then Archimandrite Philip Saliba stood before the electoral assembly on March 17, 1966, in Brooklyn, New York, following the death of Metropolitan Antony Bashir, and so stirred the audience with his speech of such humility and persuasiveness, it was natural that he received an overwhelming majority. He has continually inspired this archdiocese with his vision, and it began with a *word*.

Can one imagine the thirty-five year old Archbishop moving into the old archdiocese house on 239-85th Street in Brooklyn, New York, with no staff, no structures, limited files and a massive challenge ahead of him to pull together the widowed archdiocese? Undaunted, he literally plunged into the trenches and began visiting every church. It did not take him long to harness the archdiocese by his *word*, and persuade the Board of Trustees to provide the resources needed to purchase the new headquarters, now housed in Englewood, New Jersey. This was a giant step in itself, because of the emotional ties to the past.

Until felled by his original heart attack in Washington, D.C., in 1968, he energetically began to chart a course of action that would bring unprecedented renewal to the archdiocese. Even during his various hospitalizations and recovery, his focus remained steadfast.

I was appointed to establish the second Pan-Orthodox Church in Chicago, to which, incidentally, Metropolitan Philip was so committed that he paid a portion of my salary for years. This new parish would soon host the Twenty Fifty Annual Archdiocese Convention in 1970. His Eminence charged me to head the Department of Convention Planning and Credentials and Statistics, with an insistence on altering the way business was being done. In the early years, Wednesdays were devoted to seating of the delegates. With his commitment to reform, the entire process was streamlined and a convention manual was published. It was sheer joy to work with a person of exceptional gifts and the ability both to listen and to implement changes.

Dreaming Dreams

The theme song of the early years of Saidna's ministry was from *The Man from La Mancha*—*"To Dream the Impossible Dream."* Soon after the convention, Albert Joseph and I were charged to develop the first stewardship book that would raise awareness of the financial needs of the archdiocese. This book was presented at the Louisville Convention in 1975. By this time constitutional changes had been made that eradicated the upstairs/downstairs theology that plagued the archdiocese, and Antiochianism became the theme. The word "Syrian" was dropped from the title of the archdiocese, to be replaced with the biblical, universal designation, "Antiochian"—reminding the faithful of the depth of our heritage.

His Eminence, wishing to change the landscape of the archdiocese, wanted an international organization that would pool together the nascent spiritual, intellectual and financial resources of the archdiocese, which was at that time exemplified by an inactive laity, scattered across North America. The Order of St. Ignatius of Antioch was born in the mind and heart of Metropolitan Philip. Gathering together Protosyngelos Ellis Khouri, Archpriest Paul Schneirla, Al Joseph, Ernest Saykaly, Robert Andrews, Robert Laham, Theodore Mackoul, the treasurer and myself, His Eminence charged us with the task of laying the foundation for this organization to come into being. As the First National Chaplain of The Order, I witnessed an excitement among founding members under the primacy of Metropolitan Philip that was extremely tangible; it is no wonder that we can see the amazing success of The Order of St. Ignatius of Antioch over so many years.

Solving Problems and Making History

In the middle of the night in October 1969, while His Eminence was resting at our home in Chicago en route to California, a call came: "Est-que Monseuir Saliba est la?" It was the shaky voice of the late Metropolitan Elia Saliba of Beirut, who urged His Eminence to return to Lebanon, for another "storm over Antioch" was brewing and the ailing Patriarch Theodosius VI was then living at St. George Hospital. This was one among my many trips accompanying Saidna Philip for meetings at the Holy Synod. They needed the force of his *word* to resolve the emerging conflict. And so it was.

In Charleston, West Virginia, on Labor Day of 1973, it again was his *word* to the throng in attendance that was the igniting power that finally ended the nightmare of division between Toledo and New York. The struggles between these two archdiocese had consumed much time and energy over the years. This agreement between Metropolitan Philip and the late Archbishop Michael was sealed in 1975. Over the ensuing decades, from his consecration until the present, it has been the charismatic *word* of His Eminence that healed divisions, united dissenting parties and nudged the Holy Synod into the realities of the twenty-first century.

When writing *Ancient Church on New Shores, Antioch in North America* and the article for the book *The First One Hundred Years,* I tried to capture the essence of Metropolitan Philip's impact at home and abroad. Not constricted by narrow parochialism, he prophetically saw the larger picture of Antiochian Orthodoxy in North America and in the world. His sturdy place in history is ensured because no living hierarch in recent memory achieved as many milestones as Metropolitan Philip: the Antiochian Women, Clergy Education and Retirement, the Antiochian Village and Heritage Center, caring for the dispossessed, the consecration of bishops, the youth programs, the pursuit of Orthodox unity… and on goes the list *ad infinitum*. He incarnates the *word,* "overseer," par excellance.

His shadow looms large over the history of the church in this era. Others have written articles that will cover various aspects of his ministry. However, from a deeply personal perspective, having traveled this journey with our most beloved Metropolitan for forty years—from the day he married Lynn and I in Cleveland, Ohio, to my elevation to Economos—this has been a most treasured period in my ministry. One final note: Saidna Philip challenged and inspired me, as he did others, toward excellence in all things. This is a gift and an immense legacy for one to bear in his heart. In all things, Saidna fulfilled the words of Nicholas Berdyaev, who once mused: "Man makes history, not the reverse."

In Saidna's own words:

> *We may know the human only where we are*
> *Confronted with the divine;*
>
> *We may know the temporal only when we ponder the eternal;*
>
> *And we may know the depth of the valley only when we look*
> *At it from the peak of the Mountain.*   —*Metropolitan Philip*

 ## IN THE VIEW OF

JULIANA SCHMEMANN
WIFE OF THE LATE FATHER ALEXANDER SCHMEMANN

HIS EMINENCE, THE MOST REVEREND METROPOLITAN PHILIP holds a very special place in the Orthodox Church in America. His quest for unity of all Orthodox Christians in America has inspired all those for whom this quest is a hope, a goal and a necessity to be relentlessly pursued.

He and Father Alexander Schmemann, of thrice-blessed memory, shared—and continue to share—a firm belief that all Orthodox Churches in this land should be united in order to accomplish her mission and become a strong presence.

When he generously welcomed the members of the Evangelical Orthodox Churches into the ranks of the Antiochian Church, he showed his prophetic vision of Orthodoxy in America. He knew how much they would contribute to American Orthodoxy, since they were born and bred on this land.

As I write these words, our beloved Saidna is recovering from his illness and deserves a period of rest and peace. But I know that he will continue serving our Lord and forge ahead as our guiding light.

I am personally grateful to Saidna for his kindness to me after Father Alexander's demise. I am praying that he be given strength to continue in his work for the glory of our Lord. With infinite respect and gratitude,

I am Saidna's faithful servant,

—Juliana Schmemann

 **IN THE VIEW OF**

THE VERY REV. GEORGE RADOS
DIRECTOR, CHILDREN'S RELIEF FUND

Forever and a Day

Those were the days my friend, I thought they'd never end, I though they'd last.

THE DAY HAS COME—A DAY OF REFLECTION, A DAY OF NOSTALGIA, A DAY AMONG DAYS! These have been the days under the *omophoria* of our revered and beloved Archbishop Philip. I am privileged to have been asked to write some reflections about Saidna Philip, whom I have know for over fifty years.

The Early Days
It all started in 1955 when Deacons Philip Saliba and Emile Hanna arrived in the United States to study at the Holy Cross Greek Orthodox Seminary in Boston, Massachusetts. There were seven other Antiochian students (Father Tom Ruffin, Fred Shaheen, Raymond Ofiesh, Michael Azkoul, Louis Mahshie, George Rados and George S. Corey) who were already enrolled in the school and who were overjoyed to be joined by brothers from our Mother Church of Antioch. Little did we realize what the

future held for each of us, much less the fact that we were classmates of the future archbishop.

My mind is crammed with agonies and ecstasies over the past years as we all ministered to the Church and did what had to be done in our own inimitable way. The legendary Metropolitan Antony Bashir, of thrice-blessed memory, who inspired our awe with enthusiasm and dedication, ordained us all. Upon his falling asleep in 1966, there was no doubt, at least in my own mind, who would be his successor. I carefully observed Deacon Philip during our days together in seminary, and always had the premonition that he was destined to serve a higher reality.

Well, it all came about on August 14, 1966. After some trials and tribulations, the episcopal miter was placed on the head of Fr. Philip Saliba at St. Elias Monastery in Dhour Shweir, Lebanon—proclaiming him the unanimously elected Metropolitan Archbishop of New York and All North America.

Saidna's Sense of Charity

Neither time nor space allows me the privilege of filling in the pages of his visions and accomplishments. There are, however, two events to which Saidna and I are significantly related. The first relates to the Archbishop's keen sense of charity.

For many years I administered a program known as Project Loving Care which was a sponsorship program in support of needy Palestinian children. With Saidna's blessing, I inherited the administration of this program from a befriended blind professor at Indiana University in Kokomo, Indiana, by the name of Dr. Rajae Busailah. For many years Dr. Busailah and his wife built this project until they could no longer handle the volume of work that had to be done. Once introduced as a project within our archdiocese, the sponsorships continued to grow and later had to be turned over to the United Holy Land Fund.

In the meantime, I recommended to Saidna Philip to create a department within the archdiocese dedicated to charity. There was no hesitation on his part. He immediately assigned me as Chairman of the Department in charge of a newly created Children's Relief Fund (initially a program of child support in war-torn Lebanon). He also assigned a co-chairman, Robin Nicholas, to administer the newly initiated program known as Food For Hungry People. Both programs have been very successful in their endeavors. It was a good beginning and an inspiration to expand our charity where necessary. At Saidna Philip's behest and appeal, all catastrophic events throughout the world have been, and are now, addressed through contributions from all congregations within the archdiocese. Literally millions of dollars have gone to the coffers of the poor and needy.

Reunification

The second significant accomplishment to my recollection, and to which I had a part to play, was the reunification of the archdiocese. It all started in the mid-70s at the conclusion of the SOYO Convention in Toledo, Ohio. Toledo was the residence of Archbishop Michael Shaheen, of thrice-blessed memory, who was a lifetime acquaintance and distant relative of mine, coming from the same hometown of Canton, Ohio. This was a golden opportunity, since we were in Toledo at the time, for both bishops to greet one another and perhaps explore the possibility of a union. Saidna Philip picked up on the idea and ordered me to call Archbishop Michael to request a friendly visit, which eventually turned out to be an historic moment. Years of division seemed to melt in the atmosphere of love and concern for the future of the Church. Both bishops immediately assigned commissions to dialogue on a possible union, which eventually culminated with the signing of the Articles of Reunification on June 24, 1975, in Pittsburgh, Pennsylvania. This restored administrative unity between the Archdioceses of New York and Toledo. Now there is only one archdiocese, that being the Archdiocese of All North America.

It has been my blessing to play a small part in these two achievements that head the list of Saidna's prioritized accomplishments. They are what make him what he is: conscientiously charitable and unifying. In other words, he is possessed of love—always protecting, always trusting, always hoping, always persevering. *Eis Pola Eti.*

—Fr. George Rados, Ss. Peter and Paul Church, Potomac, Maryland

IN THE VIEW OF

The Very Rev. John Estephan
Former Vicar General

One Man of Courage Makes a Majority

My first connection with you, Saidna, was in October 1972. You were recovering from your open-heart bypass surgery. I was then the Vicar General of the Toledo Archdiocese. I wrote to you expressing my prayers for a speedy recovery so that you would lead the archdiocese towards God and cleanse the Antiochian Orthodox family from the cancer of hatred and bickering that had been destroying it and blemishing the picture of the Lord Jesus Christ in their hearts. A few days later I received a note in which you thanked me for my letter. You made a remark that has been engraved in my memory ever since: "Our destiny," you wrote, "is to unite all Orthodox people in the American hemispheres." You added: "For me, to live is to do, produce and achieve."

And you produced and achieved! You are continuously doing so, with untiring efforts.

Forty Years of Prodigious Achievements

The text of *And He Leads Them*, which the scholarly and celebrated writer Joseph J. Allen edited, is a source of inspiration. It echoes your vibrant orations and enumerates, with accurate dates, your accomplishments. I hope this masterwork of J. J. Allen will be included in the curriculum for all theological students and Church school students.

In your consecration address on August 14, 1966, you cried aloud with boldness: "It is impossible for Antioch to recapture its past glory unless it elevates itself from the stagnant swamps of cheap politics to the esplanades of truth, goodness and beauty." Your voice resounded like the voice of John the Baptist who was the greatest among "those born of women." Riveting your eyes upon the Patriarch, you stressed: "We shall never bargain with the truth."

You tackled with wisdom the issue of bringing the Antiochian Orthodox Christians together. It was not easy. Two archdioceses, one under New York and the other under Toledo, Ohio, were competing. Though they were both claiming to be the most faithful to the Holy Synod of Antioch, they were not. Instead they were turning their backs towards each other. The split was acute. Bitterness and alienation paralyzed the two wings. None of them could move, could expand, could flap or flutter.

Brotherhood among the Antiochian Orthodox in the USA and Canada became extinct after the falling asleep of Bishop Raphael Hawaweeny, of thrice-blessed memory, in 1915.

You couldn't tolerate such divisiveness or live in peace with God while disunity was raging. You appointed priests to feel the pulse of Archbishop Michael Shaheen concerning reunification. They failed. Instead of narrowing the gap, they widened it. With the visit you paid to Archbishop Michael in Toledo, Ohio, on Sunday, June 24, 1973, the ice was broken and the relations between the two entities began to warm up.

On June 24, 1975, you, Saidna, and Archbishop Michael, signed the healing agreement in St. George's office of Pittsburgh, Pennsylvania. It buried into oblivion forever, the discords, irritations and anger that had festered for years in the minds of hundreds of thousands of Antiochians. You are, Saidna, a champion of unity and a "balsam" for the aching hearts.

Saidna's Care for His Archdiocese

You have not been to your clergy only a Metropolitan whose hands they kiss with awe, to whom they burn incense and who they commemorate in every church service. You have been a loving Father for them. You established for them a retirement plan, so when they are aged and disabled they may rely on it. In addition, you urged the parishes to pay them housing, transportation, health insurance and a fair monthly stipend. The priests of your jurisdiction live comfortably and with dignity.

In 1975, you established The Order of St. Ignatius. You started with thirty-nine members. These thirty-nine have been growing and increasing continuously. The Order is not a club of the ostentations and affluent people, as a few gossip. It consists of members who pledge to support with money, time, effort and service the various projects of the archdiocese, of which the retirement plan of the clergy is at the top of the list. Before your time, Saidna, we were solicitors for help, now we are, thanks to your guidance, a charitable and open-handed community.

Plagued with the Mosaic law of discrimination and bigotry, women in the Orthodox Christian houses of worship were isolated from men and stored like bags of potatoes in the church attics. You brought, Saidna, women from the dark tunnels to where light shines on them, and where they, on the other hand, shine in dedication and devotion. The Antiochian Orthodox Christian Women you established in 1973 witnesses to their effectiveness and worthiness.

You learned from our Heavenly Master and Savior Jesus Christ to feed and teach simultaneously. In the Lord's Prayer we ask God to give us bread before we ask Him to forgive us. Insurance for the priests and a proper salary package for the servers of the Word were followed by the St. Stephens Course of Studies and the Antiochian House of Studies, which you created. Thus you upgraded and renewed the ministry of the clergy by providing them with a theological and pastoral education and with a good living at the same time.

Saidna's International Concerns

You repeatedly say, Saidna, that you are American by choice. But you can never conceal or mask the Lebanese in you. The land in whose bosom your father and mother repose and your ancestors lay will never cease ringing in your ears. This is what prompted you, when the civil war was consuming Lebanon, to initiate and chair the Standing Conference of Middle-Eastern Christian and Muslim Leaders. You appealed with them to the Lebanese people, both Christians and Muslims, and to the Palestinians, to stop the bloodshed. As a last resort you visited the then President Gerald Ford and urged him to bring the war to an end.

The blood in your veins coagulates the minute you forsake any of the states of the Middle East.

You don't live for yourself, Saidna, you live for your fellow man. A tear in the eye of an infant that invaders have orphaned, brings tears to your own eyes. A homeless refugee makes you shiver and tremble. Your heart sinks within you at seeing a missile shattering a building. Fire burns your muscles when storms and earthquakes ravage. You don't remedy the calamities with sighs, but you issue appeals to the parishes to collect monies to send to the victims where destruction seeds death, fear, hunger and horrors. "Feed the Hungry," the Lord says, "and clothe the naked." Thus, you urge us, in compliance with the heavenly teachings of the Lord and in accordance with your directives, to do what we are called to do.

Born to Rule

You were born to rule! Your orations are a magnet that draws the crowds to the cause you defend or promote. You don't minister to the passions of people or flatter their prejudice. Your devotion to the Holy Church is undeviating, and your zeal to preserve its unity is unbending.

You want the Church to be like the heart of our Savior and Redeemer—open to all. There are in your life too many gifts for me to capture and mention. But this you have shown us: *One man of courage makes a majority!* And you, Saidna, are that man! I ask God on bended knee to grant you many, many years. And I ask you to know how grateful I am for the monumental and historical works you've completed and continue to complete.

I am most sincerely yours,

—Archpriest John Estephan

 **IN THE VIEW OF**

The Very Rev. Joseph Purpura
Chairman, Youth and Parish Ministries;
Youth Director, North American Council Teen SOYO

A Developer of Disciples: Archbishop, Spiritual Father, Pastor and Youth Worker

Building the Youth

METROPOLITAN PHILIP HAS DEVOTED MUCH OF HIS MINISTRY to the well being of the young people of the archdiocese. Saidna has always wanted the young people across the archdiocese to know one another and to build life-long relationships in Christ, as a way of joining together our whole archdiocese as one united family here on the North American Continent. This godly desire is most powerfully embodied in Teen SOYO, which serves as a strong social, humanitarian and spiritual force in the Antiochian Archdiocese of North America. Through our teen ministries, the Metropolitan has demonstrated his understanding that the youth, much as the rest of humanity, is "tired of hearing about God" and rather desires to *participate* in divinity and godliness. Through our Teen SOYO Movement, His Eminence has created a living chance for our youth to participate in the community and spiritual life of the Church in ways they will treasure, literally, forevermore.

The members of Teen SOYO, nurtured and inspired by Metropolitan Philip to be a generation of disciples and leaders in the Holy Orthodox Church, have gone out and multiplied their efforts by becoming faithful disciples and leaders in virtually every aspect of the life of the Church.

Those Who Bear Witness

Fr. Anthony Yazge, who was a Teen SOYO president in 1978, has served for many years as one of our parish priests, and who currently serves as the Antiochian Village Camp Director and Spiritual Advisor of the North American Council Teen SOYO, stated:

> While in college, my cousin Ken and I presented an idea to Metropolitan Philip to use one week at the Antiochian Village for the teens of the archdiocese to minister to the least of our brethren by conducting a camp for Special Olympics.
>
> Most adults that heard the idea thought we were nuts. However, Metropolitan Philip encouraged us and supported our efforts 100%.
>
> More than twenty-six years later, our teens are still providing this wonderful ministry to the Special Olympics Athletes.

Guided by the conviction that "youth can and must affect their culture," Metropolitan Philip saw the need to organize and empower the teens of the archdiocese into a vibrant and life-giving movement. In 1968 he organized the teens on the regional (now diocesan) level, and in 1969 he organized them on the archdiocese level, with the election of Robert Laham Jr. as the first North American Council Teen SOYO President. During the first Clergy Symposium in 1980 His Eminence reminded us of the reasons the early Church gathered—he stated: "One: To worship the Triune God and celebrate the Eucharist. Two: To preach the Good News and experience a genuine Christian *koinonia*. Three: To glorify Jesus Christ through a life of witness and service." He impressed upon us throughout his ministry that the Orthodox Faith is to be lived out daily in real people's lives; it must be rooted in the person of Jesus Christ and not simply be theoretical. Therefore his ministry has taught us and inspired the current youth ministry platform—"Living the Orthodox Faith in Christ through Worship, Witness, Service and Fellowship." Thus our archdiocesan youth ministry platform was based upon Metropolitan Philip's vision and inspiration. Indeed, Metropolitan Philip has always inspired our young people. First he established Youth Month, where, during the month of October, teens take on leadership roles in the Church by ushering, collecting, giving sermons, etc. Then, in July of 2005, he established the SOYO Leadership Conference to help raise up a generation of disciples and leaders for the Orthodox Church.

Father Timothy Baclig, one of our past NAC Teen SOYO Spiritual Advisors, states:

A priority in Saidna Philip's episcopate has been the development of youth leadership through the programs of Teen SOYO: Programs which involved young men and women in humanitarian projects, participation in liturgical services, festivals which encouraged expressions of their faith through art, writing, poetry, orations, and catechism/bible bowls, all of which aim at deepening one's personal understanding of our Tradition.

Creating Opportunities for Our Youth
Metropolitan Philip stated:

We Orthodox must realize once and for all that we are on this continent to stay, and that we should integrate our old cultures into the new cultural reality of this land. Moreover, we must not stifle the creative and artistic spirit of our young people, but rather encourage them to experiment in all matters related to the cultural expressions of Orthodoxy, strictly under the supervision of the Church.

Across our archdiocese, His Eminence has tilled the spiritual soil to prepare it for the creative visions, inspired by the Holy Spirit, in himself and in our young people. He has made the fields of this archdiocese fertile for our young people to experience prosperous lives rooted in Christ.

His Eminence has created real opportunities for our young people to learn their faith, opportunities to learn to give expression to their faith and opportunities to grow closer together. So many young people have stayed in the Church through the relationships built during their Teen SOYO years, through our camps and through our other youth ministry programs and events. Many teens met and married one another through the youth programs. Many of our families in this archdiocese can credit Metropolitan Philip's nurturing of our youth ministry programs for their existence as Orthodox Christian families rooted in Christ. Many of the past Teen SOYO members now serve as priests, deacons, khourias, youth workers, Church school teachers, Parish Council members, Archdiocese Board Members and members of The Order of St. Ignatius.

Inspiring Teen SOYO

Throughout its history, Teen SOYO has been inspired and motivated by Metropolitan Philip to minister to the poor and needy. Teen SOYO has done this over its past thirty-six year history, reaching out to the homeless, the needy, the poor, the lonely, to special Olympians and our neighbors across the North American continent. His Eminence blessed and encouraged the teens to raise their level of outreach on the North American Continent and hence Orthodox Youth Outreach (OYO) was born as a ministry to raise the level of teen outreach, enabling our teens to have greater impact in the communities in which they live. OYO, a ministry inspired by Metropolitan Philip's love and concern for others, truly raises the level of Teen SOYO outreach to new heights.

Educating and enabling our young people to bear witness to their faith continues to be important in the Metropolitan's ministry. He has blessed and encouraged the establishment of the St. Stephen's Youth Ministry Concentration, a graduate program designed to educate parish youth workers in Orthodox Youth Ministry. Through such efforts he has encouraged our young people to explore and understand the Church's teaching on critical moral and ethical issues confronting our young people and families across the North American nations. This year teens across the archdiocese led workshops, sermons and talks on the Church's teaching on the sacred gift of life—understanding and explaining the Church's position on abortion and the preciousness of human life from the moment of conception.

His Eminence has always cautioned those of us who work on the archdiocesan and diocesan levels that unless what we do impacts the local parish communities, our efforts will have been in vain. Metropolitan Philip once said: "Our young people are searching with anxiety and intellectual curiosity for new spiritual horizons and for a more meaningful life in Christ. I am very much encouraged by their search." Our young people likewise have been very encouraged and free to search and reach new heights precisely because of the Metropolitan's encouragement and guidance.

May the youth of our archdiocese nurture these seeds of spiritual renaissance to fruition, may they continually add new fields of spiritual endeavor, and not be satisfied until we have restored the Americas to our Lord and Savior, Jesus Christ! To our father in Christ, Metropolitan Philip, on this his fortieth anniversary to the Holy Episcopate, we say "Thank You!" Thank you for inspiring us, thank you for protecting our freedom to grow, thank you for your foresight, your vision, your fatherly love and for leading us to make our God given dreams a reality.

May God grant you, our chief shepherd, "Many Years!"

Your son in Christ,

—Archpriest Joseph Purpura and

The Officers, Advisors and Members of Teen SOYO

# IN THE VIEW OF

THE VERY REV. MICHAEL ELLIAS
CHAIRMAN, DEPARTMENT OF CLERGY INSURANCE AND RETIREMENT,
AND CO-CHAIRMAN, DEPARTMENT OF CONVENTION AND
CONFERENCE PLANNING

I HAPPEN TO BELONG TO A GENERATION OF CLERGY AND LAITY who may have lived for some time during the metropolitanate of Archbishop Antony Bashir, of thrice-blessed memory, but who really have only known His Eminence Metropolitan Philip as our father in Christ and as Archbishop of the Antiochian Orthodox Christian Archdiocese of North America.

My earliest recollection of Saidna Philip is from one of his early archpastoral visits to my home parish of St. George Church in New Kensington, Pennsylvania. As His Eminence was meeting and greeting the faithful in the church hall, our pastor, Fr. Ted Ziton, introduced me, a child of little more than ten years of age, to the new Archbishop. Saidna made it a point of asking my name and inquiring about my interests before giving me his blessing, and I distinctly remember his saying: "When you are ready, come to me, and I will give you a scholarship to the seminary." At that moment nothing could have been farther from my mind, but he both planted a seed that would later come to fruition, and at the same time demonstrated the care and concern he has always shown for the youth and the clergy, current and future.

I now have the privilege of chairing the Department of Clergy Insurance and Retirement and of co-chairing, with Mr. George Darany of Dearborn, Michigan, the Department of Convention and Conference Planning for the archdiocese. Metropolitan Philip has had a profound impact on both of these departments, which have critical missions in and for the Antiochian Archdiocese.

Department of Convention and Conference Planning

When His Eminence became the Metropolitan of North America in 1966, the archdiocese consisted of approximately sixty-five parishes spread out across the continent in six geographically dispersed "regions." In those days each region would hold an annual Society of Orthodox Youth Organizations (SOYO) convention of its own, in addition to the annual convention of the entire archdiocese. Remarkably, Metropolitan Philip would personally attend each regional convention as well as the archdiocesan convention. Not only was his personal attendance vitally important to the unity and progress of the archdiocese, but the sheer energy required to undertake such extensive travel in such a condensed time frame was a testament to his complete dedication to the welfare of his flock, possibly even to the detriment of his own well being.

Progressively, Saidna began to refine the nature of these gatherings and to improve their efficiency. Many will remember the landmark decision to change the frequency of the archdiocese conventions from an annual to a biannual schedule. This change not only streamlined archdiocesan operations but allowed the regions to focus more effectively on regional worship, fellowship and aspirations. He also gave his blessing for the "SOYO Conventions" to evolve into "Family Life Conferences," in an effort to minister more broadly to a wider constituency within the church; moreover, these conferences further evolved into the current "Parish Life Conferences," which take place in our newly formed dioceses under the presiding local hierarchs.

The original intent of the conventions and conferences was largely to provide a social context for our Orthodox youth to meet and greet (indeed many romances, marriages and families emerged from those early gatherings), as well as to provide an incarnational expression of the Church's unity in worship and dialogue. As the archdiocese grew and matured, the regional and diocesan conferences expanded and improved as well.

In addition to the former SOYO meetings, the current conference format strives to include and address every aspect of parish life. Every conference and convention is framed in the context of our communal worship. All the recognized organizations of the archdiocese—the Fellowship of St. John the Divine, Teen SOYO, the Antiochian Women and The Order of St. Ignatius of Antioch—gather in fellowship and deliberation. Many of the archdiocesan departments now provide workshops and training. Both Church School and continuing adult education have become prominent features of these gatherings. Perhaps the highlights, however, have become the Bible Bowl and the Oratorical Contest, events in which Metropolitan Philip particularly delights. He always supports these festivals personally and has repeatedly emphasized their importance as opportunities for our young people to deepen their understanding of the Faith and to articulate and to bear witness to their closely held values and beliefs.

While the main function of the biannual archdiocese conventions is to transact the "business" of the archdiocese in accordance with the will of God and under the direction of the Holy Spirit, these gatherings have taken on greater and greater importance in manifesting God's movement within the Church. Conventions have been the official locales for greeting and receiving the blessings of our fathers in Christ, Patriarachs Elias and Ignatius; conventions have received Presidents of the United States and other high ranking officials; conventions have debated the pressing issues of the day; and conventions have adopted budgets and policies to carry out Christ's continuing ministry in our day and age.

Recently, Metropolitan Philip has guided archdiocese conventions to address the timely question of the self-rule of our archdiocese within the Patriarchate of Antioch, to approve the amendment of the archdiocese constitution in order to reflect the new diocesan structures, to elect candidates to the episcopacy and to participate in our local synod of bishops. Indeed, in many ways, through the history of the conventions, His Eminence can mark the progress of this archdiocese from a scattered group of sixty-five parishes in six "regions," to a thriving and robust archdiocese of approximately 260 parishes and missions in seven stable dioceses.

Department of Clergy Insurance and Retirement

Saidna Philip has always had a special love for his clergy. In the same way that he was prescient in offering a seminary scholarship to an innocent ten year old, he has consistently nurtured vocations, supported the clergy and advocated for their families. I have heard senior priests recall the days when they were paid in chickens, or with groceries left on the doorsteps. His Eminence has raised the level of clergy compensation and the accompanying employment benefits so that his clergy can function effectively in their parishes without unreasonable concern for their families' material welfare. His support was not only material, but he has always wanted his clergy to share Christ's Holy Priesthood in dignity, both in their active years and in retirement.

As long ago as 1980 Saidna appointed a commission to make a thorough study of the stipends and support systems available to the clergy of the Antiochian Archdiocese. One of the earliest chairmen of that commission, Mr. Ernest Saykaly, who would later become the distinguished Vice Chairman of the Archdiocese Board of Trustees, recently departed this life and was lovingly eulogized by His Eminence.

The work of that early commission produced a report in November 1983, which formed the basis for all subsequent policy guidelines in this vital area. Successive archdiocese conventions have updated the "Guidelines for Basic Monthly Stipends and Benefits," and the commission evolved into the current department. His Eminence entrusted much of the department's work as a priority to His Grace Bishop Antoun and to my predecessor in this capacity, Fr. John Badeen. The most recent edition of the "Clergy Compensation Manual" should be in the hands of clergy and Parish Councils at this point; it brings together all the pertinent policies necessary to make informed decisions about salaries and personnel matters.

Although many of our clergy, particularly those men and their families in missions and small parishes, still make substantial sacrifices in order to serve Christ's Holy Church, Metropolitan Philip has worked tirelessly to lighten their load so that the clergy can propagate the Holy Gospel and minister effectively to God's holy flock. In addition to a livable wage, His Eminence has also made provision for housing and car allowances, life and disability insurance, retirement planning, affordable health insurance and the availability of a confidential assistance program. The current situation is a far cry from the early days of Saidna's episcopacy when chickens were considered currency in some places!

On behalf of these two departments, and all the clergy and laity they serve, I extend our filial gratitude to our beloved Metropolitan Philip on this glorious occasion of his fortieth anniversary as Archbishop of New York and Metropolitan of All North America. I join the faithful of the entire Antiochian Archdiocese and the wider Orthodox world in praying that God will continue to bless us with his visionary and dynamic leadership, his inspired gifts of effective and efficient management and his paternal concern for all the clergy and laity.

Many Years, Master!

—Father Michael Ellias

# IN THE VIEW OF

THE VERY REV. JOHN ABDALAH
EDITOR OF *THE WORD*

METROPOLITAN PHILIP'S ACTIVE ROLE IN *The WORD* is evident by the magazine itself; the oversight of this man of letters is invaluable. Metropolitan Philip's life-long love for literature and poetry is well known, especially since he often uses illustrations from literature when preaching and teaching. What is perhaps less known is how Saidna's love of literature and publishing impacts his ministry through *The WORD*.

Saidna Witnesses Through Media

Saidna Philip often teaches that theology needs to be "practical." By this, he means that God's presence needs to be experienced in everyday life. We need to witness to Christ where He is, and this witness needs to meet God's people where they are. In this age of technology, God's people are used to receiving communications through modern and sophisticated media. They are accustomed to print media with color images and pleasing layouts. Metropolitan Philip insists that our Church magazines present a witness to Christ that modern readers will find appealing. Our Church magazines cannot look like medical or academic journals, without photographs or illustrations. They must be appealing enough for their audience that people will read them, and thus be impacted by the God who loves them and calls them to Himself.

Metropolitan Philip is very sensitive to what kinds of materials are printed in *The WORD*. While he gives the editorial staff much freedom in selecting which materials are to be printed and which illustrations will accompany articles, he has been clear about wanting *The WORD* to be useful to the parishioners. He wants the theology to be practical, the parish news to share useful ideas and the Orthodox world news to be enlightening to the readers. Saidna wants *The WORD* to reflect our Antiochian vision for Orthodoxy and America. I expected this kind of input from the start, but what surprised me was his keen interest in where and how things should be positioned, what colors and fonts are aesthetically attractive and what illustrations he finds helpful. Saidna Philip has a keen artistic eye.

Saidna's "Personal Touch"

Metropolitan Philip influences *The WORD* at every level of its production. He shares his vision for the Church and what the magazine should look like with the editors, layout artists and writers. Although his time constraints prevent him from being the editor himself, he has shown himself to be competent in all the areas of production. Saidna genuinely seems to enjoy publishing and editing. Any success of this magazine surely reflects his leadership, vision and his special touch. I am personally appreciative for all that Saidna has taught me concerning publishing and editing over this last decade, and about God and ministry over the past four decades. Many years, Master!

IN THE VIEW OF

Carole Buleza
Director, Department of Christian Education

Saidna's Dedication to Christian Education

My "journey" to the directorship of the Department of Christian Education began a decade or so before I was Antiochian Orthodox. In the 1980s, I met a man who was wearing an Orthodox cross, as was I. We explained what Churches we were affiliated with by mentioning our bishops. He explained that he was Antiochian Orthodox, and then said: "We're the ones with the great new bishop, maybe you've heard of him—Philip Saliba."

My First Meeting

I met Metropolitan Philip in 1996. We spoke about educating the children, and I recall being impressed with the force of his remarks, and his energy. In 1999, I went to the chancery for two interviews. I recall being taken off guard when he laughed, since I had expected him to be formal and stern, as he appeared in the portrait at our Church. During lunch, he posed a few questions that kept me "on my toes." Perhaps he was just making conversation, or maybe he was testing my ability to handle challenges. I recall one of these—"Do you think the Antiochian Archdiocese should have its own seminary?"—but not my answer! Later, during the interview, he asked slowly and carefully: "So, can you travel every weekend?" I know what I responded to that. As I explained about my children, in particular, about my two-year-old son, I saw his expression soften. I would do the necessary traveling.

When given the opportunity at the end of the interview to ask questions, I mentioned that some proponents of Orthodoxy sharply criticize other denominations. I said that I could not do so and hoped that it was not expected. After a pause, he said: "You are not to disparage other faiths; you are to teach Orthodoxy."

During my interview days at the chancery, I met, and was made welcome by, Kathy, the Metropolitan's Executive Secretary. I have come to appreciate, through the years, the "efficiency with grace" that she embodies; she has been of inestimable value to our archdiocese. I also met Archdeacon Hans and journeyed to the basement to tour the Archdiocesan Bookstore. I was introduced to the Middle Eastern custom of sipping rosewater after lunch, while chatting informally with the Metropolitan and other guests of the day. I witnessed and smiled at the ongoing banter between the Metropolitan and his beloved friend, Bishop Antoun.

My Tenure and His Directives

I began my tenure January 1, 2000. In appointing me to the position, Metropolitan Philip took a risk. Although my education and experience pointed directly to a position such as this, I was not born into this archdiocese, and I was a woman. (The latter characteristic caused a bit of a stir when I attended the Clergy Symposium on the directive of Metropolitan Philip, since I was the only woman with the men in black during that week). Indicative of his personality, he has a well-known penchant for decisive acts of calculated risk. In a very personal way, I was the beneficiary of this trait.

I was only "summoned" to the chancery on one occasion. This is not a pleasant way to arrive, and to make matters worse, I arrived quite late. The problem was that I had not responded to his letter of months earlier, asking me to create a program to teach tithing to children. I explained that I had many tasks to complete before I could turn attention to this. He explained that it was to be moved to the top of the list. My reprimand was firm, but not unkind.

Professionally, the Metropolitan has impacted my cause, that of Orthodox Christian Education, in two important ways: by word and deed. He has made it one of the three most important departments in the archdiocese, and he has provided the Department a budget. The latter is of utmost importance. I have been able to accomplish a great deal more than others in similar positions in other archdioceses because of my budget. I would be remiss at this point if I did not mention the financial support for the Department given by The Order of St. Ignatius, founded by our metropolitan. We are the envy of other jurisdictions because of that organization which has no equal, possibly, anywhere in the Orthodox world. It is one thing to have visions, but to convince others of their validity, and the need to contribute money to achieve them—that is the gift God has given to His Eminence.

Shaping Attitudes with New Ideas

Metropolitan Philip has shaped my attitude towards what needs to be done in my field. My endeavors are pan-Orthodox, and have met with greater success because of this direction. I know that I can be bold in expressing new ideas, because he has set that tone in giving to all of us the vision of a strong Orthodox Church on this continent. Because he is my hierarch, I am respected when I speak at Orthodox meetings.

At another visit to the chancery, I was with the Executive Director of the Orthodox Christian Education Commission (OCEC)—the Metropolitan is the liaison to the OCEC on behalf of SCOBA. I was appointed the Curriculum Department Chairperson, and needed validation for what I was proposing as the curriculum revision. The Metropolitan listened carefully to my nascent ideas and asked questions. We knew we could count on his support. Two years later, I was pleased to offer His

Eminence the first book of the new series that was developed under my leadership and his support, *The Way, the Truth, and The Life*. Written for high school students and adults, the book presents the basics of our Faith and nurtures spiritual maturity. On behalf of the OCEC, I presented a plaque to the Metropolitan, and read this letter:

Your Eminence,

On this occasion, as you bring a message of hope from the Holy See of Antioch to the members of your Archdiocesan Board of Trustees—a message that affects the lives of all Orthodox Christians in North America in a positive way—we have asked Carole Buleza to present this citation to you on behalf of the members of the Executive Board of the Orthodox Christian Education Commission.

Your steadfast commitment to Orthodox unity on our continent speaks for itself. However, on this occasion as you meet with the members of your Archdiocesan Board of Trustees, we also wish to express our appreciation for your devotion to furthering the cause of Orthodox Christian education for both the younger as well as older members of our Church.

Please accept this citation as a symbol of our gratitude and love. For so many years, you have served as the Chairman of the Orthodox Christian Education Commission. Now, as we begin the development of the new series of materials designed to impact minds and hearts in the twenty-first century, we thank you for your dedicated example and episcopal leadership.

We ask God's blessing upon you. May he grant you many, many years of good health as well as the opportunity to see God-given progress leading to an administratively united, spiritually vibrant and well educated, One, Holy, Catholic and Apostolic Church witnessing the Orthodox Christian way of life on this continent.

With Gratitude,

Archpriest Paul Kucynda,

Executive Secretary, Orthodox Christian Education Commission of

The Standing Conference of Canonical Orthodox Bishops in the

Americas (SCOBA)

Two Personal Memories

I have two personal memories that I cherish. During a chancery visit, a small group of guests was asked to review a presentation on our Faith. It was very factual and professionally done. However, I didn't find it expressive of the beauty, glory and life-giving richness of Orthodoxy. When asked my opinion, I honestly shared my assessment. Metropolitan Philip quickly responded: "I knew you were going to say that!" I sensed that he agreed with me, and understood the essence of who I am. Moreover, I felt that decades of administrative work, political savvy, war in the Middle East, wounds in our church and the battle for self-rule had not eclipsed in him that same sense of Orthodoxy that I had expressed. Dare I say I felt him to be a "kindred spirit."

My second memory is from the November 2004 Board of Trustees meeting. At that meeting, I listened to him share the story of his recent trip to Damascus to "discuss" self-rule with the Holy Synod of Antioch. I gained insight into the difference between the "old world church," and our own archdiocese. I was struck with his intellect, wisdom, past achievements and his leadership for self-rule and the unity of the church in North America. I sensed the toll that these goals had taken on his emotional and physical strength. During that meeting it dawned on me that I was privileged to be hearing first-hand about this historic trip, from this history-making man. Acting decisively with strength for the good of the Church, looking for the grace of the Holy Spirit and not fearing the future, he reminded me of St. Basil. I felt, and still feel, that I am in the presence of greatness when with His Eminence. My second memory is not so much of his recollections of the trip, but rather, of a few minutes together after the meeting, when I was lucky enough to encounter him in the hallway. I was able to look him in the eye and express my admiration of and my love for him.

Every Christmas, His Eminence signs his greeting card: "With sincere appreciation and heartfelt gratitude." While I am certain that I am not alone in receiving this sentiment, I take it personally and work each new year with the intent of earning those words once again. Now I have the opportunity to send those words to him. Saidna Philip, for the opportunity to hold this position and share in your vision, and for your kindness and patience, I offer my sincere appreciation and heartfelt gratitude. May you continue to guide us as the Holy Spirit guides you.

—Carole Buleza

# IN THE VIEW OF

RON NICOLA
CHAIRMAN, DEPARTMENT OF STEWARDSHIP

Champion of Stewardship

A Vision for Growth

A REVIEW OF THE 2006 DIRECTORY for the Antiochian Orthodox Christian Archdiocese will reveal a total of twenty-four departments. Some of these departments predate Metropolitan Philip's tenure as Metropolitan of the Antiochian Archdiocese, but many were established in the years following his consecration in 1966. Successful and history-making leaders are characterized by many strong qualities, but certainly vision is a characteristic needed in order for a person to recognize what steps must be taken to maintain forward momentum. In many ways and in many forms, Metropolitan Philip has demonstrated that his vision for the growth and development of the Antiochian Orthodox Christian Archdiocese in North America has guided us on not only the right path, but also the kind of courageous and challenging path needed to establish greatness. The fact that the Antiochian Archdiocese is seen within the Orthodox World as a visionary and courageous entity is due, in no small measure, to the faith, wisdom, knowledge and strong will of our leader for the past forty years, His Eminence Metropolitan Philip Saliba.

Faith and Works: the Basis for Stewardship

Saidna Philip founded the Department of Stewardship in 1975, and he named Ernest Saykaly of Montreal, Quebec, as its first chairperson. The department's initial charge was to make the word "stewardship" part of the vernacular in the Antiochian Archdiocese. Mr. Saykaly began this process by modifying a parish program he helped develop in Montreal. Based on the phrase, "I Believe," the program's message was that what we do after expressing our belief in God and in the teachings of the Holy Orthodox Church is what stewardship is all about. Stewardship brings to life this passage from James 2:17-18:

> Thus also faith by itself, if it does not have works, is dead. But someone will say, 'You have faith, and I have works.' Show me your faith without your works, and I will show you my faith by my works.

In 1977, Ernest Saykaly was elected to serve as the vice-chairperson of the Antiochian Archdiocese Board of Trustees. The enormous responsibilities of this position resulted in Metropolitan Philip turning over leadership of the Department of Stewardship to Dr. George Dibs and myself, Ron Nicola. George and I both lived in California, we were both members of the Archdiocese Board of Trustees and we were both educators. With the word "stewardship" now firmly entrenched in the vocabulary of the archdiocese, George and I utilized our training as teachers and as educational administrators to explore ways of incorporating the meaning of stewardship into the actions and practices of our parishes and its parishioners. Together with a team of regional stewardship coordinators, the Department of Stewardship sought out and accepted invitations from parishes and regions throughout the archdiocese to conduct workshops and seminars designed to explore ways to teach that our Orthodox Christian Faith carries with it the inescapable fact that our time, our talents and our resources must be used to produce actions based on our expression of faith. With the Department of Stewardship continuing to offer workshops and writing articles for *The WORD*, the Antiochian Archdiocese has taken large strides toward institutionalizing practices of Christian stewardship within the lives of our faithful and of our parishes.

It can be truthfully stated that all the work conducted by the Department of Stewardship, from 1975 to 2006, would not have been possible without the support, encouragement and direction of Saidna Philip. This statement goes far beyond the obvious fact that it was Metropolitan Philip who established this department. It is not at all coincidental, for example, that a contemporary of the Department of Stewardship is The Order of St. Ignatius, which was founded in 1975. Given Metropolitan Philip's vision for the Antiochian Village, the Antiochian Women, expanded roles for SOYO, continually growing charitable endeavors, campus ministry, missions and evangelism, marriage and parish family ministry and many other new initiatives within the archdiocese, our traditional practices about and understanding of giving would not be adequate to fulfill these goals. In addition, the traditional giving practices at work in most of our parishes were not consistent with teachings found in the scripture and in the teachings of the Orthodox Church. By creating the Department of Stewardship and The Order of St. Ignatius, Saidna Philip was not only developing vehicles for giving, but also processes which would allow the joys of giving to be learned and for the teachings about giving, unknown to many, to be discovered and embraced.

Three Examples

Three specific examples dealing with the Department of Stewardship serve to illustrate the impact of Metropolitan Philip's mentorship of our work. First, he saw the need to introduce the concept of Christian stewardship into the life of this archdiocese in a more direct and conscious manner when the department was created in 1975. Second, it was at Metropolitan Philip's urging and encouragement that we began the practice of holding biennial parish council symposia in 1992 at the Antiochian Village Heritage and Learning Center. These gatherings have allowed a clearer picture of what it means to be a parish council member to emerge throughout the archdiocese, and for a more enlightened parish council ministry to further the goal of teaching about member giving and other stewardship practices in a manner consistent with scriptural truths. Third and finally, it has been Metropolitan Philip's leadership, example and encouragement that have moved our archdiocese toward incorporating the practice of scriptural-based giving, in the form of tithing and proportional giving. These are practices are consistent with traditional church teachings, but have long been ignored in most of our parishes. The recent move to institute proportional giving by our parishes in their annual assessments to the archdiocese serves as a clear example of how individual parishioners should give to their parishes.

Giving is not an act based solely on the secular needs of the Church. Rather, giving is largely a practice that is reflective of our Faith and our understanding of what God expects from His children. Beyond the work of the Department of Stewardship and The Order of St. Ignatius in this field, we now have the Department of Planning and Future Development to help shepherd our people toward a clearer understanding about what the Scripture teaches about giving. These three entities within the archdiocese, along with the Department of Christian Education, which has developed a lesson series on tithing, serve to illustrate the manner in which Saidna has formed the archdiocese into an organizational model which, at its heart, is driven by a clear and abiding understanding of the teachings and principles of the Holy Orthodox Church.

Personal Memories

In 1977, my parents, Nick and Helen Nicola, God rest their souls, traveled with me to the Archdiocese Convention in Washington, D.C. Prior to the start of the convention, we spent a few days in New York City and paid a visit to the archdiocese headquarters in Englewood, New Jersey. Our family was honored on a number of occasions to host Metropolitan Philip in our home in Oakland, California. Each visit carried with it an opportunity to enrich our lives and deepen our respect and admiration for Saidna Philip and the work he was doing as leader of the Antiochian Archdiocese. His Eminence welcomed my parents and me into his home with great warmth and joy; he was so pleased to be able to entertain my parents with the same love and friendship that they had showed toward him. Not only is Saidna the unquestioned leader and shepherd of this archdiocese, he is also our friend and a "member of the family" to many throughout Canada and the United States. It was during this particular visit in 1977 that Saidna Philip took me quietly into his office to ask me to serve in the Department of Stewardship. With an expression of confidence in my ability, with a sincere handshake and with a prayer for God's guidance in this new lay ministry, he gave me the courage to accept this assignment and work diligently to serve our Lord and this great archdiocese.

All we can do to express our congratulations to Metropolitan Philip on the occasion of his fortieth anniversary as leader of the Antiochian Orthodox Christian Archdiocese is to pledge our continued support for his initiatives and to serve the church in a manner well pleasing unto God. Congratulations Saidna, and may God grant you "Many Years" of good health and happiness in your ministry. In the truest and deepest meaning of this holy expression, we say: *Axios, Axios, Axios!*

 ## IN THE VIEW OF

ROBIN L. NICHOLAS
CO-CHAIR, DEPARTMENT OF CHARITIES

A True Shepherd

IT IS A VERY SPECIAL HONOR TO BE A PART OF THIS FORTIETH ANNIVERSARY TRIBUTE to our great and dynamic spiritual father, Metropolitan Philip. He has led our archdiocese to unprecedented heights, and we are still in the forefront of bringing Orthodoxy to America. May God continue to grant him many years!

We Have Witnessed His Compassion

In 1966, I was blessed to attend Saidna's first Archdiocesan Convention as our metropolitan. I remember how he inspired all of us, young and old, men and women. His energy and enthusiasm was infectious. He met with us, prayed with us, taught us and inspired us. He welcomed our thoughts and ideas, and our questions were always answered. He challenged us all to do the work of our Faith and put our ideas into actions.

As Co-Chair with the Very Rev. Fr. George Rados of the Department of Charities, I have personally witnessed Saidna's love and compassion to unfortunate people all over the world. He has seen the needs of those less fortunate who have suffered through wars, earthquakes, hurricanes, tsunamis, famines, floods, tragedies and catastrophic events. If there is a need to help, we help!! Because of Saidna's love and compassion, over fifteen percent of the budget of the archdiocese is given to charity. As our shepherd, Saidna has instructed us in the teaching of the Church, and we live those teachings by showing our love and commitment to care for those less fortunate.

The bread in your cupboard belongs to the hungry man; the coat hanging unused in your closet belongs to the man who needs it; the shoes rotting in your closet belong to the man who has no shoes; the money which you hoard in the bank belongs to the poor. You do wrong to everyone you could help, but fail to help.

(Saint Basil the Great, +379)

Our Five Programs and Saidna's Leadership

The Department of Charities consists of five programs:

1. *Children's Relief* — We assist in adoptions of babies and children from all over the world and provide yearly sponsorships for needy children.
2. *Middle Eastern Relief Fund* — We support Orphanages, Convents, and Schools for the Handicapped throughout the Middle East. We provide medical assistance and scholarships for countless families in need.
3. *Emergency Relief Fund* — We have collected and distributed millions of dollars for disaster and emergency relief victims in North America and all over the world.
4. *Special Parish Community Ministries* — Each local parish provides aid and assistance to their

own communities, whether through food banks or clothing drives, mentoring programs or neighborhood schools, nursing homes or homes for unwed mothers.

5. *Food for Hungry People* — This special program began when the world took notice that 700 million people lived in absolute poverty, lacking food, shelter and clothing. In the autumn of 1974, an international conference convened in Rome, Italy, to formulate a program aimed at alleviating world hunger.

Our own Archpriest James Meena, of thrice-blessed memory, presented the idea of creating a Food for Hungry People program within our archdiocese. With the encouragement of Saidna Philip, the members of NAC SOYO adopted a program that would afford every individual in our archdiocese an opportunity to personally help bring food to their hungry brothers and sisters throughout the world. The first campaign was planned for the Great Lent of 1975.

Saidna has instructed us that in the spiritual tradition of the Church, it is the teaching that what one saves through fasting and abstinence, should be given away to the poor. The first few years we collected about $5,000.00, now we collect nearly $200,000.00 annually. And, our program runs for just forty-nine days during Great Lent every year.

The Work We Have Done

Under the guidance and leadership of Saidna Philip we have collected almost four million dollars to date. We have given much needed relief to the hungry poor in the United States, Canada, Mexico, South America, the Middle East, Africa, Asia and Europe. The Food for Hungry People funds have been used to meet the needs of people all over the world for thirty-two years.

For thirty-two years, Saidna has:

- Helped the homeless and the sick;
- Fed starving babies, children and adults;

- Sheltered and guided run-away and thrown-away teenagers;
- Aided and visited those in prison and cared for their families;
- Brought food, clothes, assistance and hope to the homeless; and,
- Provided food, medicine and aid to war-torn and disaster struck victims.

For thirty-two years, Saidna Philip has touched the lives of thousands of people because their needs touched his heart.

When we read the thank you notes from the families and organizations we have helped, we realize that we CAN make a difference in this world and this inspires us to work harder and give more of ourselves to those in need.

> When you see a poor person, remember the words of our Lord Jesus Christ by which He declared that it is He, Himself who is fed. For though that which appears be not Christ, yet in that person's form it is Christ Himself who receives and begs.
> (St. John Chrysostom, Homilies on Matthew #78)

Loved by God, Loved By Saidna

The world of hunger, poverty and homelessness touches us all. Hunger is one of the world's most pressing problems, affecting over one billion people. Behind the grim statistics are children and families loved by God, who are deprived of their right to a full life because they do not have enough to eat. Whenever there is a need to help anyone, or any emergency, our metropolitan is there to help. Over the years we have helped thousands of men, women and children in an attempt to improve their lives and alleviate their suffering. And until the day comes when God's children are all well cared for, we will continue to Feed the Hungry, Clothe the Naked, Shelter the Homeless, Visit the Sick and in Prison and give Hope to the Hopeless.

Thank you Saidna, for allowing me to assist you with this life changing, humanitarian Department of Charities.

Your servant in Christ,

 —Robin Lynn Nicholas

 Co-Chairman Department of Charities

 **IN THE VIEW OF**

Dr. Anthony Bashir
Director, Department of Lay Ministry

Saidna's Leadership and Integrity

IT IS AN HONOR TO CONTRIBUTE TO THIS COLLECTION OF ESSAYS in celebration of the fortieth year of Metropolitan Philip's episcopacy. May God continue to bless him and sustain him as he cares for the vineyard God has planted here in the United States and Canada. The unity, integrity, diversity and growth of this blessed archdiocese are a testimony to his vision and leadership.

It Began In Chicago

My first recollection of you, Saidna, dates to February 1970, at a meeting of the North American Council (NAC) of SOYO (now the Fellowship of St. John the Divine), held in Chicago at the Hilton Hotel. You'll remember we had a fire in the hotel from which we all safely escaped. You were so worried and concerned about each of us and when, later that morning, we were in Liturgy with you, you found each of us with your eyes and heart. It was my first glimpse of what I would come to understand as your compassionate and caring nature.

The NAC met in Chicago to discuss the future of the youth movement; so many of the ideas that motivated SOYO had been fulfilled and it was urgent that we develop new perspectives and programs. You urged us to be bold in our work and from our ideas that we discussed with you, Jack Hanna and I developed the Awareness and Commitment Program of the archdiocese, a program that would later become the Parish Ministry Program of the Fellowship.

Many of us young people (at least, young back in the 70s) were very interested in acts of social ministry based on Jesus' teaching. I was particularly impressed with you because you supported us in our desire to build outreach programs into our communities as well as offerings for our parishes, i.e., The Special Olympics initiative which still occurs today under Fr. Anthony's directorship. From that first meeting in Chicago I deeply appreciated your commitment and support for the diversity of ministries that you clearly saw and encouraged around you. St. Irenaeus of Lyon notes: "Those who are truly His disciples receive grace from Him and put this grace into action for the benefit of others, each as he has received the gifts." I think that your deep sense of compassion and caring love for those who suffer and those in need has been a persistent theme throughout your episcopacy—one that I have admired and from which I have taken heart.

The Ministry I Learned

One of the great lessons I have learned from you over the thirty-six years I have served you and the Archdiocese Board of Trustees, is that all ministries are spiritually derived and must become spiritually driven action. In this regard, all ministries are intentional and revealed as services and acts within the world. My ministry, indeed my maturing processes as an Orthodox Christian, was shaped by my father and mother, and equally by you, the late Metropolitan Antony and Aunt Adele. I have learned from all of you to bear witness to the fact that our lives as Orthodox Christians are centered in Christ, in whom we are sustained and transformed as we progress on the inner path.

As I am writing these words to you, I realize the many accomplishments of your episcopacy, and how much we, as your spiritual children and members of your Board of Trustees, have been through with you. We have benefited from your initiatives—from the constitutional changes, to the development of new and vibrant organizations, to a unified archdiocese, to the development of the Antiochian Village and Heritage Center…the list goes on. I had first hand knowledge of the suffering and deep sense of betrayal experienced by Metropolitan Antony over the existence of two archdioceses in the United States. You took on this "ministry of reconciliation" and through your vision of unity, and your effective use of negotiation, realized for the Church, and for all of us, a longed for experience of oneness.

I suspect that the commonly held opinion of leadership is tied to such ideas as "in charge," "gets direct and immediate results," and "brings about defining moments." I'm sure that is all true of you and your episcopacy. But I think to end there would miss the example of the leadership you provided to this archdiocese and indeed to each of us. Your leadership has come about because you are motivated and led by a vision for the Church in the United States and Canada.

You are always learning and teaching; I really enjoy listening to you and engaging with your ideas. While you and I sometimes use different process approaches to problem solving, our relationship is sustained through our mutual trust and respect for each other. I so appreciate the opportunities you have given me to work with John Dalack in the Department of Lay Ministry and now with Ron Nicola in the Department of Stewardship. This collaborative work has molded me and the ability to mold men and women as you have done is a mark of a great leader. Your trust in the work you allow me to do with others is deeply appreciated and acknowledged; it means a great deal to me.

Qualities of Leadership

Perseverance in the face of challenge is the mark of an extraordinary leader. I so very much respect your perseverance, whether with ideas or in the face of your health challenges. When I go for my cardiac visit, I cannot help but think of you, take from your example and say a little prayer for all of us who have followed there. In your perseverance you have shown great ambition for achieving some really big goals—another mark of a great leader.

Innovation in your approach to challenges, as well as devotion to excellence in yourself and in others, has resulted in the emergence of ideas and programs that are exemplars to others in the Church. Working under your leadership and in the face of your trust is an awesome experience and one that I have never taken lightly. Finally, leadership remains open to new ideas. The coming into our archdiocese of the Evangelical Orthodox group is a fine example of allowing the wind of the Holy Spirit to enliven and refresh us all—but then so are the Antiochian Women and The Order of St. Ignatius of Antioch.

We have much to be thankful for in your episcopacy. For me the most precious gift is the opportunity to know you as a man of integrity and good spirit, whose mind is set on building up the Body of Christ. It is a blessing to serve you and be trusted. God grant you many years! I look forward to the endlessly wonderful outcomes of your mind as it unfolds though your maturing process on the inner path.

—Anthony S. Bashir
Department of Lay Ministry

 IN THE VIEW OF

EDWARD ASSILE
NORTH AMERICAN CHAIR, THE ORDER OF ST. IGNATIUS OF ANTIOCH

I BECAME ORTHODOX IN 1982, SO, ALONG WITH MANY OTHERS, I was not involved with the archdiocese when The Order began in 1975. I have had the honor and the privilege to serve on the Governing Council since 1989, but I needed the insight from the beginning of The Order to reflect on Metropolitan Philip's incredible vision of this wonderful ministry. I spoke with Fr. Anthony Gabriel, The Order's first North American Chaplain, who guided me to an excellent brochure entitled "A Call to Greatness Through Service." Dn. Hans was kind enough to find the brochure in the archdiocese archives and I read it with a deep sense of appreciation and awe to see where we were and where we are now!

This brochure, published in 1975, answered the questions: What is the archdiocese? What does it do? Today we could publish the same brochure, adjusting the dollar amounts to today's budget, which would be, obviously, much larger, but the same needs would certainly be evident. In 1975, the archdiocese was receiving $5.00 per baptized soul and servicing twenty-one departments. The young Metropolitan understood that to grow our archdiocese, he would need serious amounts of money to unleash Antiochian Orthodoxy in America.

Providing for Growth

In the book, *And He Leads Them,* the Metropolitan states: "It [this brochure] describes through simple words, figures and fine art the various departments of the archdiocese and demonstrates clearly what we have and what we lack. If you read this brochure, you will find that some of our departments have no budgets at all, and whatever others budgeted for other departments is far from being adequate; we cannot serve you properly without the necessary funds." In clear simple words, this is why Saidna Philip created The Order: "We cannot serve you properly without the necessary funds."

Many times we have heard Saidna Philip say we do not have an "upstairs/downstairs" approach in our archdiocese. Rather, we have a symphony of hierarchs, clergy and laity working together. One of the greatest strengths of our archdiocese is the strong clergy/laity partnership. It was this partnership, through many meetings, that helped form The Order. The Very Rev. Anthony Gabriel, Albert Joseph and their committee created a foundation, slightly modified over the years, that has stood the test of time and allowed The Order to flourish into one of the most important accomplishments of Metropolitan Philip's episcopacy.

Saidna: Never Satisfied

Saidna Philip often tells us he suffers from never being satisfied. That is why at many hierarchical liturgies he has asked how many new members are being inducted and when he receives the answer, no matter what the number, he then says: *Baas?*—meaning, "Is that all?" He says this because he knows the needs are great and will continue to be great; therefore, he constantly challenges both the clergy and laity to do more for our archdiocese.

Saidna has said on many occasions that the history of our archdiocese will be written based on what happened "before" The Order and what happened "after" The Order. He says this because during the past thirty years, The Order has funded approximately twenty-five percent of each archdiocese budget. Where Saidna used to say: "The Order is the best kept secret in the archdiocese," now we ask: "where would the archdiocese be without the seventeen million dollars contributed since 1975?"

The Work We Do

As we reflect back on the thirty years of The Order and see the difference The Order has made in our archdiocese, Saidna reminds us that we must remember that today the needs of the Church are, in fact, greater than thirty years ago. The challenges of our open society dictate that we have a strong Church. The Order of St. Ignatius is the interface between the real world and the Church. Order members not only give of themselves financially but also participate in many aspects of archdiocese and parish life: the choir, Church school, parish council, teen advising, the Camp, prison ministry, volunteering in the community, etc. The work we do allows us to answer St. Matthew's judgment in the Gospel, for we do feed the hungry, clothe the naked, visit the sick and help those in prison.

As a member of the Governing Council for all these years I have had the privilege of being in the Metropolitan's company many times. I have heard him speak, understood his reasoning and always felt we are blessed to have him as our Metropolitan. May God grant him many years.

 **IN THE VIEW OF**

JOAN FARHA
PRESIDENT, NAC FELLOWSHIP OF ST. JOHN THE DIVINE

Saidna Philip's Impact on the SOYO, the Senior SOYO, and the Fellowship of St. John the Divine

Our Evolvement Now

THE TITLE OF THIS ARTICLE INCLUDES THE PAST AND PRESENT NAMES of this dynamic organization of the laity. As you can see from the title, the history of this organization has not been static. We began in our regions as SOYO, eventually becoming Senior SOYO, in order to differentiate ourselves from the Teens. Now, we have evolved into the Fellowship of St. John the Divine, an organization that is mobilized for twenty-first century ministries.

The North American Council (NAC) of the Fellowship of St. John the Divine is comprised of presidents and delegates from each Diocesan Fellowship. Our members may vary in age and experience but they are unified by their commitment, love and service to God and His Holy Church. Over the years we have developed, implemented and administered numerous projects, including many that have grown into archdiocese departments: Christian Education, Communications, Conference and Convention Planning, Creative and Oratorical Festivals, Food for Hungry People and Sacred Music.

Saidna's Encouragement

While we are still directly involved with many of these Departments and Programs, we are also striving to effectively redefine ourselves as an organization of this God-protected archdiocese. Today, we are focusing our efforts on three areas. First, we are working towards Orthodox unity by spearheading efforts to promote cooperation on a local level. Second, we are re-emphasizing our commitment to missions, outreach and evangelism…locally, nationally and internationally. Finally, we will always seek to continue our spiritual growth, individually and collectively. How do we do it? Quite simply, we look to His Eminence Metropolitan Philip for his vision, while he prays for us, supports us, has faith in us and trusts us to faithfully serve our Lord through the archdiocese.

> I believe that the Fellowship of St. John the Divine has grown in its mission over the past several years due to the encouragement and motivation of His Eminence Metropolitan Philip. (Kh. Gigi Shadid, NAC President 2001–2005)

Before writing this article, I asked my predecessors and other longtime active Fellowship members about the impact they believe Metropolitan Philip has had on this organization. Their answers pointed to His Eminence's leadership, trust, direction and wisdom.

> He believed in his people and challenged us to work with him toward achieving his visions. He empowered us through his example of leadership. (Kathy Abraham, NAC President 1995–1999)

> The legacy of the Metropolitan is surrounding himself with people who are more than equal to their tasks. The programs of the Fellowship have succeeded because Saidna challenges people to be strong leaders. (V. Rev. Michael Abdelahad, active member since 1975)

His Trust, Direction and Wisdom

When reflecting on why His Eminence gives us his *trust*, I have come to the conclusion that it is because of his own complete and total trust in God, and his love for us. Whether reading one of his books or listening to him speak, this trust and love shines through. And gratefully, we are the ones who benefit.

> Saidna Philip expects great things from us because he knows that with God's help, we can accomplish much. (Kh. Gigi Shadid)

This brings us to Metropolitan Philip's *direction*. Through His Eminence's direction, the Fellowship helps brings the family together—each individual family, as well as the archdiocese family. In the past, Regional conventions were social events, not intended for families and certainly not children. I remember eagerly awaiting my fourteenth birthday when my parents would allow me to attend the "SOYO Convention." Today we gather for Diocesan "Family Reunions." Children are not only welcomed, but also encouraged. While we still enjoy the social fellowship of the Parish Life Conferences, it is secondary to worship and spiritual growth.

As I look around the NAC Fellowship table, I clearly see how His Eminence's *wisdom* has affected the Fellowship. The Antiochian Village, Camp St. Nicholas and the diocesan camps have inspired a new generation of faithful, active leaders. Many of our Fellowship Presidents are camp alumni. This legacy will provide the Holy Orthodox Church with priests and monastic and lay leaders for generations to come. The Fellowship is blessed to be one of the beneficiaries of Metropolitan Philip's visions of Orthodox camps.

Childhood Memories

Reflecting on the last forty years, I realize that I know no other Metropolitan. I was too young to be aware of the struggles of the past. What I do remember, however, is the excitement and anticipation of my elders when the Metropolitan would come to town. I can still see him standing next to my grandfather, as they burned the mortgage on the Educational Building at the "old" St. George. The song being sung was "The Impossible Dream." A few years later my older cousin became involved in Teen SOYO, where His Eminence was affectionately called "Your M & M's."

These childhood memories more accurately depict our beloved Metropolitan than one might think. They describe a leader with a tender spot for the young, a visionary with a gentle heart, a loving father surrounded by his children.

On behalf of the Fellowship of St. John the Divine, Saidna, we thank you for your constant love and support. We wish you a most blessed fortieth anniversary. We pray that the Almighty God will continue to bless us with your leadership, and may He grant you many, many years.

Many Years, Master!

—Joan Farha, President

Fellowship of St. John the Divine

 **IN THE VIEW OF**

LAILA FERRIS
PRESIDENT, ANTIOCHIAN ORTHODOX CHRISTIAN WOMEN OF
NORTH AMERICA

Born of a Vision

THE ANTIOCHIAN ORTHODOX CHRISTIAN WOMEN OF NORTH AMERICA was "born" of a vision of one of the most prominent visionaries of our time—our beloved Metropolitan Philip. Saidna Philip founded the organization in 1973, due to his belief that the women of this archdiocese had so much more to give. He saw in us a great ability to lead, to serve causes greater than those at the local levels. With this in mind, he announced the formalization of a new organization, fully chaired and run by women. This "Sisterhood of Charity" would use their dedicated energies and leadership abilities to serve those in need, at home and around the world.

Our Purpose is Eternal
It was at the Archdiocese Convention, in Los Angeles, California, that Metropolitan Philip first announced his visionary plans, for the women of this archdiocese. After watching the diligent work and loving care of these women, through his own service to the Faith and the archdiocese, the realization

came to him that the women should formally come together from all over North America to work together as one body, one Sisterhood, in order to perform acts of service for those in need. He named the purposes that he believed the women would fulfill, along with the first President and Spiritual Advisor. The purposes, which have now become the Mission Statement of the Antiochian Women, are timeless, but showed the great wisdom through which they were developed. They are as follows: to develop among women throughout the archdiocese a spirit of Christian leadership, awareness and commitment; to foster among women a genuine expression of love and service through works of charity; and, to instill in women a large sense of fellowship and a deeper understanding of the heritage and traditions of the Antiochian Archdiocese and the Orthodox Church. His Eminence also showed his great belief in the leadership abilities of the Antiochian Women, in that, through the Archdiocese Constitution, he has granted a seat on the Archdiocese Board of Trustees to the President of the North American Board of the Antiochian Women. His faith and trust in the Antiochian women is fully visible, for he gave us a voice within the ruling laymen's leadership of this archdiocese. His vision of leadership, service and spiritual growth for the Antiochian Women is solid and forever strong.

Saidna's Lead: To Serve Others

Not only would the Antiochian Women ensure continued support for each other and their own spiritual growth, through the persistent acquisition of knowledge of the Orthodox Faith, but they would also be allowed to serve those in need through many venues. Through Metropolitan Philip's understanding and knowledge of the world around him, he was able to challenge the Antiochian Women to support many entities who were in need of their love and care. These challenges have come to be known as the Antiochian Women's Projects. Some of the Antiochian Women's Projects in the past have been: Pastoral Education, the Balamand Seminary, the Antiochian Village, the Married Seminarian Fund, St. George Hospital in Beirut, the IOCC, the Antiochian Village Camp, the Antiochian Village Dining Hall expansion, the Orphanages Around the World, the Orphanage Endowment Fund and, presently, the Retired Clergy Fund. Through His Eminence's support, the Antiochian Women have raised approximately $2,000,000.00 to support these projects over the past several years. This great achievement would never have been accomplished without Metropolitan Philip's foresight and challenge for the Antiochian Women to serve those in need through these projects, as one body, one Sisterhood.

Again, through his desire to support those in need through the good works of the Antiochian Women, perpetual funds have been established within the archdiocese such as the Married Seminarian Fund and the Orphanage Endowment Fund. All one has to do is to review this list of projects to know the great and sincere care Metropolitan Philip has for people around the world who are in need of the service that has been provided through his vision and the Antiochian Women. All these projects are so worthy and have ensured that someone's life has been made a better one just because one great man, our beloved Metropolitan, had the foresight to provide the care that would come to them. He has truly allowed the Antiochian Women to fulfill our motto: "The Antiochian Women: A Sisterhood Serving Christ through Serving Others."

His faith and belief in the good works and the leadership roles of the Antiochian Women can be seen in so many ways. A few years ago, during dialogues with the Antiochian Women, Metropolitan Philip stated to them that he felt they were the "heartbeat of the archdiocese." This due to: their charitable works, love and care for others, especially those in need; to their commitment to work as one body, one Sisterhood, with all those around them; and to never say "no," nor feel that their jobs are done. Throughout the years, he has continued to show his support and trust in the Antiochian Women, has watched this organization grow and continue to accomplish whatever has been placed before us. His Eminence's belief in all that we do is the greatest compliment that can be given to any organization. He has been our advisor, our supporter, our cheerleader and our role model.

"Many Years, Master!!"

—Laila Ferris, President, Antiochian Women, North American Board

# IN THE VIEW OF

CHARLES ABDELAHAD
PRESIDENT, NAC TEEN SOYO

Saidna Philip and His Love for Our Work

WITH LITTLE MORE THAN THIRTY SECONDS LEFT TO PLAY, THE SCORE WAS TIED during the championship soccer game of Special Olympics Pennsylvania. The referee blew the whistle and the ball was thrown into play. It was passed back and forth, slowly making its way up the field as time continued to count down. Suddenly, Billy Wusner was on a breakaway! He confidently dribbled toward the goal, his Superman cape flapping violently in the wind as he sprinted up field. Billy brought his foot back and kicked the ball as hard as he could, but the ball only glanced off the side of his foot. The ball rolled slowly on the ground towards the goal…right past the unsuspecting and baffled goalie. The referee blew the whistle signaling the end of the game. It was over, and Billy Wusner had won the game for his team. He came running across the field, tears streaming down his face. He jumped into my arms, buried his face in my neck and gave me the biggest hug of my life, as I tried to fight back my own tears. After four years of failing to score a goal, Billy had finally achieved what he had been training so hard to do. What made the scene even sweeter was the fact that the athletes on the other team were not downtrodden and depressed at their defeat. Rather, they were beaming, their grins reaching from ear to ear as they joined Billy's teammates in congratulating him. It was like a scene straight from a movie as he was carried off the field while the crowd chanted: "Billy! Billy! Billy!"

Special Olympics and Abiding Optimism

The Special Olympics Sports Training Camp in Pennsylvania is held at the Antiochian Village Church Camp located in the Laurel Mountains, near Bolivar, Pennsylvania. The athletes look forward to annually returning to "God's Mountain," the place where miracles really happen. The North American Council of Teen SOYO (Society of Orthodox Youth Organizations) funds Special Olympics Pennsylvania, so that the athletes can live their dream for one week. With coaches from Special Olympics Pennsylvania, members of NAC SOYO volunteer to be coaches and counselors for a week.

The mornings were cold and everyone gathered early to run around the track. Training continued as the day got progressively hotter. Athletes broke up into their primary sports after breakfast. Despite intense heat and the demanding tasks before them, the athletes worked hard and always had smiles on their faces. No matter how well they performed, they were always happy and willing to help one another. They returned to their cabins after a grueling day of training, their bodies exhausted yet their faces radiant with joy.

As a coach, I helped the men in my cabin, who were older than me, with tasks that are second nature to us. I helped them dress and undress, get into bed, wash up, take showers, shave, etc. As scary as it was, I had to calmly deal with occasional seizures. You would think that this life is disappointing to these athletes, but that is not the case. No matter what they had to overcome, these Special Olympians were always optimistic. My friend and fellow counselor put it best: "You know, being here is a humbling experience. Take us for example. We get so upset over material things, like a girl losing her bottle of nail polish. Then I look at these athletes who are the kindest, happiest, most laid-back people I have ever seen; then I become ashamed for being so self-centered."

Saidna's Dream Realized

This opportunity would not have been given to me if not for Metropolitan Philip Saliba. The Antiochian Village was the vision of Metropolitan Philip. His dream of providing this camp for our youth has molded me into the person I am today. It is primarily a Church camp during the summer months and serves as the site for Special Olympics Pennsylvania. I have learned so many lessons about my faith and about myself while attending the Village as a camper, counselor and Special Olympics Coach. Metropolitan Philip is directly responsible for the success of all of these programs that are a part of everything that I am. In addition to the Antiochian Village Camp and Special Olympics Pennsylvania, there is also Teen SOYO and its various outreach programs. Hosting the Special Olympics at the Village is one of the main projects of Teen SOYO. Through Witness, Worship, Fellowship and Service, Teen SOYO strives to uphold Christian values in the youth of this archdiocese in today's turbulent society. As President of this organization, I can directly appreciate all that it has done for my fellow teens and me. Together, Teen SOYO and the Antiochian Village are producing a generation of good Christian leaders. On behalf of NAC Teen SOYO, I cannot thank Metropolitan Philip enough, not only for all that he has done for this God-protected archdiocese, but also for my organization and me. He is a very dignified man who I look up to, and I am so thankful he has had such a profound impact on my life. May God grant him many more years as our leader, teacher, father and friend. Thank you Saidna!

In Christ,

—Charles Abdelahad
NAC Teen SOYO President

 **IN THE VIEW OF**

BRUCE JOHN JABBOUR
GENERAL MANAGER, ANTIOCHIAN VILLAGE

IT WAS A SPRING DAY ON SATURDAY IN 1967 AT ST. GEORGE CHURCH in Boston, Massachusetts. As children, in Sunday school we were all instructed by teachers and parents to meet and greet Saidna by having our palms upward to receive his blessing, as well as a gift from the Metropolitan, as we kissed his hand. I approached, looked up, turned, and said: "This is not the Metropolitan!" Embarrassment spread over everybody's face as I exclaimed again: "This is not the Metropolitan!" Metropolitan pulled me close and asked: "Why do you say I am not the Metropolitan?" I replied: "Because you are smiling."

> Then He took a little child and set him in the midst of them and when He had
> taken him into His arms, He said to them, 'Whoever receives one of these little
> children in My name receives Me; and whoever receives Me, receives not Me but
> Him who sent Me.' (Mark 9:36-37)

Let us go to the spring of the early 70s. It was a very hot and humid day, fans were blowing, doors and windows were all open, the congregation was in prayer, the choir was singing. Then Saidna

Philip, with cross in hand, turned to bless, only to find an unnoticed vagrant with knife in hand standing before him! Ushers and chanters attempted to apprehend the man when Saidna gave instructions not to harm him, but instead gave the man blessed holy bread to eat, and told him to kiss the cross and to depart in peace. We were all awe struck as the man did exactly what Saidna had asked. "Blessed are those who hunger and thirst for righteousness, for they shall be filled" (Matthew 5:6).

These are very important memories that poured the foundation and placed the stamp of Metropolitan Philip on my life—founding my belief in the Church by his living and teaching God's word.

His Vision

Metropolitan Philip has been characterized in many different ways, specifically as a practical visionary. Proverbs 29:18 reads: "Where there is no vision, the people perish." And so, in the short life of a man, no lost time can be afforded.

In 1973, Metropolitan Philip commissioned Fr. George M. Corry and Board Trustee member George S. Koury to find a place where the faithful of the archdiocese could escape the noise of this world and spend time rediscovering themselves through prayer, retreat, meditation and meaningful human encounters. Five years later, in 1978, Camp Fairfield was purchased and hence the Antiochian Village Camp was born. In 1986 it entered the first full year of operation as the Antiochian Village Heritage and Learning Center.

Saidna Philip's dream became a reality with the Camp and Phase I, Phase II and Museum Phase III of the Heritage and Learning Center. Imagine the long term thinking of Metropolitan Philip for such a retreat to come to fruition. There are many questions posed about the Antiochian Village. The two I would like to address here are: Who we are and what the Center has to offer the local, national, and international Orthodox and non-Orthodox communities. The Antiochian Village Heritage and Learning Center is a house of prayer through Saints' Peter and Paul Chapel; a place of learning through the 25,000-volume library; a museum of religious and cultural artifacts; as well as the location of many auditoriums and indoor and outdoor spaces for pilgrimages, symposia, lectures, meetings, physical training and concerts. It is an establishment that provides temporary lodging and dining experiences. The following is a list of only the Antiochian groups and events at the Village: College Conference; Winter Camp Session I; mid-winter meetings held by the Antiochian Women, the Fellowship of St. John, Christian Education and Teen SOYO; Winter Camp Session II; Byzantine Chanting Workshop, Diocesan Clergy Retreat; Antiochian Women Lenten Retreat; Spring Delegates Meeting; Clergy and Lay Leadership Training; Orthodox Christian Fellowship; spring meetings of the Board of Trustees, The Order of St. Ignatius and the Village Council; Village Alumni Weekend; Sacred Music Institute; Clergy Symposium; Summer Delegates Meeting; summer meetings; Teen SOYO Leadership Training; House of Studies; St. Stephen's Course of Studies; Missions and Evangelism; St. Thekla and St. Raphael Pilgrimage; Parish Council Symposium; Orthodox Institute; Youth Workers Conference; and personal or family reflective reunions. Look! A Village created from an idea that Metropolitan Philip refused to allow to be consumed by any wind. Saidna has afforded people the opportunity to "Come Pray and Play."

This is without question dynamism and synergy.

I am eternally thankful to have in our midst such a spiritual leader heading the Antiochian Orthodox Archdiocese of North America. I am so impressed with Metropolitan Philip's choice in surrounding himself with so many dedicated and wise advocates. These clergy and lay people work diligently together within the archdiocese, and then reach out as humanitarians to the world, under the guidance of His Eminence. In the fall of 1994 a very important historical meeting took place at Antiochian Village, with Orthodox bishops discussing Orthodox unity in America. Once again, a concept that was so simple for our metropolitan to see and to look beyond, to visualize a much more glorious icon.

His Call to Me

In the spring of 2005, I was summoned from Las Vegas, Nevada, and honored by the appointment of

Saidna and Mr. Bob Laham, Chairman of the Village Council, to the position of General Manager. I was challenged not to "come into retirement," but rather to "toil into retirement!" I am the newest steward watching over this establishment that God has blessed through the perseverance of Saidna Philip. Under their direction, part of the marketing plan was to aggressively pursue the SMERF (Social, Military, Educational, Religious, and Fraternal) markets, including Corporate and Motor Coach, all of which have a good core of value. The plan was also to work with the Camp in developing one website. These combined strategies have increased activity at the Heritage and Learning Center by almost one third. This successful exposure was achieved as the direct result of Metropolitan Philip's "business sense" of fruitful freshness.

Often leaders are lonely. However, Metropolitan Philip has never left our sides, nor have we failed to show abundant love for him. I acknowledge that it is better to be loved than it is to be honored; I believe Saidna to be both, as he has always accepted the great tears of the Church faithful to be joyful praises.

On behalf of the entire staff (with which I am so proud to be working as a team), I promise that we will remain committed to sincere service, ultimate cleanliness, genuine safety and, of course, pleasingly delicious meals, as we welcome you to your spiritual oasis and your second home, the jewel of the archdiocese, which you planted upon good soil. We invite all to take advantage of a journey to western Pennsylvania, since the only situations that are overlooked are the Laurel Highlands.

IN THE VIEW OF

WALID KHALIFE
HONORARY MEMBER, ARCHDIOCESE BOARD OF TRUSTEES

Saidna Philip, the Guiding Light

ABOUT 18 YEARS AGO, I RECEIVED A CALL FROM METROPOLITAN PHILIP requesting that I serve on the Archdiocese Board of Trustees. Little did I know at that time my involvement on the Archdiocese Board would lead me to a new discovery and learning experience that far exceeds the knowledge of the ordinary layperson.

With this involvement, I extended my horizons to learn about our archdiocese, its departments, missions and charities. Saidna Philip encouraged me to use my assets, my business experience and my love for the Church in order to help in the financial support of the church and her missions. Through Saidna, I developed many strong friendships as he encouraged my involvement in many major projects within our archdiocese. Foremost among these involvements was when I was invited to accompany him to the Holy Synod in support of pursuing our self-rule. I experienced, first hand, the knowledge with which Saidna is blessed and the respect he received from all concerned, from the deacons to the hierarchy. This included ministers, prime ministers and presidents, who expressed their sincere appreciation for the leadership Saidna demonstrated, and especially for his efforts in bringing Arab Americans together with their Christian and Muslim leaders in North America. I also learned that the model of practical theology, as expressed by Metropolitan Philip, is revealed in his leadership of bringing both clergy and laity together, and incorporating them to work for the welfare of the Church. Saidna's leadership focuses on establishing a balance between the material and spiritual needs of the Church. I pray he will continue to be a catalyst in these endeavors.

I would like all to know that my friendship and love of Saidna knows no bounds. He has always given great support to my family, in times of trial and in times of celebration. He personally supported my late father, Khalil, in rebuilding our church in Lebanon.

From a layman's point of view, Saidna has endeared himself not only to my family, but also to our local parishioners of St. George of Troy, Michigan. He is always there for us, a "guiding light," giving us encouragement, love and leadership.

May God grant him "Many Years!"

—Walid K. Khalife

IN THE VIEW OF

NICOLA M. ANTAKLI
CHAIRMAN AND CHIEF EXECUTIVE OFFICER
INTRACO CORPORATION

A Lifetime Friend

PHILIP SALIBA IS AN INSPIRATIONAL LEADER, A VISIONARY, A DYNAMIC SPEAKER and the Metropolitan of the "Church of the straight thinkers." *He is a lifetime friend.*

I knew Philip as a student at the Orthodox High School in Homs, Syria, from 1947 to 1949. At that time he was a deacon at the Church of Forty Martyrs in Bustan Al-Diwan. The Homs Boy's High School was then recognized as the best academic high school institution in Syria and Lebanon for both resident and non-resident students.

Deacon Philip Saliba was associated with a trio of deacons who were famous for the most beautiful voices in the Byzantine Church chanting style. I recall that during the Lenten season, the Church of Forty Martyrs and its large yard was crowded with people. Especially on Wednesdays and Fridays, during the chanting of *Al-Madayeh*, the whole community came to enjoy the beautiful voices of the trio of deacons: Philip, Demitri and Mesaeel. Even Metropolitan Alexander Geha of Homs enjoyed the chanting of the trio and the great choir under the direction of Mr. George Rizk.

The Homs Orthodox School, both teachers and students, was also known as a hub of political involvement during the period from 1947 to 1949, right after Syria gained its independence from France in 1945, and beyond. There were three main political groups at the school: the Syrian Nationalists, the Communists and the Arab Nationalists. Deacon Philip was a leading figure and influential peacemaker among the different groups.

Philip was fortunate because he resided in Homs at the archdiocese residence, which is located next to the Church and the girl's Orthodox High School. I remember quite a few young ladies who always admired the handsome young Philip Saliba; however, we were living in a society where girls and boys could only look and smile!

Saidna at Wayne State

After six years of separation, I was surprised and extremely pleased to see my friend Philip as a student at Wayne State University. He was an "A" student, with admiration from the entire faculty as well as the Arab-American students. Philip Saliba, Zaki Khzouz, Hani Fakhoury, Habib Fakhoury, Emil Najm, Claude Romain, Sam Zawaydah, I and many others were always together for lunch at the corner table at the Wayne State Student Center, discussing Mid-East politics. Of course, many American young men and young women tried to join us at that famous roundtable; they called us the "table of elites."

The year 1956 was one of activity and crisis. We formed the first Arab Student Club at Wayne State University and we elected Philip Saliba as president. A major crisis took place in Egypt—the occupation of the Suez Canal by the British, the French and the Israeli. Philip Saliba called for a meeting of the club to consider the possibility of the Arab students in the United States volunteering to go to Egypt to fight for the liberation of the Suez Canal. A group of six students, representing Arab students in the United States, traveled to Washington, D.C., to visit the Arab Ambassadors and offer our willingness to go to Egypt and fight for the liberation of the Suez Canal from the occupiers.

However, the occupation did not last long because the United States, under the leadership of President Dwight Eisenhower, requested the end of the occupation and the withdrawal of the occupiers from the Suez Canal.

The college years at Wayne State University were memorable for studying hard, struggling to make ends meet our needs, celebrating at the Alcove bar with our many activist friends and discussing politics back home and in the United States. I recall one time we boycotted certain public places because they were segregationists and did not allow our black student friends to join us. Of course, Philip Saliba was always the leader for freedom in the United States and back home in the Middle East.

From Deacon to Priest to Archbishop

In 1959 Deacon Philip was ordained a priest for Cleveland, Ohio—residing in Parma Heights. I still remember the beautiful days we spent together at his residence during the holidays.

In 1966 I was in Lebanon, spending the summer at Kassouf Hotel in Dhour Shweir, and was surprised to see Fr. Ruffin, Fr. Gabriel and other priests at the hotel. They were coming for the great celebration to see our dear friend Philip Saliba elevated to Metropolitan, as the Archbishop of New York and All North America, overseeing more than sixty parishes. We were all so proud of his accomplishments and celebrated for many days.

Years passed, until one day I attended a major celebration to burn the mortgage of St. George Church in Detroit at the Silverdome in Pontiac, Michigan. Metropolitan Philip was also attending the celebration and he greeted me enthusiastically when he saw me among the audience. This event was the beginning of many meetings that allowed us to renew our friendship and revisit many years of experiences, from Church to business to life. Metropolitan Philip convinced me to again become active in the Church, and we met as often as possible. As a result of these meetings, I was amazed by the growth of the Church under his leadership, and I wanted to work with the distinguished group of leaders on the Archdiocese Board. Along with this privilege, I have been graced with long-lasting, meaningful friendships, and the blessed experience and opportunity to work for the glory of God through the Orthodox Church. Metropolitan Philip and I have spent days and weeks during the last twenty years discussing the future of the Church of Antioch and its role throughout the world; of course, the North American Church was the pinnacle of most of these conversations.

The Great Visionary for Future Ages

The great visionary, Philip Saliba, would like to see the Orthodox Church united in North America in order to have a powerful voice in Washington, D.C. He would also like to see the Antiochian Orthodox Church strong in the Middle East, as well as among its congregations throughout the world. He encouraged the leadership of the Church to make fundamental changes that would enable the Orthodox religious community to have a paramount effect in the modern world. At the same time we must maintain the old world meaning and teachings of the Church, as these are the laws and the message blessed by God to remain forever.

Saidna Philip has dedicated his life to strengthening Orthodoxy, and the Antiochian Orthodox Church in particular. His devotion, inspiration and vision, which have led to the astounding growth of the North American Archdiocese, will remain forever engraved in the hearts and minds of the faithful for generations to come.

 IN THE VIEW OF

CHRISTOPHER HOLWEY
CHAIRMAN, DEPARTMENT OF SACRED MUSIC

Saidna Philip as a Source of *Dynamis*

I CANNOT IMAGINE WHAT STATE OF EXISTENCE WE WOULD BE IN TODAY in this archdiocese, or in the Orthodox world, for that matter, if we had not had Metropolitan Philip at the helm for the past forty years. Working together with his brother bishops, his many priests and deacons, his Board of Trustees, the chairmen of our departments and the beloved faithful across this great North American continent, his leadership and guidance, his wisdom and insight, his courage and determination to bring Orthodoxy to America, has allowed us to grow tremendously in Life and Faith and Spiritual Understanding. He has given us the opportunity to make our Faith a living Faith of service and ministry to God's holy people.

A Man of Power and Strength

If I had to choose one term, one word, to describe his leadership, I would have to say it would be the word "*dynamis!*" *Dynamis* is a Greek word that means power or strength. It is where we get the English word dynamic. It is a very important word to him, and it became a very important word to me as well back in the early 1980s. Let me explain.

I think it was during the summer of 1982, after I had finished one year of seminary, when I was the Midwest Region Choir Director, and the Region had come together for the Parish Life Conference. It was Thursday morning, at the first Divine Liturgy. I had about 80 sopranos in the choir with only a few other voices in each of the sections! It was very hard to get the choir to sing together, to keep it all moving and balanced. This also was the first service for many different singers to sing now as a group, without any rehearsal time together. It was not going well. I guess our struggle through the Cherubic Hymn was all that Metropolitan Philip could take at that point, and he decided that it was time to send Deacon Hans back to the choir to put us out of our misery. So, after singing the final Alleluia, Deacon Hans came up to me and said: "Chris, the bishop is very displeased. He wants you to stop singing." Of course, my first thought, as I was turning how many different shades of red, was: *Well, who's going to sing the rest of the Liturgy?* He then told me that the clergy would take over and do the chanting. How embarrassing!

Well, after the Liturgy was over, the bishop welcomed us all to the Conference, gave us a few remarks and comments, and at the end said, in front of everyone, that he wanted the clergy to stay after for some directions for the week, and that he wanted to see me as well. (*Oh, boy!*) Then, sitting there with the clergy, he looked at me and said: "Chris, do you know what the word *dynamis* means?" (*Oh, great!* I thought. *I mess up the Liturgy and now he's throwing Greek at me. Well, I'm a first year seminarian. I should be able to figure this out. It sounds like the word dynamic.*) In my nervousness, I said: "Yes, Saidna. It means something like dynamic, or powerful." While nodding, he replied: "Yes, Chris." Then, after pausing for a brief moment, he looked at me and said: "Chris, there was no *dynamis* in the Liturgy this morning." And I sighed.

From that moment on, I realized what this man was all about—what was so very important to him with regard to the music of our liturgical services. There needs to be a dynamic movement in what we sing and how we sing it, reflecting the power and gift of the Holy Spirit breathing and acting within all of us. The music is the means by which we pray. It is the *dynamis* of our offering to God. It is the soul of our liturgical services, which breathes life into the hearts of all the faithful believers, and lifts us up to join with the angels in the worship of our God.

Even though it was a very difficult experience for me to go through, being told to stop singing in front of all the clergy and laity of the Midwest Region, I very much appreciated his doing so. It helped to shape me not only in my own relationship with God as I continued on in the seminary, but also in my future ministry to my parishioners as a priest in the archdiocese, and even now in our ministry in the Sacred Music Department.

A True Musician

Speaking of which, let me share with you a few thoughts from some of the other people in this department, who have also been influenced by our beloved Metropolitan Philip. Our former chairman James Meena has always recognized that although our Metropolitan may not call himself this, he is a true musician who is extremely well versed in Byzantine chant, and knows full well the connection between music and prayer. More importantly, he understands the need we have to allow our musical tradition to continue to grow and take shape as it becomes more American. It is this latter aspect that became a big part of his ministry, and which directed this department during his three years as chairman. It is summed up by the mission statement that became a part of our letterhead.

Our Vice-Chairman, Michael Farrow, has been working in this department for over fifteen years, and has appreciated the bishop's insight and direction in guiding the music development in this archdiocese. Michael shared with me that it was Metropolitan Philip who "initiated and supported the Kazan project so that we would not forget our Byzantine musical tradition." This project was taken on by Ray George, former Chairman of this Department, and Basil Kazan—may God rest their souls. It involved the composition, typesetting and printing of all the music in Byzantine chant for Vespers,

Matins, the Triodion, Holy Week, the Pentecostarion and the Menaion, all of which Ray did by hand in the basement of his house. Then, with the establishment of the Antiochian Village, the bishop helped us to provide "a forum for the Sacred Music Institute, which has had over twenty-two years of training musicians, choir directors, chanters and clergy." This was important to the life of the Church, since, as Michael said, the bishop always "encouraged the selection of hymns and proper conducting of the hymns, conducive to keeping the Liturgy moving, so that the continuity of meaning was not lost due to an excessively lengthy Liturgy." Finally, when the bishop accepted the Evangelical Orthodox back in 1987, "the onus was placed on the Department of Sacred Music to issue a greater variety of music in a shorter period of time."

Bearing Witness to His Leadership

Elizabeth McMillan was one of those who came into the Church back in 1987. She recalls being awestruck when she first met the bishop, and was honored when she and her family were chrismated personally by him. She was also one of those who attended the Sacred Music Institute, and remembers weeping "at hearing the thundering voices singing Vespers, Divine Liturgy and Matins." "There are no words to describe how I felt hearing Byzantine Music for the first time." Without Metropolitan Philip's courage and direction, she may never have had the opportunity to come into the Orthodox Church, let alone become so inspired by our music and tradition. She now serves as our Diocesan Choir Director for the Diocese of Miami and the Southeast.

As the choir director of St. George Orthodox Cathedral in Wichita, Kansas, for over twenty years, and the Director for the Diocese of Wichita and Mid-America, Chris Farha recalls quite a history with the Metropolitan. He would visit them on the Sunday of the Myrrh-Bearing Women, and he was in Wichita for both the groundbreaking and the consecration of their new cathedral—both of which occurred on that Sunday as well. It was also very memorable to have the consecration of Bishop Basil there in Wichita, also during the Paschal season. She remembers singing that beautiful hymn "The

Angel Cried" by M. Balakirev, that we all know and love, and which the Metropolitan loved to hear. He even asked that it be sung at one of the Sacred Music Institutes that he attended. He also gave us direction and insight as to what kind of music we should be developing. "His keynote that evening [at the SMI] was centered around making our own tradition of music in [this] archdiocese, using both Byzantine music and music from other Orthodox traditions." We could very easily sum up how important our music is to the bishop by his words to Chris following Bishop Basil's consecration: "The music during the Liturgy today created a spiritual experience for me."

Finally, Venise Kousaie, our Diocesan Director in the Diocese of Ottawa, Eastern Canada and Upstate New York, has appreciated the bishop's great interest in this Department; he "without fail thanks the efforts of the choir director and choir members whenever he serves Liturgy." Her sense is "that he likes the Liturgy to move, to be alive and not to drag. . . . He likes 'God Grant You Many Years' to be upbeat and not sung as if someone has just died!" When the bishop was asked about why we sing in four-part harmony when our tradition is Byzantine chant, she recalls him explaining it as an adaptation to our "North American Culture, that music that leads people to prayer is what is acceptable." In her words: "he is a diplomat and a visionary to whom we owe a great debt of gratitude."

So to you Saidna Philip, on behalf of Ray George and James Meena, and all of those who work for the betterment of our liturgical music in this archdiocese, we thank you for your guidance, your courage and dynamic leadership. Thank you for inspiring us to provide the *dynamis* we need in the development of our music on this North American continent, as we continue to sing to the glory of our God, who has given us this life.

With much love in Christ,

—Christopher A. Holwey, Chairman

Department of Sacred Music

IN THE VIEW OF

RUTH ANN SKAFF
DIRECTOR, PLANNING AND FUTURE DEVELOPMENT DEPARTMENT

Saidna's Hope for the Future

My Earliest Memory

YEARS AGO, A HANDSOME AND ENGAGING YOUNG DEACON STAYED WITH MY FAMILY at our parish home on weekends. That is my earliest memory of Metropolitan Philip, dating back to 1958–1959.

My father, the Very Rev. Thomas Skaff, and my mother, Khouria Elaine, were serving St. George Orthodox Church in Parma Heights, Ohio, located in metro Cleveland. At the behest of Metropolitan Antony Bashir, of thrice-blessed memory, then Deacon Philip Saliba was preparing to assume the pastoral duties there. During the week, he studied at Wayne State University in Detroit, Michigan. He spent the weekends at our house, then bustling with four active youngsters.

I was 10 years old and liked him very much. Years later he readily recalled that my kid sister's boisterous running up and down the stairs early on Saturday mornings would invariably awaken him. I like to think that this noisy wakeup call may have influenced the wake up calls Saidna Philip has given us for four decades.

For in truth, Saidna Philip has awakened *us* to the life-saving vibrancy and fullness of our Holy Orthodox Faith, and to our responsibility to vigorously share our Faith and bring America to Orthodoxy.

Paths Crossing Again: 2004-2005

In December 2004, our paths crossed again, this time at his home, in the archdiocese office in Englewood, New Jersey, when he interviewed me as an applicant for a newly created position. For me, the reconnection with Saidna Philip has been profound, deeply meaningful and spiritually renewing.

In January 2005, Saidna Philip appointed me to be the Director of the newly established Department of Planning and Future Development. The Department's primary responsibilities are to initiate fundraising programs in support of the archdiocese's thirty-plus departments, programs and projects. The Department seeks to raise substantial additional operational and endowed funds, as well as increase the number of contributors for these programs which benefit all our parishes.

For forty years His Eminence *was* the Department of Planning and Future Development. He has raised millions of dollars to build and support our churches, strengthen and grow our parishes, educate our seminarians and our youth, care for our clergy and establish enduring institutions. During these four decades, through God's grace, the number of Antiochian Orthodox faithful has increased, as has the number of parishes. Of necessity, the projects and programs to meet the manifold needs of the faithful and teaching the Faith have also increased quite extensively.

Saidna's Forward Looking Vision

To continue Saidna's forward looking vision, it is essential to institutionalize and expand the fundraising, or, more properly described, the sacrificial giving and almsgiving that is a tenet of our Faith. To assist him, and to effect a successful transition, every single one of us must take ownership of this department's mission. "Remember this: whoever sows sparingly will also reap sparingly, and whoever sows generously will also reap generously" (2 Corinthians 9:6). Every bishop, every priest, every layperson must sow generously in the fertile field of America so Orthodoxy grows ever more abundantly. The Metropolitan's gift to us is a vibrant Church in North America, which serves our life-saving Faith. It is our duty to nurture and advance the Orthodox Faith. Funds are an essential tool to this service.

At the Metropolitan's direction, the Department has begun soliciting individual major gifts to complete three previously established endowed funds, each with a goal of $1 million: Christian Education Endowment; Missions and Evangelism Endowment; and Youth Ministries Endowment. Endowment revenue (interest earned on the *corpus*) will provide a dependable portion of the annual funding needed for each of these departments, and help them advance their work.

The Department of Planning and Future Development is the newest department, but had its roots in a detailed analysis and report made more than a decade ago. In 1993, Metropolitan Philip commissioned the Task Force on the Church in the Twenty-First Century. Their report, "An American Orthodox Vision: Charting a Course of Action for the Church in the Twenty-First Century," included hiring a full-time Director of Development, among its numerous recommendations.

Doing to the Least of the Brethren

My reaction at time of appointment remains the same today:

> To serve our Holy Orthodox Faith and faithful professionally is a dream come true. It's definitely time to enhance our fundraising efforts and realize our capacity as an Orthodox Christian community so we can better evangelize and 'do unto the least of these.' I'm grateful, humbled and excited.

Danny Thomas used to say: "Takers eat well, givers sleep well." By takers, he meant those with means who never returned any of what they themselves had been given. Along that same line, we remember what Jesus said to Sir Launfal in Longfellow's poem: "Who gives of himself of his alms feeds three: himself, his hungering neighbor, and me."

Metropolitan Philip loves us very much, and is deeply engaged in all aspects of our journey to salvation. I am struck by the constancy of his vision, especially as I reread *And He Leads Them: the Mind and Heart of Philip Saliba*, the thirty-fifth anniversary tribute edited by the Very Rev. Joseph Allen. The issues he addressed and the path he charted then still resonate loudly today. He chose the name Department of Planning and Future Development because he emphatically stresses that we must plan for the future. He often cites Matthew 28:20: "And lo, I am with you always, even to the end of the age."

For forty years he has held a vision for the spiritual growth of America through the evangelism of Orthodoxy. This department is merely the most recent of his truly visionary leadership. I'm extraordinarily privileged and grateful to have this responsibility. Thank you, Saidna Philip. "Many Years!"

—Ruth Ann Skaff, Director

Planning and Future Development Department

IN THE VIEW OF

THE VERY REV. MICHAEL NASSER
DIRECTOR, ANTIOCHIAN VILLAGE CAMP

The Dreamer and his Dream

IN 1874, THE BRITISH POET ARTHUR O'SHAUGHNESSY wrote in his poem *Ode*: "We are the music makers, / We are the dreamers of dreams." Exactly one hundred years later, Metropolitan Philip was doing just that: dreaming dreams. One of the amazing things about dreamers is their ability to see past current limitations, or even more amazing, to see things before most can even imagine why the dream might be important in the first place. The dream of what would become the Antiochian Village did not begin when the first campers arrived in June of 1979. Nor did it begin when the property was purchased a year earlier, or even when, after a long search, the property was found. The reality and experience that we now know as the Village began in the mind and heart of Metropolitan Philip long before, as a simple dream, but one which held the potential to be a dream-come-true for generations of our children.

Saidna's Vision of the Camp
I first heard Saidna Philip speak in depth about his vision for the Antiochian Village when I was called

to meet with him in November, 1996, as he considered me for the position of Camp Director. Sitting in his office in Englewood, New Jersey, he probed me to see if I would be a good fit for this vital position, testing me to see if I recognized the unparalleled opportunities for spiritual growth that he knew the Village could provide our children. Between his questions, he reminisced and reflected back on the earliest days of his dreaming of what would become the Antiochian Village. He sat back in his chair and with closed eyes he remembered days gone by, recounting the embryonic beginnings of his dream.

The time was the mid 1970s. The nightly news, he said, was filled with images of war around the world and moral decay at home—in our cities, our schools and our homes. He grew tired of these destructive influences and worried about their effect on the young people in the archdiocese. Then he did what he's done whenever a challenge has presented itself: he dreamed, and as usual, dreamed big. He reminisced about his hope for a "home away from home" where the children of the archdiocese could come for rest, retreat and education. A place they could find ultimately true recreation: being created anew amid the beauty of God's creation. He wanted something beyond a place to get away from the noise and confusion of modern life. He did not want his children to merely leave behind the distractions of this world; he wanted them to experience the beauty, peace and joy of the life of the world to come. He wanted them to taste the Kingdom.

As we sat together on that gray November morning in the warmth of his office, he would occasionally glance out at the starkness of leafless trees. He reflected on his original vision for the Village, returning to a concern that has never seemed far away. As I had heard him say so many times before and since, he expressed his desire to see his people live out their Christian Faith not merely on the surface, but rather to "plunge to the depths" of the Faith. The unencumbered life lived throughout Christian history in the villages of Syria, Greece or Russia was a lifestyle suited to living in true community. God's own handiwork was seen in the beauty of His creation, and Christians in days gone by had the peace and quiet needed to see and hear God. This was what our children needed. Even if for only a short week or two, they needed the chance to live that "village life."

To find a location in which this vision of village life could become a reality, Saidna told me he looked to Fr. George M. Corry and Mr. George Koury, both of St. Michael parish in Greensburg, Pennsylvania. Ultimately, the former Camp Fairfield was chosen, principally for its location right in the middle of the heaviest concentration of Antiochian parishes—stretching from Chicago, Illinois through New England and into Eastern Canada. Its lush, pristine setting in the Laurel Highlands of western Pennsylvania reminded Saidna of his own home village in the mountains of Lebanon, and this inspired him as he walked around Camp Fairfield, trying to imagine his vision coming to reality in this proposed location. As he spoke to me, his closed, reminiscing eyes quickly opened. With a glimmer of success in them and a proud smile, he added that the $300,000 price for 280 acres and over thirty-five buildings made the decision that much easier.

With his vision fully formed and a location found in which to see it become reality, Saidna told me how he turned to Fr. John Namie, at that time the pastor of St. George Church in Houston, Texas, to be the Village's first Camp Director. He gave Fr. John the task of fleshing out his vision into a living experience. Though both Saidna and Fr. John shared much about just how the Village experience would be designed, they also had their differences. Would there be pews in the chapel? Would there be formal Christian Education as part of the program or would the Christian Education simply be the lifestyle that would be lived? Saidna recounted how he and Fr. John had shared some rather open, honest and occasionally heated discussions; although, as Saidna reiterated to me many times, and as Fr. John later confirmed, their disagreements were never stronger than the respect each had for the other.

From Wish to Reality

In June of 1979, what began just a few years before as a wish for his young people became reality when those first pioneer campers arrived. As I sat listening to Saidna Philip tell the story of those early days, it was obvious to me that this was not simply a trip down memory lane for him; I was being commissioned to continue carrying out the vision which had already inspired almost two decades of camping at that point.

As I now complete ten years as the Camp Director of the Village and look back on the decade of ministry with which Saidna Philip entrusted me, I see so many aspects of the Village experience which have only become more important with each passing year. The youth come to the Village, coming up the mountain and bringing with them everything life has thrown at them: hopes, successes, worries, insecurities and disappointments. In days gone by, layers of loving communities wrapped our young people in relative security and stability. Aunts and uncles, teachers and coaches, and a generation or two of extended family were a part of the "village" that it took to raise a child. With our modern society's "development," many of these layers of support no longer exist for our children. For some of our children, none of them do.

When the young people come to the Village, it's as if they're making a visit to a bygone era. The day is marked at its beginning and ending with the community being called to worship, not with the buzzing of an alarm or beeping of a computer, but with the peaceful toll of a bell. Meals are eaten together in cabin groups around a common table, and surrounded by the entire larger community. Technology is purposefully removed (with increasing resistance with each passing year) and in place of personal stereos, CD players, Game Boys and iPods, children can be found passing time in conversation with each other or with the adult staff, or playing checkers or a card game.

Saidna's Children and His Dream for Them

Perhaps most importantly, the children are surrounded by staff members who have come to spend their summer at the Village with one purpose: to love them. They love them by keeping them safe, by making sure they're fed and rested, by challenging them to learn new activities and sports and most of all by just accepting them as they are. I see this blanket of love in which our young people are wrapped during their one or two weeks at the Village each year, and I am increasingly convinced of the essentiality of this experience. Seeing this, and reflecting back almost three decades since the dream that would become the Antiochian Village was born in the heart of Saidna Philip, I ask myself this question: is it possible that so many years ago he could have known how important the whole endeavor would be? Could he possibly have foreseen the changes in society, in our country, in our parishes and ultimately in our families that would make the "Village experience" that much more crucial as time progresses? I do not know the answer to that question, but as I have grown in my understanding of the man over the years, one of the qualities I recognize with increasing clarity is His Eminence's ability to see where life is leading, and to act in the present to be able to meet the future once it arrives.

Of the many things I have learned from listening to Saidna Philip over the years and observing him in action, I think the most valuable lesson I've learned is to dream dreams. We can only prepare for the challenges and opportunities that await us down the road by dreaming dreams now and being ready to meet those challenges and opportunities when they arrive. Our dreamer and chief shepherd has provided us with the best example of what can happen when God's Grace meets our willingness to receive His love and strength and to do His Will.

"We are the music makers, / We are the dreamers of dreams."

—Father Michael Nasser, Director

Antiochian Village Camp